Hope

www.**transworldbooks**.co.uk

Hope

A MEMOIR OF SURVIVAL
IN CLEVELAND

Amanda Berry and **Gina DeJesus**

WITH

Mary Jordan and Kevin Sullivan

BANTAM PRESS

LONDON · TORONTO · SYDNEY · AUCKLAND · JOHANNESBURG

TRANSWORLD PUBLISHERS
61–63 Uxbridge Road, London W5 5SA
www.transworldbooks.co.uk

Transworld is part of the Penguin Random House group of companies
whose addresses can be found at global.penguinrandomhouse.com

Penguin
Random House
UK

First published in Great Britain in 2015 by Bantam Press
an imprint of Transworld Publishers

'Gina DeJesus' disappearance has changed her neighbourhood' by Ariel Castro,
Plain Press (Cleveland), June 2004. Reprinted by permission of the publisher.

Photograph credits:
Insert page 1 (top): © FBI/Splash News/Corbis
2 (top), 14 (top): AP Images/Tony Dejak
4 (top): The Plain Dealer/Landov
5 (top): © Aaron Josefcyzk/Reuters/Corbis
13 (top): © David Maxwell/epa/Corbis
14 (bottom): © John Gress/Corbis
15 (top): © SGusky/Cleveland PD/handout/Corbis
16 (top): The White House/photo by Pete Souza
Other photographs courtesy of the authors

A CIP catalogue record for this book
is available from the British Library.

ISBN 9780593075142 (cased)
9780593075159 (tpb)

Typeset in Warnock Pro
Printed and bound by Clays Ltd, Bungay, Suffolk

Penguin Random House is committed to a sustainable
future for our business, our readers and our planet. This book
is made from Forest Stewardship Council® certified paper.

MIX
Paper from
responsible sources
FSC
www.fsc.org   FSC® C018179

1 3 5 7 9 10 8 6 4 2

A Note to Readers

We have written here about terrible things that we never wanted to think about again. But our story is not just about rape and chains, lies and misery. That was Ariel Castro's world. Our story is about overcoming all that.

We want people to know the truth, the real story of our decade as Castro's prisoners inside 2207 Seymour Avenue in Cleveland, Ohio.

For years we could see on TV that our families were looking for and praying for us. They never gave up, and that gave us strength. We video-taped news coverage of them holding vigils and replayed those tapes on our most desperate days. When it was very hard to believe we would ever be free again, and no longer enslaved by a cruel man, just writing the word "hope" over and over helped keep us going.

Now we want the world to know: We survived, we are free, we love life. We were stronger than Ariel Castro.

While we lived within feet of each other for years inside a very small house, our experiences were very different. Castro was a master manipulator who lied to each of us about the others so we wouldn't trust one another and band together against him.

To tell our distinct stories, parts of this book are in Amanda's voice and parts are in Gina's, and we have clearly marked each.

Amanda kept a diary of more than 1,200 pages, and its entries are a key source for this book. They were written on McDonald's napkins and takeout bags, on loose-leaf paper, in a kid's dime-store journal, and even on the inside of empty cardboard boxes of Little Debbie cakes. Ariel Castro also shot many hours of home video over the years, and together with Amanda's notes they form a vivid record of life inside that house, which has enabled us to write precisely about what was happening on specific dates and times.

Amanda was only seventeen when she started writing down her thoughts, and especially in the early years they are written in a teenager's shorthand. A week after her abduction, for example, she wrote: "I asked him when he's takin' me home—he said MAYBE the last wk of June. I just don't want no one 2 4-get about me. Ima go 4 now. PRAY 4 me!" To make it easier on readers, we have expanded that shorthand, and use italics when we quote Amanda's diary exactly as written.

Other parts of this book involve matters that were taking place outside the house that we could not possibly have known about. To explain those, we have relied on Mary Jordan and Kevin Sullivan, the journalists who helped us write this book. Their reporting has enabled us to learn about law enforcement's search for us, the school bus driver who stole a decade of our lives, his violent relationship with his common-law wife, and his long history of domestic violence.

Mary, who grew up on the west side of Cleveland, and Kevin reviewed thousands of pages of police reports and court transcripts, watched hours of Castro's videotaped interviews with police, visited Castro's hometown in rural Puerto Rico, and interviewed Castro's family members and scores of other people to help investigate how our kidnappings happened and went unsolved for so long.

Michelle Knight was also a captive in Castro's house and we invited her to join us in writing this book, but she decided to tell her story by herself. She appears throughout our account when she had significant interactions with us. We wish her only the best as we all try to recover and rebuild our lives.

We are inspired every day by Jocelyn Berry, who was born on a Christmas morning in the house on Seymour Avenue. She made a dark place brighter, and in many ways helped save us.

Amanda Berry and Gina DeJesus
Cleveland
February 10, 2015

Preface

September 3, 2013: He Is Dead

Amanda

My phone chimes. A text message.

Who could that be? It's after midnight, and I'm in bed. Jocelyn is asleep next to me, just like every night since she was born six years ago. That's about the only thing that hasn't changed in the four months since I kicked my way out of that hell house.

I'm staring at the message from my aunt Susie: *Did you hear that he killed himself?*

I freeze. A minute passes, then another. Can this be real?

I start to feel sick. The phone rings, and it's my aunt Theresa: "Did you hear? It's breaking news on Channel 19 that Ariel Castro killed himself."

I slip out of bed so Jocelyn doesn't wake up, and I run downstairs and turn on the TV.

His mug shot takes up the entire screen.

"Cleveland kidnapper Ariel Castro is dead. He apparently hanged himself in his cell tonight. He had served a little over a month of his sentence: life in prison plus a thousand years."

My stomach knots up. It's hard to breathe.

How dare he do this? How dare he?

He kidnapped me, chained me like a dog in his house, and raped me over and over. Because of him, my mother died without knowing if I was dead or alive. She was only forty-three, and I can never forgive him for breaking her heart.

But he was Jocelyn's father. She loves him, and he loved her. He never hurt her. He took her to the library, to the mall, to McDonald's. He even took her to church. I hid the reality of 2207 Seymour Avenue from her as best I could, hoping that she would think her home was no different from anybody else's.

Ariel Castro deserved to be in jail, forever. But now that he's suddenly dead, I don't know what to feel, and that confusion is running in rivers down my cheeks.

Gina

I'm sitting on the floor in my living room, talking to my mom and my brother, Ricky. Since I got out of Ariel Castro's prison four months ago, I am with my family night and day. I hate to be by myself. I'm still afraid.

I was walking home from the seventh grade in April 2004 when he tricked me into his car. I turned fifteen locked inside Seymour Avenue, and then sixteen, seventeen, eighteen, nineteen, twenty, twenty-one, twenty-two, and twenty-three. He made me want to kill myself, and I felt so sad and alone that for months at a time I barely got out of bed.

A big "Breaking News" bulletin comes across the TV screen: ARIEL CASTRO IS DEAD.

Everyone in the living room stops talking.

I don't feel anything, but only stare at the TV, numb.

I just had a dream a couple of nights ago that two prisoners got into his cell and killed him, and that his body was found naked in a pool of water.

Now he's really dead.

Or at least the prison officials being interviewed on TV say he is. I'm not sure I believe it. Maybe they are claiming he's dead so people will stop talking about him. Our story has been nonstop bad news for Cleveland. Maybe they think pretending he's dead will quiet things down.

Or maybe he's behind this somehow. He's so sneaky and clever, anything's possible with him. I learned that the hard way, and I don't trust anything about him. But on TV they keep reporting that he's dead, so maybe he really is gone.

I call Michelle, and we both agree that it would have been better for him to suffer in prison for the rest of his life.

I text Amanda, not wanting a call to wake up Jocelyn, and she calls me right back.

"I didn't want him to die this way—nobody should. I wanted him to be in prison like we were," I tell her. "I wanted him to be locked up and left with his thoughts, because his thoughts would eat him alive."

I can tell Amanda is upset, and I know that dealing with this is going to be more complicated for her.

When I hang up, I start thinking that it might actually be good that he's gone. Now he can't hurt anybody else.

I start crying—not because he's dead, but because he hurt me so badly for so long.

Amanda

The phone keeps ringing. I know it's news reporters, so I don't pick up. What could I say? I don't know what I think or feel.

I start remembering all the times he talked to me about his fear of prison, how he said he would kill himself before going to jail. He said he would rather die in a gunfight with police than let them put him behind bars. But I never thought he would have the guts to hang himself.

And so soon. After holding us prisoners for years, he couldn't stand being locked up for even a few months? And his mom was allowed to visit.

My sister, Beth, is sleeping upstairs. She's not feeling well, and I don't want to wake her up, so I sit alone.

My aunt Theresa calls again.

"Think of everything he did to you. It's good that he's gone."

Maybe she's right.

But all I can really think of is that Jocelyn never got to say good-bye to her daddy. After we escaped from Seymour Avenue in May and drove away in an ambulance, we never saw him again. Now it's September and he's dead.

When Jocelyn turned eighteen she would have been able to visit him in prison and ask him all the questions I know she will have. It's cruel that he took away her chance to face him one day.

I wonder which was harder for him: being behind bars, or knowing that his grown kids and the whole world learned of his sick double life. What others thought of him mattered a lot to him. He craved respect. He thought he deserved it as a self-taught musician and because he had grown up in poverty but now owned his own house and drove nice cars.

After Jocelyn was born, he began to pretend we were a normal family, and I think he actually convinced himself we were. He locked me in his house but took Jocelyn out to help him pick flowers for me. For a decade he was my whole life and often the only person I had to talk to.

Now he's dead.

Right now that feels like more pain, more sadness, and more loss.

Hope

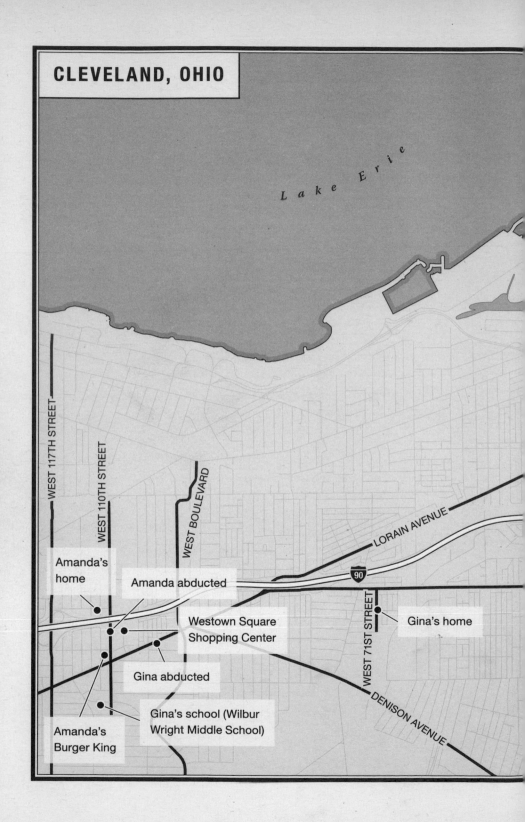

CLEVELAND, OHIO

Lake Erie

WEST 117TH STREET

WEST 110TH STREET

WEST BOULEVARD

LORAIN AVENUE

90

Amanda's home

Amanda abducted

Westown Square Shopping Center

Gina's home

WEST 71ST STREET

Gina abducted

DENISON AVENUE

Gina's school (Wilbur Wright Middle School)

Amanda's Burger King

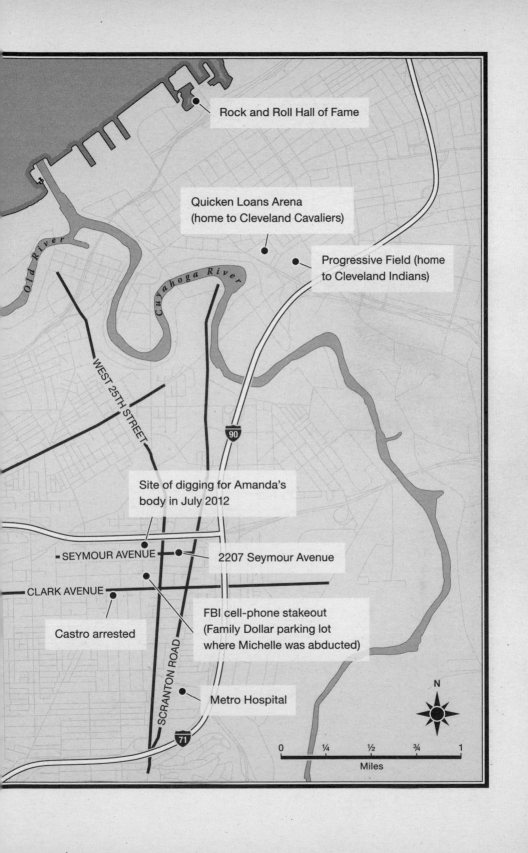

Rock and Roll Hall of Fame

Quicken Loans Arena
(home to Cleveland Cavaliers)

Progressive Field (home
to Cleveland Indians)

Old River

Cuyahoga River

WEST 25TH STREET

90

Site of digging for Amanda's
body in July 2012

SEYMOUR AVENUE

2207 Seymour Avenue

CLARK AVENUE

FBI cell-phone stakeout
(Family Dollar parking lot
where Michelle was abducted)

Castro arrested

SCRANTON ROAD

Metro Hospital

71

N

0   ¼   ½   ¾   1

Miles

Part One

April 21, 2003: Maroon Van

Amanda

I wake up at noon on the day after Easter. I was up late again listening to Eminem. His song "Superman" usually cheers me up: *"They call me Superman, I'm here to rescue you."* I have his posters all over my bedroom—on the walls, my mirror, the closet door. But today even Em can't help me feel better.

My mom pushes my door open and sticks her head in. I'm still in bed, upset.

"Mandy, I'm off to work. See you tonight. Love you!"

"Love you, too. See you later."

We live in the upstairs part of a duplex at West 111th Street and Belmont Avenue, near Cleveland's Westown Square Shopping Center. It's not a bad place, except for the noise from all the cars and trucks whizzing by on I-90, the highway just beside the house. My older sister, Beth Serrano, lives downstairs with her husband, Teddy, and their two little girls, Mariyah, age four, and Marissa, age three.

Teddy is the reason I'm so miserable. He and my sister are having a fight. She's furious. Teddy is the manager of the Burger King where I work and I don't want to see him today because he's made my sister so upset.

Outside my window I hear Beth drive off with my mom in her old Chevy Lumina. They work together at a tool and die factory over on Brookpark Road assembling metal parts: a thirty-nine-year-old mom and her twenty-three-year-old daughter standing side by side, putting little metal pieces together like a puzzle. No one ever told them what the part they make is for, but when they fill a box with a hundred of them, they start over on a new box.

A lot of parents in my neighborhood do hourly work like my mom, and then their kids drop out of school and join them in the same jobs, getting by but not going far. My dad moved back to Tennessee with another woman, so my mom works minimum-wage jobs and I try to pitch in and pay for things like my schoolbooks.

I blast more Em in my room. My stereo speakers are on my dresser, next to my porcelain angels and Nativity set. I keep the angels and baby Jesus out all year, not just at Christmas, because they make me happy.

I jump in the shower and stay under the hot water for an extra-long time, wondering if I should quit my job because of this mess with Teddy. I don't want to. It's the first job I've ever had and I've met some nice friends there. I started nearly a year ago when I turned sixteen, and I've already gotten a raise to six dollars an hour, almost a dollar more than when I started. Lots of people work there a long time and never get raises, so I guess they like me. It's nice, too, to hear customers tell me I have a pretty smile.

I need money because one day I'm going to go to college. I'm not sure exactly what I'm going to study—maybe clothing design. I love clothes and obsess over every detail, right down to my shoelaces, which I make sure always match my shirt.

If I did quit today, I wouldn't miss this Burger King uniform: burgundy shirt, black jeans, and black sneakers. I drew the line at those nasty polyester pants. The shirt was bad enough, but they weren't going to get me to wear those pants, too.

I pull my work shirt out of a drawer and leave two identical ones folded there. I like everything ironed and orderly. I have a system for hanging up my clothes: light pink shirts together, close to, but not mixed with, darker pinks. All my whites are together. Pressed jeans are organized from light blue to darker. I arrange my shoes on the floor by heel height, starting with flats and sneakers and moving up to wedges and high heels.

Tomorrow is my seventeenth birthday, and a few friends are coming over to celebrate with me, so I should be excited. I check my money hidden in a glittery pink box in the back of my bra drawer. I have a hundred dollars tucked away, and to celebrate I'm going to splurge on a new outfit and get my nails done.

Why not call in sick? It might be nice just to stay home and read my magazines. I have subscriptions to *Entertainment Weekly*, *People*, and *Rolling Stone*, and keep old copies stacked neatly in my room.

But I don't want to work on my birthday, so I guess I should just go. It's only the four-to-eight shift. I can do this.

I'd better hurry; it's ten minutes to four.

I pick up my black Burger King baseball cap and carry it, because there's no way I'm wearing that on the street. I pull on my black sweater and head out the front door into a gray April afternoon.

Work is a ten-minute walk. After I pass a couple of houses and turn right onto West 110th Street, I can see the traffic light ahead at the corner of Lorain, where the Burger King is.

I cross the long bridge over I-90 and watch the cars whizzing by, carrying people going places. Someday I'm heading somewhere better. I am not going to live like my mom, always worried about how to pay the bills. She has been a clerk at Kmart, a BP gas station, the deli counter at the Finast grocery store, and even the Burger King where I work now. Because she dropped out of middle school, she hasn't been able to get anything better. After I graduate from college I am going to earn enough money to buy my own house. My mom can live with me, and then maybe I can make her life a little easier.

I pass Westown Square, where we buy just about everything: food at the Tops grocery store, movies at the Blockbuster, clothes at Fashion Bug. Beth has found cute outfits for the girls at the thrift shop, Value World.

Right at four I arrive at work. God, that smell. French fries and burgers. Grease. It never comes out of my uniform, even after I wash it. I feel as if it's soaked into my skin.

I drop my sweater and my purse in the back, where the head manager, Roy Castro, hangs out. I'm working "back cash" today, which means I take the orders and money at the drive-through window.

After Roy sets up my cash drawer I walk over to my work station. My friend Jennifer is working "front cash," at the main counter, and I see Teddy standing there. Our eyes meet, and I shoot him daggers.

I plug in my headset.

"Welcome to Burger King. May I take your order?"

Here we go again.

Time ticks by slowly. It would be easier if we were busier, but it's the Monday after Easter, and it's dead. I try not to talk to anybody. Roy knows I'm having a hard time, so around seven fifteen he asks if I feel like going home early. He doesn't need to ask me twice. I'm so ready to get out of here.

I grab my things and sit down at a table to call my boyfriend, DJ, to see if he will pick me up. No answer. I call him again, but still no answer. I would love to see him tonight. We've only been dating for a month, but I like him. He holds my hand and opens doors for me. I first saw him when he ordered food at the drive-through. Jennifer knew him and said he was nice. He kept coming back and asking about me if I wasn't there, then finally we went out.

Right now I just wish he would answer his phone. Where is he?

I almost never walk home. For one thing, more people are around in the evening, and I don't like being seen in my Burger King uniform. But the big reason is that my mom doesn't like me coming home alone at night. She never learned to drive, so she has Beth pick me up.

But Beth and Mom are still at work, and I am definitely not hanging out in this soap opera one minute longer than I have to. It's seven thirty, still light outside, and I start walking.

My phone rings as I head home. Beth says she is cutting out of work now, and I tell her I'm doing the same thing.

"We can get you. What time should I pick you up?"

"No, don't worry. I'm already walking home."

As we start discussing Teddy, I see an old maroon van blocking the sidewalk ahead. A guy has turned into a driveway on West 110th, but hasn't pulled all the way up.

I walk around the front of the van to get by. Because I'm still on the phone I'm not paying much attention, but I notice that the girl in the passenger seat looks familiar. I'm pretty sure she used to work at Burger King with me. The driver—it must be her father—is looking right at me and smiling. I smile back as I keep walking.

A minute later his van pulls up alongside me, and he rolls down his window. No cars are coming in either direction, so he's just stopped in the middle of the street.

"Hey, you need a ride home?"

Now I can see him more clearly and definitely remember having seen him before, but I'm not exactly sure where. I'm halfway home, maybe a five-minute walk, and don't really need a ride, but it's nice of him to offer.

Still talking to Beth I nod "yes" to him and start walking toward the van.

When he reaches over and opens the front passenger door, I notice that his daughter is not in the car anymore. I rush Beth off the phone as I climb in.

"Beth, I gotta go because I'm getting a ride."

He starts to pull away as I hang up the phone.

"Where is your daughter?" I ask, as I suddenly realize I am alone in a car with an older guy I don't really know.

"So you work at Burger King?" he says, not answering the question but smiling and friendly. I'm still in my uniform, with my "Amanda" name tag, so it's an easy guess where I work.

I'm starting to get a weird feeling, but he seems nice enough. He's dressed cooler than guys his age: he's all in black, from his T-shirt to his jeans to his boots, and he's listening to 107.9, hip-hop and R&B.

"My son used to work at Burger King. Do you know him? Anthony Castro?"

That's who he is! He's Anthony's dad. Anthony is no relation to Roy Castro, the manager, but I know Anthony, and so does my mom.

"Oh, yeah, I know Anthony. He came to my house one time. He's friends with a friend of mine."

I tell him I also went to Wilbur Wright Middle School with his daughter Angie. "How's she doing?" I ask, more relaxed now that I know who he is.

"She's good," he says. "She's at the house right now. Would you like to go see her?"

"Okay. I haven't seen her in a long time."

Why not go see her? I wasn't looking forward to going home anyway.

He makes a few turns away from my house and then pulls out onto I-90, cheerfully talking about his kids.

"That's a nice phone," he says, looking over at the little blue phone in my hand. A few of my friends have cell phones, and I just bought this one a week ago, used, from a girl at work.

We turn off the highway at West 25th Street, take a few more turns, and then pull onto Seymour Avenue.

I know this neighborhood. It's only about a ten-minute drive from my house, and I have cousins who live close by, on Castle and Carlyle. There are so many Spanish-speaking people here that they call it Little Puerto Rico.

We pull into the driveway at 2207 Seymour. It's a white, two-story house. Nothing special, that's for sure. He drives to the back, where a big, mean-looking dog is barking like crazy right outside the passenger side of the van. It's one of those Chow Chows, with a huge bushy head. The dog is chained to a tree, but the chain's long enough to reach the van. I'm glad I'm inside.

He mentions my phone again.

"That's really nice; let me see it for a minute."

I hand it to him.

"Wait, let me hold the dog back so you can get out," he says, taking my phone with him as he jumps out of the van and pulls the dog away by its collar.

"Angie's inside," he says. "Let's go see her."

We walk to the back door. He unlocks it and we step inside a small enclosed porch cluttered with boxes. Then he unlocks yet another door into the house.

I follow him inside.

He turns on the light in the kitchen. It's so messy. Definitely could use some cleaning up.

He points to the closed bathroom door.

"Angie must be taking a bath right now," he says. "While she's in there, let me show you around the house."

"Oh, okay," I tell him. "That's very nice of you."

We walk into the small dining room, then into the living room, which has dark wood paneling and a black leather couch. He has a big stack of old phone books, family photos all around, and the two biggest stereo speakers I have ever seen. I'm five-foot-one, so they must be four feet tall.

"C'mon, I'll show you upstairs," he says, when he's already halfway up.

As I reach the top landing, I see that it's pretty dark up there. There are a couple of closed bedroom doors, and he points at one of them.

"My roommate is in here," he says. "She's sleeping."

That's weird, I think. Maybe he got divorced from Anthony and Angie's mom? I guess he has a roommate now to help with the rent.

"Take a look," he says.

The doorknob is missing, and I bend down to look through the big hole where it should have been. A girl is sleeping there, with a TV on. I look only for a second, because it feels strange to peek into somebody's room.

We walk into a big bedroom and then a smaller one beyond it. And when I turn to leave, he suddenly blocks the door.

"What are you doing?" I ask him, startled.

"Pull down your pants!"

"No!" I shout. I am panicking and can't believe what he just said. "Take me home! I want to go home!"

There is a girl across the hall, and his daughter is downstairs, so what could he be doing?

I look directly at him for the first time. He's maybe in his forties, older than my mom. He has curly brown hair, dark eyes, a receding hairline, and a goatee. He's about five-foot-seven and stocky, with a bit of a beer belly. If I passed him in the mall, I'd never even notice him.

"Pull down your pants!" he orders again.

He has suddenly turned so scary—his voice, his eyes, his manner—and I do what he says. I stand there, crying, my jeans around my ankles. Why didn't I see this coming? How could I be so stupid? Just because I know his kids doesn't mean I should have gone with him to his house.

He pulls his pants down and starts playing with himself. It's disgusting.

There's a window behind him with lace curtains. He glances outside and says something about police. I look out and see a police car parked across the street. The cops are so close! He says he'll hurt me if I make a sound.

He hurries what he's doing and when he finishes, his voice changes back, and he sounds like the nice guy who was talking to me in the car.

"I'm going to take you home now," he says and tells me I can pull my pants back up.

"Please," I beg him. "Please take me home."

I start praying, asking God to get me out of here.

We start toward the door but then he suddenly stops.

"Turn around, get on the bed, and take your pants down."

"No! No!" I scream. "If you don't take me home right now I'm going to call the police!"

I blurt that out even though I know I can't call anyone. He still has my phone.

"Help! Help me!"

Doesn't his roommate hear me? What's going on in this house?

I run back into the bigger bedroom and try to open the door to the hallway but there's no knob. I see a doorway next to it and run into it, but it's a closet.

I'm cornered, crying, when he grabs me by the arms and drags me over to the bed, where he yanks off my pants and rapes me. He must be fifty pounds heavier than me, and it hurts so bad.

When he is done, he gets up and says, "I'm going to take you home now, but you have to be quiet."

I'm terrified and I know he is lying.

"I'm going to tape your mouth so you don't scream any more until I get you home," he says as he reaches for a roll of gray duct tape, tears off a long piece, and slaps it over my mouth from ear to ear.

He slams my wrists together and tapes them, too, and then does the same to my ankles. Then he takes out a leather belt, and I freeze. Is he going to beat me with it? Hang me? I don't move as he slowly wraps the belt around my ankles, over the tape.

He takes a motorcycle helmet from the closet and pulls it over my head. I can see out of the visor until my tears make everything foggy.

"Don't worry," he says, as if he is actually trying to help me. "I'm just doing this so I can carry you to the van and take you home."

He picks me up and throws me over his shoulder. My head is dangling down by his butt, and every part of my body hurts. He carries me down to the first floor, then takes me into the basement.

He sits me down on the cold concrete floor and props my back against a pole. He takes a thick rusty chain, like a tow truck might use to pull a car, and wraps it around my stomach and the pole. He clamps it shut with a padlock and puts the key in his pocket. We are not going out to the van.

He pulls off the motorcycle helmet and turns on a little black-and-white TV, setting it on a tiny stool.

"Be quiet. Don't scream. Don't try to get away," he says in an oddly calm voice as he switches off the one bare lightbulb and walks back upstairs.

I look around and see piles of clothes, boxes of junk, and dusty shelves filled with knickknacks. It smells like wet dirt, like the basement hasn't been aired out in years. It is so creepy.

I have to break out of here. I put my taped hands up to my face and use my fingertips to pick at the tape across my mouth.

"Somebody help me! Somebody help me!" I scream when I get it loose. "Please! Someone hear me!"

I bite into the tape on my wrists and begin to chew it off, bit by bit. It takes forever, but I finally get my hands free and quickly pull the belt and tape off my ankles.

Now my nails are broken and my fingertips are bleeding. I struggle to get this chain off my waist, but it's so tight I rip my shirt trying. My jeans are kind of thick, so I wriggle out of them, hoping that if I have that extra bit of room I can slip out of the chain. But I can't.

Somebody please help me!" I scream over and over, not knowing what else to do.

He's going to come back and kill me, and I'm going to die because I took a ride from a dad who turned out to be a psycho.

I have no idea what time it is, but while I have been fighting with the chain many TV shows have come and gone, so hours must have passed. *Cops* is on as I finally fall asleep against the pole.

I wake to the sound of heavy footsteps. My body tenses up. He's back. How long have I been asleep?

"I told you not to try to get away," he says in a cheerful voice, looking at all the ripped tape.

It's so strange how nicely he's talking to me, like we're friends playing a game.

"I brought us breakfast," he says, holding out a Burger King bag. "But first we're going to take a shower."

He unlocks the padlock, loosens the chain, and helps me stand up. Since I couldn't get my jeans back on, I'm wearing only my shirt and underwear. He walks me up the stairs, staying close behind, and guides me into the bathroom off the kitchen, where he tells me to undress and get in the shower. Then he takes his clothes off and comes in, too, and with a washcloth rubs away the sticky stuff from the tape around my mouth and ears.

"Here, let's get this off," he says sweetly, like he's washing a baby, and then he begins to shampoo my hair.

I am disgusted by his touch. I want to run away from him, but I'm trapped.

I'm afraid he is going to attack me again, but instead he climbs out of the shower and finds some Band-Aids for my bloody fingers. He gets dressed and gives me a pair of jogging pants and one of his shirts, then takes me into the living room. We sit on the couch, and he hands me a cold ham-and-egg croissant.

He's talking, but I'm in shock and can't focus.

"It's time to go upstairs," he says after I finish eating.

What choice do I have? I follow him up the stairs and into the bedroom where he raped me.

"Just lay down and relax," he says, pointing to the mattress, which has no sheets.

He lies down beside me, and I brace myself for what's next, but he seems exhausted, like he was up all night. At least an hour passes, maybe more. He is inches from me, asleep, or pretending to be. I'm afraid to move or make a sound. My mom and Beth must be losing their minds, so scared about what has happened to me. I am so scared about what is happening to me.

Then, suddenly, he opens his eyes, stands up, and says, "Let's go downstairs."

He walks me back down to the basement, sits me against the pole, and locks the chains tight around my stomach. I cry and cry, but he only turns up the volume on the TV, shuts off the light, and walks back upstairs without a word.

It's so dark.

Then I remember: It's my birthday.

April 25, 2003: Alone in the Dark

Amanda

He has moved me upstairs into the bedroom where he first raped me. It's not pitch-black like the basement, where I spent the first two nights, but it's still dark. There are two small windows covered with heavy gray curtains that were probably white once.

I have to lie sideways on the queen-size bed, my toes hanging off the edge, because of the way he has me chained to the radiator. The padlock on the rusty chain around my stomach feels like a big rock. Its weight makes it hard to sleep, and it's giving me huge purple bruises.

He came in yesterday and put some old socks around the chain so it wouldn't hurt me so much. I don't think he felt bad for me but was just tired of me complaining. He fastened them with plastic zip ties, and now those are digging into me.

The chain is just long enough that I can stand up next to the bed to use my "bathroom"—a tall, beige plastic trash can. He put a trash bag over the top, but it still smells so bad that it's making me sick.

The chain isn't long enough to let me open the curtains, or reach the switch for the overhead light. So when he leaves for work in the morning and turns it off, I have to sit in the dark until he comes back. He told me that he kept the light out of my reach so that I couldn't flip it on and off to attract the neighbors' attention.

He's careful. He constantly peeks out the window to check if anybody is watching the house. Whenever he leaves he keeps a radio blasting in the upstairs hallway. That way, he says, nobody can hear me if I scream. It's hard for me to even hear my TV. Is that girl he called his roommate still here? Who is she and why isn't she helping me? After the first nights in the basement, I lost my voice screaming, so I don't bother anymore. I know nobody can hear me over the radio. Sometimes he stays out all night, and that means it's impossible to sleep with the noise, or even to think. I have a constant headache.

He has a weird mannequin, a woman's torso with black hair that he dresses in a red fishnet tank top and props up in the kitchen. Sometimes he lays it down on the living room couch when he goes out. He says if a burglar tries to get into the house, he'll see it and think somebody is home.

I still don't know his first name. I can't believe I know his kids. I met Anthony only once, and I haven't seen Angie in a while. Why did I agree to come here to see her? I was having a bad day and made a bad decision. Now I will probably die because of it.

I hate wearing his ugly, baggy clothes. I even have to wear his underwear—big, nasty briefs. It's like I'm wearing a prison uniform. The only thing I have left of my own is the bra I was wearing when I got here. I used to hate my work uniform, but now I'd give anything to have it back.

I eat once a day, if I'm lucky, McDonald's or Burger King that he brings for me when he comes home. Often that's at five or six in the evening, but sometimes it's midnight, and I am so hungry.

After I finish eating, he tells me to strip, and he does it again.

When I've been here four days he asks, "Do you want to come downstairs and watch TV?"

The last thing I want to do is spend more time with him. But I'd love to get out of this room and away from the smell and these chains, even for a few minutes.

"Okay," I say, trying not to look at him.

He unlocks the chain and walks me downstairs. The door to his roommate's bedroom is closed.

We sit on the couch and he turns on the news. My mom and Beth are on Channel 5, being interviewed in our house.

"It's been a hard week, and it's getting harder," my mom tells the reporter, wiping her eyes with a tissue. She's sitting on the couch, where I used to cuddle up beside her. "She never made it home. Somewhere between there and here, something happened, and nobody can figure it out."

Beth is crying. "I'm hoping she's out there somewhere," she says. "I hope nothing happened to her. Maybe somebody's got her, drugged her or something. Just bring her home."

I'm crying, too, but glad I'm on the news, because that means people are looking for me. Maybe somebody will see this interview and remember something.

"Your mom looks really upset," he says. There's no sympathy in his voice, it's just an observation, as if he had nothing to do with her misery. He flips around the channels looking for other news reports about me and finds them on Channel 8 and Channel 3. He can't take his eyes off the TV.

I look at him. He has an odd expression on his face, and then I realize what it is: He's proud. He's admiring his work, he feels like he's done something big.

This makes him feel important.

April 27

It's Sunday. I've been gone six days. And so far, he's raped me at least twenty-five times. It's been four or five times every day.

He's out the door at five a.m. to go to work. Then he's back around eight or nine and strips off his bus driver's uniform—black jeans and a burgundy shirt with a little yellow logo for Cleveland Public Schools. After he's done with me, he goes back to work and drives little kids until lunchtime, when he comes home and forces himself on me again.

Then in the evening, he does it again—sometimes several times. He always leaves my chains on.

He slobbers on my face and is obsessed with my breasts. He's always touching my chest and telling me, "These boobs are mine."

I am learning that the more it hurts me, the more he likes it, and that it's over quicker when I don't fight. What would be the point, anyway? I'm chained to a radiator, so where could I go?

I told him I would like something to write on, and he asked if I wanted a journal. I said yes, and he came home today with a blue diary with flowers on its cover.

"You can write what you want," he says, "but don't write any names."

I know he might read this, so I have to be careful about what I say. But I'm going to write to my family. Maybe that will feel like talking to them on the phone or sending them a letter. I miss them so much. I want to let them know I'm alive.

When he leaves I begin my first entry, by the light of the TV:

4/27/03. Sunday. One week.

I never thought I would miss my mom sooooo much! But it's sooo true. You never know what you got 'til it's gone! I just can't wait to go home. I'm 17 now, but don't have a life. But he told me I'm young and will go home before summer. Another two months! Tomorrow it will be a week I've been here—so I've survived this long. I'll just try not to think about it. But it's hard.

I saw my mom and Beth crying on TV. My mom said, "Mandy I love you" and I started bawling. I love you Mom. See ya sooooon! Love, Amanda.

It feels good to write that. I am glad they don't know how horrible it is here.

Eminem's new song, "Sing for the Moment," is on the radio. I can't believe it has some of Aerosmith's music in it, the chorus from "Dream On," my mom's favorite. As I listen to it I get lost in the music, and it takes me back home for a few minutes. I can picture myself there with my mom, safe and free.

I know I haven't always been the best daughter. Sometimes I would argue with her over some pretty stupid stuff. I wish I hadn't. When I get out of here, I won't do that anymore.

He controls when I eat, what I see, what I hear. But he cannot control what I think, so I am going to take my mind somewhere else when he climbs on me.

I have almost nothing in this room, but I have an idea. I have a few pictures of my mom, dad, and nieces in my purse, and I'm going to make a family album. To make a frame I carefully rip apart an empty box of Crunch 'n Munch that he got me. I chew a piece of gum and then separate it into tiny pieces that I stick on the back of the pictures and press them into the cardboard from the box. Then I prop it up on the table next to my bed.

When he is doing horrible things to my body, I look at my mom's face. I imagine her laughing. I picture her smoking her cigarettes and gabbing on the phone, or cooking in the kitchen. I look into her eyes and lose myself in her.

And my mom and I get through it.

April 28

I see my mom on the noon news. She is showing a reporter my bedroom and the pink box where I keep my money, insisting that there's no way I could have run away from home. Who would run away in a Burger King uniform, leaving all her clothes at home and a hundred dollars in her dresser? She says I'm not the runaway kind of kid, anyway. And I'm not.

It's so weird to see pictures of myself on the news, and my mom giving strangers a tour of my room. I never thought I'd ever be on TV. We're a normal, nothing-special family, kind of messed up like everybody, no different from all the other families around here just struggling to get by.

Now everybody knows my name, and they're all looking for me. I'm in a big city, close to downtown and the crowds at the Indians baseball games and the Rock and Roll Hall of Fame. Didn't anybody see me getting into his van? Maybe a neighbor on Seymour saw me come in here? Someone has to rescue me.

The news says it's nice outside today, but there could be a tornado and I wouldn't know. The only light comes from the screen of the little black-and-white TV, the one I had in the basement. It's maybe twelve inches and has rabbit-ears antenna. I have it on a little chair at the foot of the bed and watch *Maury* and other shows my mom likes. It's comforting to think that we might be seeing the same shows at the same time.

All day long all I can hear is that annoying radio in the hall. When he's home in the evening, he turns it off, and then I can hear lawn mowers and cars going by. I keep trying to make my mind wander away when he forces himself on me, but it's hard.

"You said you'd take me home—when are you going to do that?" I ask as he gets dressed.

"You're young. You have plenty of time. What's a few months?"

I am furious but I reply quietly, "Maybe it's nothing to you, but it's a lot to me. This is my life you have taken."

"Maybe the last week of June," he says. "You just gotta be patient."

Another two months, if he's not lying. I don't trust anything he says, but it helps me to think it will be over in two months. I can make it that long. I choose to believe him.

I never went to church much, but I know there is a God and I know he must have a different plan for me than this.

One day he comes in at midnight and sits at the end of the bed, holding my cell phone.

"I called your mother," he says. "I told her that we are in love, and that you are my wife now."

Shocked, I start crying and ask, "You talked to my mom?"

"Yeah, I called her with your phone," he says. "She asked when you would be home, and I told her I didn't know. I told her you were safe."

"Can I talk to her?" I ask. "I want her to know that I'm okay."

He ignores me. "I talked to your sister, Beth, too. I told them you were okay. I said you were with me now."

Maybe this is good; they know I'm alive. Or maybe it's bad, because they'll think I've been taken by some crazy guy and are scared about what he's doing to me. Why did he call them? Does he think that if they believe that I ran away, they won't search for me? He doesn't know my family. They'll never stop looking for me. But he's such a liar. I bet he didn't even call them.

He lets me listen to a couple of the voice messages on my phone. One is from my little niece Mariyah, telling me, "Please come home." Another one is from my friend Mary from Burger King. I guess she didn't know I was missing, because she left a message saying, "Which one is your house? I'm trying to find it for your birthday party."

Hearing their voices makes me cry so hard I can barely breathe.

"Can I please call them and tell them I'm alive?" I ask, begging him.

"You can write to them," he says. "But there are rules. You have to tell them that you ran away. You left on your own and you're okay, so they shouldn't worry about you."

"I won't do that," I tell him. "I'll never tell my family that I ran away. That would hurt them so much. I would rather have them wondering what happened to me than think that I would leave them."

"Okay," he says.

He rapes me again.

April 29

They haven't shown me on the news at all today. Over and over they run a story about bad lettuce making people sick. I don't think he actually called my mom. If he did, that would be bigger news than lettuce.

I heard on the news about Elizabeth Smart, the girl in Utah who was kidnapped and released last month. The lunatic who took her also said she was his wife. He kept her nine months! If she can survive for that long, I know I can, too.

He's back and he says he wants to stay with me all night long. He keeps calling me his "temporary wife."

I move over to the very edge of the bed, as far away from him as I can get. But he cuddles up behind me and reaches around and takes my hand. It's like he thinks we're a couple.

I lie still until he falls asleep, then I slip my hand out of his.

He has ruined my life and my body. I'm filthy. My toilet is a trash can. I'm hungry and cold and chained up.

And he wants to hold my hand.

April 30

Getting to go downstairs to the bathroom is what I look forward to most. That crummy little bathroom has become the highlight of my week. I miss feeling clean. Today I finally get to shower and brush my teeth—it's been days. It feels good.

I just start to feel the water wash him off me when he steps into the shower.

I think about killing myself. But if I do, he wins.

I have to keep it together until I can figure out how to escape. To keep from sliding into complete sadness I try to focus on anything good. I felt hot water today. I heard Eminem on the radio. I found a penny in the pocket of his old sweatpants and decide it's my lucky penny. I have pictures of my mom and dad, and they remind me that I need to stay strong so I can see them again.

But it's hard. These chains are so tight that even with the socks wrapped around them they cut into my stomach. It's impossible to sleep, because I keep rolling over onto the padlock. But even worse than the physical pain is the mental torture of never knowing what's next.

I'm learning that they have TV shows that teach everything—cooking, dance, languages. I saw one that teaches meditation, how to relax, how to rid your mind of what's bothering you. I am going to look for that one. I have to get better at making my mind fly away from this place.

I close my eyes.

"Please, Lord, make this end. Please let me go home to my family. Please keep them safe and bring me home soon," I say over and over.

I turn to my photo of Mom, kiss it, and tell her good night.

Tomorrow is May 1. A new month.

This is how I'm going to think about time: Every day that passes means I'm a day closer to this being over, a day closer to being home.

Hope is my only option.

May 2003: The Woman in the Other Room

May 1

Amanda

"Do you want to help me with the laundry?"

No, I don't want to do his laundry. But I do want to get out of this room, even for a few minutes, even to wash his filthy clothes. "Okay, sure," I tell him, and he takes a key off the keychain on his belt and opens the padlock on my stomach. The chains fall to the ground, and I feel fifty pounds lighter.

We walk into the hallway, and he points at the closed door of the bedroom where I saw that girl sleeping ten days ago.

"We have to clean up this room," he says, unlocking the door.

I've been thinking about her. Why does he call her his roommate? Could she be part of this somehow? I thought about yelling out to her, in case she's still here, but I never know when he's home or not. Sometimes he pretends to leave, then creeps back up and opens my door. He tells me he's testing me and says, "I don't know if I can trust you yet."

I notice now that her door is also locked from the outside. Oh, no. She must be another prisoner.

I step inside and see her sitting on the bed. We look at each other, and I can't read her expression or tell what she's thinking. She seems in a daze. I can't see if she's chained because she's sitting under a blanket. She's tiny and looks older than me.

"This is my roommate," he says, but doesn't tell me her name. "This is Amanda," he tells her.

We both say hi. Neither of us says another word.

He hands me a plastic garbage bag and orders, "Pick up the trash."

The room is a mess. I start stuffing pizza boxes and old bags from McDonald's, Wendy's, and Burger King into the bag. Pizza crusts and dirty napkins are everywhere and look like they've been piling up for weeks. How long has she been here?

"It smells like a hamster cage in here," I say.

I'm not trying to be funny, but that makes him laugh. She just watches and doesn't say anything.

She has a TV. I've been on the news lately—my face, my name. She must know who I am. She seems as afraid of him as I am. Who is she?

"Okay, that's enough, let's go," he says when I finish filling the trash bag.

I look at the girl again, but she doesn't look back. He leads me into the hallway, locks her in her room, and stays close behind me as we go down the stairs. At the door to the basement, I stop. I haven't been down there since those first two horrible nights. I hope this isn't some kind of trick or new punishment. But I have no choice because he tells me to keep going.

"Start with these," he says, pointing to a huge pile of dirty clothes.

I guess he really does want to do laundry.

I start sorting whites and colors. As I put the first load into the machine, something catches my eye amid all the junk in the basement: on top of a stack of photos is a picture of Jesus, with light radiating from around his head and his heart wrapped in thorns. He has beautiful eyes that seem to stare directly at me. There are some prayers in Spanish on the back: *Novena al Sagrado Corazón de Jesús.*

"Can I have this?" I ask him.

"Sure," he says. "Why not?"

After he orders me back up to my room, chains me, locks my door, and leaves, I set the Jesus picture against the rabbit ears on top of the TV. Now I have my mom watching over me from the bedside table, and Jesus doing the same from the TV.

I decide to write in my diary every time he attacks me. I won't use the word "rape" in case he ever reads it. But I need a record of what he is doing to me. I want him someday, somehow, to be held responsible for every single time he steals a piece of me. I can't let him get away with this.

It was three times today—morning, lunchtime, and when he came home from work—so in the corner of my diary page, I mark *3x*. He'll never know what it means. I'll never forget.

May 2

I'm crying, blaming myself for being so stupid for getting in that van. I was minutes away from home. It wasn't that cold; why didn't I just walk? Did I bring this on myself?

The FBI is on the news, announcing that there's a reward of up to $10,000 for information about me—that makes me feel a little better. Maybe if somebody thinks there's money in it, they'll report something. I have to believe somebody saw me get in the van with him.

Help me, somebody, please.

4x.

May 3

The hours go so slowly, and I've told him how depressed I am. Today he brings me a coloring book and crossword puzzles, saying that they'll help pass the time. It's so dark, and I'm so hungry. A little after five, after I haven't eaten all day, he brings me Pringles and gross little frozen pizza rolls.

DJ was on the news. He tells a reporter I called him twice for a ride when I was leaving Burger King, but he doesn't say why he didn't answer. I guess he just didn't hear the phone. If he had picked up, I wouldn't be here.

The news report also says that the police think I was taken by somebody I knew. They think I got into a white car with some guys. Who told them that? It wasn't a white car!

He keeps coming in here. It never stops.

4x.

May 4

It's late, and I finally get to eat—a burger and fries from Wendy's. By now they're just cold grease, but I'm so hungry.

3x.

I realize that he thinks if he feeds me, or gives me anything at all that I want, even a sheet of paper, he's entitled to do whatever he wants with me. In his warped mind, he's providing for me, so my body belongs to him.

May 5

I'm watching *The Tonight Show with Jay Leno* when he comes hurrying upstairs and says his daughter Angie's going to the hospital because she has some problem with her teeth. He has to watch her son, and he says I have to help. He warns me to be quiet when she comes to drop the boy off, or else.

He's back in a few minutes with a cute little kid, maybe two or three years old. I pull the covers up over my chain, because I don't want to scare him.

"This is Angie's son," he says.

He doesn't say my name, and I know I'm not supposed to either.

I wish he were older, so that he might be able to tell someone I'm here.

He is crying hysterically. I wonder if he can tell how sad I am.

I try to coax him over to me, but he won't budge, and I can't go to him because of the chain. He picks up the boy to calm him, but the crying doesn't stop.

After a while he takes his grandson downstairs and a few hours later I hear Angie come back.

I am too scared to scream to her. I've seen how clever he is, and I'm sure he could explain it away, and then what would happen to me?

May 6

Another long day in the dark. I watch TV show after TV show, from *Days of Our Lives* to *Wheel of Fortune*. I miss talking to people. I'm going crazy alone in this room. My dinner is a Snickers and a Twix.

3x.

When he comes back into my room again, I'm praying to God that he doesn't want more.

"Here, you want to listen to your messages?" he says, holding out my phone.

"Yes!" I tell him. I hold the phone up to my ear and hear Beth, crying and telling me to please come home. Then I hear Mariyah's little voice saying, "Nandy, where are you? I love you and come home." My family calls me Mandy, but Mariyah says "Nandy."

There are messages from my cousin Crystal and my friend MJ, asking about my birthday party. Their voices shatter me.

"That's enough," he says, pulling the phone away, though I know there must be messages from my mom. He gives, he takes.

May 7

I just brushed my teeth for the first time in three days.

4x.

In my diary, I draw my heart with a dagger through it.

May 11

It's Mother's Day.

He brings me today's *Plain Dealer* and shows me an article about my mom that says she is so upset and worried that she hasn't eaten or slept since I disappeared.

"I don't know if she's out there being held, I don't know if she's out there laying on the side of the road somewhere," my mom told the columnist, Regina Brett.

The article says that when my nieces see my picture on TV, they always ask when I'm coming home, and my mom tells them, "She'll be home soon."

My mom says she is keeping everything in my room exactly how I left it, and as I read that the tears are rolling down my face.

It turns him on to see how much it hurts me to read the article.

4x.

May 13

5x.

May 15

I'm on the news every day now. That's a good thing. I know people are searching for me and I get to see my family on TV. Today the cops are saying they had dogs search DJ's car, and they found a spot of blood and a knife in his trunk.

He's watching the news with me, looking so proud, so happy. He loves that the police are focusing on the wrong guy.

May 16

He has been at his mother's house for dinner and he brings me leftover rice and beans that she made. He seems to go to her place a lot, which seems weird to me because he's always telling me how much he hates her. He calls her "whore" and "bitch" and says she beat him when he was little.

I don't know whether to believe what he says about how his mother treated him, because he lies so much. But I'm grateful to get her home-made meals instead of another cold fast-food burger. I just wish she knew her son was feeding me her leftovers.

May 21

I haven't gotten my period yet. I pray I'm not pregnant. What would I do? I can't imagine going through that here.

I've been here for a month. I can't sleep. I'm so lonely. I guess that girl is still in the other room, but I haven't seen or heard her since that day I cleaned her room. I have no one to talk to but him.

I feel dead inside. I miss the smell of fresh air. I miss being able to get a drink when I'm thirsty. I miss the feeling of rain on my face. Everything I used to think was a pain really wasn't. I even miss my mom hollering at me.

He hasn't attacked me for two days in a row. That's never happened before. Maybe things will get better.

May 30

I hear fireworks again. That means the Indians won another game tonight.

I see on the news that somebody donated money for a huge billboard with my picture on I-480, near West 130th Street. Thank God for whoever did that!

The Investigation: Searching for Amanda

Louwana knew her Mandy was never late. Never. So she and Beth were surprised she wasn't home when they got there. They checked the shower; it was dry. She always took a shower after work. There was no sign of her uniform, either, so she hadn't changed and left. They called her cell phone, but she didn't pick up.

That was worrisome—she was never out of touch.

Louwana and Beth started making calls to Amanda's friends to ask if anyone had seen her. Maybe she'd gone to see a friend after work? But no one knew anything, so they got into the car and began driving around the neighborhood. By now it was completely dark, and Louwana was becoming frantic, certain that something was wrong.

A little after nine she called 911. Police took the report but didn't seem concerned. They told Louwana to keep looking for her, that the girl hadn't been missing long and she'd surely come home soon.

By midnight, when there was still no sign of Amanda, Louwana called the police again, and this time two officers were dispatched and arrived in a patrol car just before one a.m. They took down Amanda's description—five-foot-one, 120 pounds, long, dark blond hair—and told Louwana not to worry, that teenage girls ran away all the time and almost always came back in a day or two. Amanda was probably just with her boyfriend somewhere.

Louwana Miller had a short fuse, and when something ticked her off her temper could be volcanic. "Kids don't run away in Burger King uniforms on their birthday and leave all their cash at home! Somebody must have taken her! Do something," she told the police in a loud voice salted with profanity. She told them Amanda was a good kid who would never stay out this late without calling, had never run away before and had no reason to now.

The officers stood in the living room making notes, but Louwana and Beth felt they weren't taking Amanda's case seriously. They clearly thought she was yet another runaway whose mother was overreacting and wasting their time.

The two women stayed up all night, calling every one of Amanda's friends they could think of and waiting for the phone to ring. In the morning they made flyers with her photo, a handwritten description of Amanda, and their home phone number. Louwana thought it was smarter to put her own number down rather than some police line, to make sure no tip was lost or ignored.

They drove around the neighborhood, taping the flyers on the door at Burger King, in the windows of shops in Westown Square, and on telephone poles.

Louwana's phone kept ringing, and people told her they were sure they had seen Amanda at someone's house, or in a store, or somewhere else. Louwana didn't drive, so she got Beth or her sister Theresa to take her to investigate every tip.

When she called television stations and pleaded with them to cover Amanda's disappearance, she was politely told that Amanda hadn't officially been designated as a missing person yet, and they couldn't run a story about every teenager who didn't come home for a day or two.

"Isn't anybody going to help us?" asked Louwana, who was getting angrier and angrier.

Louwana Miller grew up in the Tremont neighborhood of Cleveland, just over the highway from Seymour Avenue. She was part Cherokee, and her mother wanted her to have a Native American name, which she hated because no one ever pronounced it properly. Instead of "Lou-WANNA," people called her "Lou-Anna" or "Lou-Wanda" or Lou-something. And no one ever knew how to spell it.

Louwana left school by the seventh grade, and in 1976, when they were barely teenagers, she met Johnny Ray Berry, a skinny kid from rural Tennessee, with a wild side and a violent temper. He had moved to

Cleveland with his family from a farm in Elizabethton, not far from NASCAR's Bristol Motor Speedway.

Louwana got pregnant at sixteen and raised Beth with no help from Johnny Ray, who dropped out of school after the ninth grade and spent his nights drinking and partying. It was the same when Amanda arrived seven years later. By then Johnny Ray was working for Allied Van Lines, moving furniture. Louwana would make him coffee every morning, and as Amanda got older, he would sit and watch cartoons with her before he left for work.

There were good times during these years, but far more bad ones. Johnny Ray was in and out of jail, mainly for assaults and bar fights, and one of Amanda's earliest memories is visiting him at the old Ohio state prison at Mansfield. He often beat Louwana, usually when they were both drunk, Louwana on a twelve-pack of Busch and Johnny Ray on whiskey. The police were often at the front door, called to stop the domestic violence.

When Louwana was young, she had Amanda's thin face and high cheekbones. But by the time she was in her thirties, her face had become puffy and scarred from all the beatings, heavy drinking, and cigarettes. Because Johnny Ray drank most of his wages, she had to work one minimum-wage job after another, buying clothes at thrift shops and using layaway plans for Christmas gifts. While Johnny Ray celebrated Amanda's thirteenth birthday by bringing her a joint and getting her high, Louwana tried hard to steer her girls clear of the path she had taken. She made sure they had regular checkups with the doctor and dentist, focused them on homework, kept the house spotless, and always put a home-cooked meal on the table.

When Amanda was thirteen, she picked up the extension on the home phone and discovered that her father was having an affair. She told her mother, who informed Johnny Ray that she had had enough, and two weeks later he moved to Tennessee with his new girlfriend.

Things became more peaceful when Johnny Ray left. Amanda and her mother loved to watch Lifetime and cop shows, and never missed *America's Most Wanted*. But it wasn't always easy between them.

Amanda fought with her mother over the smallest things. Louwana would order her to turn down her music or go to bed, and Amanda would snap back and tell her to leave her alone. She called her mother stupid for having stayed with Johnny Ray for twenty-four years.

Determined not to repeat her mother's mistakes, Amanda focused hard on school and did well. By the third grade she was enrolled in Major Works, a gifted and talented program in the Cleveland Public Schools, in which she earned mainly A's and B's.

By the eleventh grade, many of Amanda's classmates had dropped out of John Marshall, a big, tough public high school near her house. Amanda eventually stopped going to classes too, sick of the drama and fights in the hallways. But she enrolled in a Cleveland Public Schools program that enabled students to study at home and send in work to be graded by teachers, paying $40 from each Burger King paycheck to cover it.

She earned a perfect 100 on her first test, in "Psychology for Life Today."

Nine days later, she was kidnapped.

When he arrived for work that morning, Detective Rich Russell was just sitting down at his desk when his secretary told him, "Hey, Rich, a Louwana Miller called checking on the status of her daughter Amanda, who went missing yesterday." Russell had been a police officer for sixteen years and he had handled hundreds of missing-child reports, and 99 percent of them turned out to be nothing—just kids spending the night with friends or off doing something they didn't want their parents to know about.

But this mother had called again, so as Russell settled into his chair, he picked up the patrol officers' notes about Amanda, which were on his desk in the routine report from the overnight shift. He looked to see if they had written "habitual" on the report, indicating that Amanda had run away before—but it wasn't there. She was a first-timer. He also saw that it was her birthday, and that she had left a hundred dollars in cash at home. None of that felt like a typical runaway case.

Russell and his partner, Detective Laura Parker, drove over to check in with Louwana. She greeted them with a blast of cigarette smoke and four-letter words, cursing the police for not caring about her daughter. But she softened a bit when the detectives seemed more concerned than the cops the night before had been, and asked questions about Amanda's friends, anybody she might be with, anybody who might have been angry enough to hurt her.

"DJ," Louwana said immediately. She didn't like Amanda's sixteen-year-old boyfriend, who never bothered to come in and say hello when he picked her up. She told the detectives that he had a bad attitude, that he sold weed, and that she didn't trust him.

Louwana had gone herself to DJ's house on West 99th Street that morning and nearly banged his front door off its hinges. DJ kept the door chained and, speaking to her only through the crack, told her he had no idea where Amanda was.

After leaving Louwana, Russell and Parker paid their own visit to DJ, who told them his phone battery had died, so he had missed Amanda's calls the night before. Though he seemed openly hostile to the cops, he let them check his bedroom. They found nothing, but the detectives agreed with Louwana that the kid seemed like trouble.

The police next interviewed Amanda's coworkers at Burger King, who mentioned a guy named Axel, a Hispanic customer in his mid-thirties who had a crush on Amanda and frequented the drive-through all the time to see her.

Almost immediately, the police had two promising suspects: Amanda's new boyfriend and a thirty-five-year-old guy who liked to hang around a sixteen-year-old girl.

On Thursday, three days after Amanda went missing, the police went to Axel's apartment, but the building owner said he had gone on a bus trip to a casino out of town. In the meantime, police interviewing people in Amanda's neighborhood got a lead from a man who had been waiting at an RTA city bus stop near Burger King on the day Amanda disappeared. He said he had seen her get into an old white car with two or three men.

A heroin addict, he was a dubious witness, but for the time being he was the only person claiming to have seen Amanda after she left work.

"White car" got the cops' attention. DJ drove a white car.

By Friday, as the "missing" posters multiplied along Lorain Avenue, the story hit the evening news, and tips started flowing in. Someone discovered a pair of sneakers in a Dumpster behind Westown Square. Somebody else found an apron they thought she might have worn at work. People reported sightings of Amanda at basketball courts, gas stations, convenience stores, and rest stops on the Ohio Turnpike.

Police looked into each tip, and none checked out.

They were nowhere.

Brian Heffernan, head of the First Division detective squad—Parker and Russell's boss—decided it was time to make DJ's life miserable.

Heffernan was the eldest of nine kids in an Irish-Catholic family, a soft-spoken tough guy. At six-foot-three, he was the 1978 Ohio state high school wrestling champion in the heavyweight division. As the father of three teenage daughters, Amanda's case felt personal to him, and his cop radar was pointing him straight at Amanda's smart-mouthed boyfriend.

DJ not only seemed to have a particular hatred of cops, but his story seemed inconsistent. He said he'd been with a friend fixing motorcycles on the evening Amanda disappeared and swore that she had called him at eleven that night. But when police had subpoenaed Amanda's phone records, they revealed that her last calls to DJ were placed before eight. Was he remembering wrong, or was he lying?

When Heffernan learned that DJ was driving without a valid license, he had patrol officers pull him over, tow his car, and get a warrant to search it. They had a cadaver dog sniff it, but it found no traces. They sprayed it with Luminol, a chemical that makes blood show up under black light, and discovered bloodstains in the trunk. But lab results revealed that it was chicken blood that had probably leaked from a bag of groceries.

They also found a receipt showing that DJ had washed his car the day after Amanda went missing. The car wash was near a big park with large wooded areas, so officers searched it with dogs. When nothing turned up, they got a court order to attach a tracking device to DJ's car to follow his movements and persuaded a friend of his to wear a hidden microphone.

"What do you think happened to your girlfriend?" the friend asked, with police listening.

"I don't know what happened to her, and I don't care," DJ said, launching into a profanity-laced tirade about the police.

DJ infuriated the frustrated cops, who finally brought him into the station and gave him a lie detector test, which he passed.

They had absolutely nothing on him.

On Monday night, Louwana and Beth were at home, crying as they watched a report about Amanda's disappearance on the eleven o'clock news.

Beth was growing worried about her mother. Louwana had never been a sound sleeper, but she had barely slept at all since Amanda had gone missing a week earlier. And while she had always been a heavy drinker, she was now drinking alarming amounts of beer.

Louwana taped a poster of Amanda over the living room fireplace, in the same place she used to hang her daughter's Christmas stocking, and put a pink butterfly on it as a symbol of freedom and hope. "We miss you, Mandy. We love you," she wrote on the poster. Every day, she kissed the photo good morning and good night.

Within minutes of Amanda's face appearing on the news, the phone rang. As Louwana rushed to answer it, Beth was picking up the extension in the dining room.

"I have Mandy," said a man's voice on the other end. "She wants to be here because we're married. But I'll have her back home in a couple of weeks."

"Please bring her home!" Louwana pleaded. "Drop her off at a store. Drop her at the corner. Anywhere! We don't care who you are, we just want Mandy home!"

The line went dead.

Louwana gasped and sat down. She and Beth were struck that he had called her "Mandy," because only family and her closest friends called her that. They thought he sounded like an older white man.

A minute later, the phone rang again.

"Don't worry," the same voice now said. "She's okay and she'll be home."

Louwana and Beth both begged: "Please bring her home!"

Without another word, he hung up.

They reported the calls to police, and a trace confirmed they had come from Amanda's phone. Louwana and Beth had new hope that Amanda was safe, but police viewed the calls as evidence proving only that Amanda had been abducted—not that she was still alive.

When Axel returned from his weekend at the casino, police searched his apartment, checked his phone records, and brought him in for a lie detector test, which was inconclusive. Though Axel had been coming to the Burger King regularly for months, after Amanda went missing her coworkers never saw him again.

Several callers told police they had seen Amanda working as a prostitute along Cleveland's infamous Broadway Avenue corridor, near Fleet Avenue. Parker and Russell showed Amanda's photo to some of the regulars there who said a blonde, who looked like her and called herself Amanda, had recently started walking their strip. So the two detectives began a stakeout, watching from their car and waiting for the young woman to appear. On the night of April 30, nine days after Amanda went missing, Parker was on her cell phone checking in with Louwana when the blond woman they were waiting for walked into view.

"I'll have to call you back," Parker told Louwana, and then called out to the young woman, "Girl, get your ass in the car."

But Parker quickly realized it was not Amanda. She had the worn-down look of someone much older.

"You look so much like Amanda Berry," Parker told her.

"Yeah, I know. That's what people keep saying to me," the woman said.

Parker called Louwana back and told her they were still looking.

When Heffernan heard that the young blond woman in the red-light district they had been tracking for days wasn't Amanda, he decided to bring in the FBI. It had been ten days since Amanda had disappeared, all leads were exhausted, and the police needed help. Police receive huge numbers of missing-children reports, most of which involve children who intentionally ran away or went somewhere without telling their parents. Police only call in the FBI when they suspect a child has been kidnapped. Heffernan called his friend Tim Kolonick in the FBI's big Cleveland field office on the shores of Lake Erie.

Kolonick had wanted to be a federal agent since the day in elementary school that he saw Secret Service agents guarding Rosalynn Carter on a visit to the west side of Cleveland. Tall, trim, and athletic, he rose quickly from Cleveland police officer to U.S. Secret Service agent to the FBI, where he worked on the violent crime task force.

As they drove up to Amanda's house, Heffernan and Kolonick saw yellow ribbons tied to the chain-link fence, and they found Louwana waiting for them in a white-hot rage. She demanded to know why they weren't working harder and why nobody had found her daughter.

She took them to Amanda's bedroom, where Kolonick marveled at the twenty-five pairs of jeans Amanda had hung neatly in her closet and the rows of perfectly lined-up shoes. Louwana went through the details yet again—the untouched money, the birthday plans, the strange call from a man who said Amanda was now his wife.

From everything Kolonick could see, he felt certain Amanda hadn't run away. He also knew that the longer she was missing, the less likely she would be found alive.

The FBI hoped the kidnapper's first mistake would be to turn on Amanda's phone again. It was 2003 and bureau engineers in Quantico, Virginia, had developed new cell phone–tracking equipment that could pinpoint a particular phone's location, as long as it was switched on, and so on May 8 an FBI engineer arrived at Cleveland Hopkins Airport with several large suitcases containing a mobile computer lab. Seventeen days had passed since Amanda's disappearance, and ten days since Louwana had received the call from her daughter's cell phone.

Amanda's phone records showed that her phone had been turned on repeatedly on the night she went missing and during the next day. Someone had been calling her voice mail and listening to the messages.

FBI agents determined that Amanda's phone had been somewhere near two cell towers on the west side of Cleveland when the call to Louwana was made. The caller might have been driving, because the signal seemed to bounce from one cell tower to the other. The towers were on either side of I-90, and they covered a radius of about forty square blocks. For all the bureau knew, the caller could have been racing along the highway when he made the call and he—and Amanda—could be in California by now.

Hoping they were still in the area, Kolonick packed into a grungy gray van with the Quantico engineer and several other FBI agents and looked for a place to park somewhere between the two cell towers. They pulled into the parking lot of the Family Dollar discount store at Clark Avenue and West 30th Street, where their banged-up vehicle was inconspicuous, and turned on their gear: a device consisting of a computer screen, keyboard, and antenna. If Amanda's phone was turned on for even a minute, they could pounce, along with an FBI SWAT team waiting in two Chevy Suburbans parked nearby.

Although Kolonick and his team didn't know it, they were parked only about a thousand feet from the house where Amanda was being held, and could have walked there in a matter of minutes. The FBI had never heard of Michelle Knight, and they didn't know that she was also being held in the same house. Nine months earlier, Castro had abducted her from the exact same Family Dollar lot where the FBI van was now parked.

The FBI agents continued their stakeout for eight days, changing shifts every twelve hours, but Amanda's phone never went on. They knew she had left her phone charger at home and reluctantly concluded that by now the battery had died and there was little chance of it being used again.

On May 16 they drove the engineer and his gear back to the airport.

Samantha Farnsley looked remarkably like Amanda: same age, same height, same build, even the same piercing over her left eye.

Everyone noticed the uncanny likeness. On city buses she would hear people whispering: "Is that Amanda Berry?" An FBI agent spotted her one day in a thrift shop and followed her around the aisles, then tailed her into the parking lot. When she confronted him, he asked her if she was Amanda Berry, and when she said she was not, he still demanded to see her ID. Police stopped her eight or nine times in the months after Amanda went missing, and the situation became so bad that the FBI finally gave her a letter to carry certifying that she was not Amanda.

Samantha ultimately left Cleveland, but not until after a sad encounter with Louwana. When police booked Samantha on a truancy charge one day, they asked Louwana to come to the station and take a look. When she arrived and saw the back of the girl's head and her long blond ponytail, she gasped. But then Samantha turned around and Louwana's face fell.

"No," she said. "That's not my child."

June 2003: First Summer

June 3

Amanda

I haven't eaten in two days. I guess he just forgot about me yesterday. I'm feeling weak.

I'm not sure why he won't spend much money on food for me, but he will buy me cigarettes and weed. Getting high dulls the pain of being here. If it weren't for the weed, I would have killed myself by now. Maybe he knows that, and that's why he gets it for me.

Before I was in here, pretty much everyone I knew smoked weed. It was just what teenagers in my neighborhood did. I liked to sit in my room, listen to music, and smoke a bowl once in a while. Now I'm smoking a lot and it takes me to a different place for a little while. But he doesn't give me anything for free.

1x.

When he finally gives me a Mr. Hero sandwich, I keep the napkin. It's very thin but has lots of white space where I can write. I'm keeping McDonald's and Wendy's bags too, because I can tear them open and write on the inside. The only paper I have is my diary, but that's filling up. So I keep every scrap of paper I can find in case I run out.

Writing things down makes me feel closer to my family.

"Are you still going to take me home at the end of June?" I ask him. "You said you would."

"I don't know," he says. "Maybe next year."

"You told me you were taking me home!" I tell him, crying. "I need to see my family!"

He complains that I'm always talking about my family like I'm the only one who is missing someone. "Soldiers don't see their families for years at a time," he says, "and they don't cry like babies about it."

I just saw a TV news story about a female soldier from Cleveland who is in Iraq and who won't be coming home before Christmas. I think about her on the other side of the world from her family and know it must be hard for her. But I also know she will make it.

Life is giving me a test. I have to pass. God wouldn't give me anything I can't handle. I can do this.

June 10

This morning Channel 19 has a story about a sixteen-year-old girl from Massachusetts, Molly Bish, who has been missing for three years. They found her body in the woods. I'm so sad and sorry for her and her family. What agony. I'm worried my mom is watching this too, scared that's how they're going to find me.

And now there's another story about five women, as young as fourteen, who were sex slaves for fifteen years. Why do so many men hurt women?

June 17

He hates the feeling of air blowing on him, so when he sleeps in my room he turns off my fan. Without it I feel like I'm suffocating. Even when he sleeps downstairs or stays out all night, he sometimes turns off my fan, though he knows I want it. He keeps it just out of my reach so he can control it.

He's back from work.

1x.

"Can you please turn the fan on?" I ask him.

"In a little while," he says.

"Why not? It's too hot."

"In a little while."

He's like a prison guard who loves taunting, punishing, and taking away privileges. I make loud groaning noises to annoy him until he finally gets up and turns on the fan.

He smacks my arm hard. "Don't be a baby!" he yells at me.

He is on me again. I don't want him to see me crying because I hate giving him the satisfaction of knowing he hurts me. But I can't help it, and my tears spill.

"You have been acting really strange lately, and you'd better stop," he says when he's done. "Stop crying so much. It's only going to make you look old. You're prettier when you laugh."

June 23

I saw Ricki Lake's show about sexual assault victims putting their lives back together. I hope when I get out of here that I am not scared of every man for the rest of my life. But I'm afraid I will be. I don't want to be paranoid. I want my life back the way it was. Can I bounce back from this? I'm fighting back thoughts of killing myself.

At some point this has to end, doesn't it? If I thought I was going to never get out of here before I died, what would be the point of even getting up in the morning? I have to believe that one day I will walk out that door, free, and it's going to be like coming back from the dead.

June 24

I wake up in the morning and I hear a girl's voice downstairs. Who is it? Another prisoner? Maybe one of his daughters?

I strain to hear over the radio, but I can't make out what they are saying.

Hours pass, and it's late afternoon when he unlocks my door.

1x.

"I had a girl here this morning," he says afterward. He keeps telling me that he's going to find somebody else to kidnap, and when he does he's going to let me go. I want to be at home more than anything, but I don't want somebody else to suffer through this.

"What happened to her?" I ask.

"You could have been going home tonight or tomorrow," he says. "But people saw me bringing her in, so I had to let her go."

He says he was driving by Meyer Pool, a public pool over by Lincoln-West High School. He went to that school, which is only a couple of blocks from here. He saw this young girl, maybe fourteen or fifteen, walking along and asked her if she wanted to get high.

She got in his car, and he brought her back here. He says that because he knew he couldn't keep her, they just smoked weed and had sex on some blankets on the living room floor. He claims she was into it. Maybe he's telling the truth. I don't think he would rape her and let her go, because she knows where he lives.

After they were done, he says he gave her a ride back to the pool. But he's mad at her because she stole his weed.

I can't believe he came that close to having another prisoner. And I can't believe there is a girl out there who came to this house and had sex with him willingly.

Girl, you don't know how lucky you are. You have no idea how close you were to being chained to a wall.

June 25

I hear him on the phone with one of his daughters. She needs a bathing suit, so he's going to bring her money to buy it. To everyone outside this house, he must seem like a nice, ordinary guy. He drives a school bus, talks to neighbors, works on cars in his backyard, buys presents for his daughters. I wish somebody would figure out what he's doing inside this house.

It must be nice to be able to go swimming in this ninety-degree heat. I can smell grilling outside, the smell of summer. I daydream of barbecued ribs. I'm always so hungry.

There's another story on the news about a soldier who won't be home until the holidays, and I take it as a sign: I've been here two months. I can do six if I really have to.

I check the calendar and start counting. It's 182 days until Christmas.

August 20, 2003: Strangle

Amanda

He wakes me up again. It's whatever he wants, whenever he wants it. Even after four months, it's still three or four times a day.

My strategy has become: Don't fight. Don't make him mad. Do whatever I have to do to stay alive and get home. But now he is making me lie on my stomach while he does that really nasty thing again. It hurts so bad. How would he like it if somebody stuck something into him that way? It's horrible and he won't stop. I can't help it, so I scream, "Let me go home or kill me!"

He stops, sits me up, and looks at me funny.

"Do you want to die?" he finally asks.

"No, but I don't want to be here!" It's hard to get the words out through the tears. "If I was dead, at least I could see my family from heaven."

He just looks at me for a while and then quietly says, "Okay."

He steps out into the hallway and returns with an old vacuum cleaner, like one from the '70s. He takes the cord and wraps it around my neck, and then starts tightening it. I feel it squeezing my throat, tighter and tighter.

I feel suddenly calm. I close my eyes. I am ready to die.

I pray silently: *Please, God, save me. I love you, Mom. I love you, Beth. I love my girls. I love you all so much.*

I feel a release. No more pain.

Then the cord suddenly goes loose, and he throws it on the floor.

"I'm not here to kill you!" he shouts. "I don't want to kill you! This is just about my sexual problem!"

He storms out of the room.

No matter what he says, I know he could kill me at any minute. His anger comes out of nowhere, like lightning. I never know what's going to set him off.

As I rub my throat and sit there thinking, I realize I have a mission, like the soldiers. This man enjoys hurting women, and I want people to know it. I don't want him to get away with it. I need to outlast him.

November 22, 2003: Numb

Amanda

I'm out of paper, so I start writing on the napkins he's brought from fast-food restaurants. I have to be very careful not to press down too hard with the pen, because they tear so easily. I take my time, because there is so much time.

I try to numb my mind with TV so I can forget that I'm shivering in this cold house: morning shows, soap operas, sitcoms, movies, Jay Leno, more movies, just filling time. The only thing I really care about is the news. Starting at five-thirty in the morning, if I'm awake, and I usually am, I flip through the channels, looking for anything about me. There's usually nothing, but every once in a while I see my family.

I listen to the radio late at night after all the local news shows are over. He gave me an old CD player and an Eminem CD and I listen to "Lose Yourself" over and over, trying to believe when he sings: *"You can do anything you set your mind to."* I've set my mind to getting to the next day. I go days without speaking.

Because the room is always dark, the light is no different at three in the morning than it is at three in the afternoon. He gave me cards and I play solitaire. I finished all the crossword puzzles in my book. I've colored every page of a coloring book he gave me. He brings me the newspaper sometimes and magazines that he must get for free because they are so boring and I've never heard of them.

Being alone is bad, but it is far worse when he comes in, and it always ends with me crying.

Today he wants to talk and is acting like he hasn't done anything wrong, like we are friends. I don't say a word to him and just keep staring at the TV.

January 2004: New Year

January 1

Amanda

"You're so pretty," he says as he starts pawing me again.

"Stand this way, stand that way, put your arms around me, you're so beautiful," blah, blah, blah. He has a whole little routine he makes me recite, about how much I love it, how much I want him. If I don't say it, he's rougher.

It's been almost nine months since he kidnapped me. He's always touching me like he owns me. He talks about the different parts of my body and says they're his, that they belong to him. He says we are "together." How can he think that if he has to lock me up to keep me here?

"You can't just take my whole life away," I tell him.

"What life?" he says, laughing. "Working at Burger King? That's not a life."

"What do you know about me? Nothing! You have no right to take my life away!"

He keeps touching me, and I feel like cutting off his hands, or something else. I hope I don't catch any diseases from him. I'm desperate to see a doctor when I get out of here.

He's raped me nine times in the past three days, but I've decided I'm not going to mark X's in my diary anymore. I want him to be held accountable someday, but when I look back at these X's, I remember every time all over again. It's more than I can bear right now.

January 9

I keep thinking about the day I was taken. This wouldn't have happened if I'd called in sick, or if I'd left work at the usual time, or if DJ had picked me up, or if I hadn't gotten into the van.

Could I actually have been able to avoid all this?

He sits on my bed. I shift a little and move the chain around so it hurts less around my waist. I hate talking to him, but the loneliness is brutal. I have to talk to somebody.

"When are you going to take me home?" I ask him. "I've been here long enough."

"You have to be patient," he says. "Maybe after three years you might get to be free."

Three years! That's forever. I can't take this for three years. I'll kill myself. I'm not going to believe him. I'm getting out of here sooner than that—I know it.

I have all my belongings lined up. My clothes, my diary, my pictures and videos. That's everything I have, and it all fits in a little box. If he said, "Okay, let's go," I could be ready in two minutes.

January 26, 2004: Cops at the Door

At around ten p.m. on Monday, January 26, 2004, two Cleveland police officers knocked on the front door of 2207 Seymour Avenue. They wanted to question the owner, Ariel Castro, because a mother had filed a complaint about how he had treated her four-year-old son on his school bus earlier that day.

That morning, Castro had punched in at 6:40 and drove his usual route, picking up sixty kids and dropping them off at two elementary schools. When he was done he volunteered for an extra midday shift and was assigned to pick up two children and deliver them to a two-hour program for children with ADHD at Wade Park Elementary School.

He picked up the children in a smaller bus and drove to Wade, where only one of them got off. The second, the four-year-old boy, was still on the bus when Castro drove to a Wendy's restaurant for lunch. The boy later told police that when Castro realized he was on the bus, he ordered him, "Lay down, bitch." It was a cold day, with heavy freezing rain and sleet, and the boy stayed in the bus alone while Castro went inside to eat.

Castro then drove to a parking lot and read the newspaper, and then went to a school building. Finally, after more than two hours, the child was taken to Wade Park Elementary, where a teacher told Castro that he should just drive him home, as school was over. Castro dropped him with a babysitter at his house, and the boy's mother called the police when she came home and heard her son's account.

When police did not find Castro at his home that evening, they got back in their patrol car and left, referring the case to detectives for follow-up.

Amanda was chained in a bedroom on the second floor, but she never heard anyone knocking. Castro, as usual, had left the radio blaring in the hall.

A month later, Castro was finally interviewed about the incident at the police station. He did not deny leaving the boy on the bus, but said it was an accident, an oversight. He said he only realized the boy was still there when he returned to the bus headquarters, and he insisted that he had never cursed at him.

He said he wasn't sure why he hadn't followed standard procedure and checked the bus at the end of his route.

"I was still mourning my father's death, and I wasn't quite right at that point in time," he told police, noting that his father had died two weeks earlier. "I am very sorry for forgetting the student on the bus."

Police referred the case to prosecutors, who declined to seek criminal charges.

The school system suspended Castro for sixty days without pay.

Part Two

Ariel Castro was born in the lush green hills of rural Puerto Rico, and his journey to Seymour Avenue began with his father, Pedro Castro, who arrived in Cleveland in the mid-1960s with big dreams and a chopped-off hand.

The elder Castro, known as Nona, joined the post–World War II flood of Puerto Ricans to the U.S. mainland. He came from Yauco, a town in the southwestern mountains, where coffee and bananas were plentiful but jobs and money were not. In the 1950s and '60s, Cleveland's steel mills, railroad yards, and manufacturing plants were drawing people from struggling Appalachian hamlets as well as eager immigrants from Ireland, Hungary, other European countries, and Puerto Rico.

Nona followed his brothers to Cleveland, where the Castro family was establishing itself as a well-regarded clan of small businessmen in the city's near west side, just across the Cuyahoga River from downtown. Nona's older brother, Julio Cesar "Cesi" Castro, had opened the Caribe Grocery, a bodega that sold Caribbean food and became a social and political hub for the growing Puerto Rican community. His brother Edwin started Isla Music, which featured Latin music and quickly became a local landmark. Another brother ran a hardware store.

Nona opened a used car lot on West 25th Street and was an unforgettable salesman, with a prosthetic left hand that he would put on and take off. He often told people that his hand had been mangled when someone accidentally slammed it in a car door. But the real story eventually made its way around Cleveland: He had lost the hand in Puerto Rico in a fight over a woman.

The man who had sliced off Castro's hand at the wrist, and left him with scars on his back and head, was named Jose "Pepe" Rodriguez, a neighbor of Castro's in La Parra, a tiny cluster of cinder-block houses on a narrow mountain road on the outskirts of Yauco.

A half century later, relatives of both men, who have since died, aren't certain of the exact cause of the machete fight, but they do remember that it had something to do with Nona's complicated relations with women.

Nona began his first family with Lillian Rodriguez in a one-story house on top of a hill in La Parra. Starting in 1958, they had three children in three years. The third, Ariel, was born on July 10, 1960.

About a year later, when Lillian was pregnant with their fourth child, Nona left her and the children and took up with another woman, Gladys Torres, who lived farther down the country lane. Both women were pregnant with Nona's children at the same time, in a village where just about everyone was related to one woman or the other.

It was around then that Nona lost his hand.

Monserrate Baez, Lillian's sister-in-law, recalled the sight of Nona driving his Jeep up the steep road with one hand, then stopping to fetch water from a communal well. He didn't let anything stop him from going about his business.

Aurea Rodriguez Torres, Pepe's niece, said that Nona and Pepe eventually became friendly again, though there were plenty of bad feelings in the village about Nona's having abandoned Lillian and their four kids.

Nona, like so many other men who had been working on farms, soon left for higher wages on the mainland. In Cleveland he quickly earned enough money to send for Gladys, who now had two children with him.

When Ariel was around four, Lillian also went north, moving to Reading, Pennsylvania, where some of her relatives had settled. She left Ariel and his siblings with her mother in Puerto Rico and got a job operating a sewing machine in a factory. She sent money and presents home and when Ariel was about six, she returned to Yauco, gathered her children, and brought them all to Reading.

But during the year or two that Ariel was living with his grandmother, he said something horrible happened.

* * *

When he was about five years old, he said he was sexually abused by a boy, about nine or ten years old, who lived nearby. He said the abuse continued for about a year, but he never reported it to anyone.

Castro would later give the same account to FBI agents and court-appointed psychiatrists examining him to determine if he was mentally competent to stand trial.

"It's known that people who are abused keep quiet, so I did," he told the psychiatrists.

Because the abuse is alleged to have taken place nearly fifty years ago, it is difficult to verify, but near the end of his life Castro talked about it frequently. Law enforcement officials believe Castro might have fabricated the story as a way to defend his own behavior, possibly in the hope that a judge would be more lenient with him.

Castro also repeated the allegations in a four-page handwritten letter that police found in his kitchen on the day after his arrest. In that document, he identified his alleged abuser by his first name and the first names of his parents.

In La Parra, relatives and friends recognized those names immediately. They said the alleged abuser, now about sixty, was a neighbor of Castro's when they were boys and he still lived in the area. When contacted by phone in the summer of 2014, the man was at first cordial and friendly, but when he heard the name "Ariel Castro," he became angry and hung up.

Castro was twelve, in the spring of 1973, when Lillian moved the family from Reading to Cleveland. She later told police that even though she and Nona had split up, she wanted the kids to be closer to their father.

Castro had virtually no relationship with his father as a young boy, and he often described his relationship with his mother as terrible. In the letter found by police, he complained of being "abandoned by my father and later my mother."

"My mother was an abusive parent," he wrote. "Her ways of discipline were very bad. For this made me grow hatred for her. There were times I wished she would die."

He told the court psychiatrists that his mother constantly hit him with "belts, sticks, and an open hand," sometimes causing bruises. He said she was always "yelling negative things and cursing at us," and "I would ask God for her to die."

But in one of the many contradictory statements he made, Castro also told the psychiatrists that his mother had done "a good job" raising him. In fact, as an adult, he spent a great deal of time with her. She lived only a few blocks from Seymour Avenue, and he would visit her often, helping her with chores and eating dinner with her. When police reviewed his cell phone records after his arrest, it included a long list of calls to her.

Lillian Rodriguez, a small woman with white hair, visited him frequently when he was in jail awaiting sentencing. She has stayed largely out of the public eye since his death.

In Cleveland, Ariel Castro attended Lincoln Junior High, where, he later told law enforcement officials, he was suspended for "touching a girl's breast."

When police interviewing him after his arrest asked him if he had ever sexually abused anyone other than his three captives, Castro said: "I had a girlfriend in junior high school. She would let me go under her shirt. I wanted to go farther, and she would say no. I tried to force her. I guess that was an early indication that I wanted to be in control."

During his years at Lincoln-West High School, he played bass guitar in the school band and worked part-time at a Pick n Pay grocery store on West 65th Street. He was a shy teenager with acne, the Puerto Rican kid who worked produce and didn't have that much to do with his coworkers, many of whom were Irish American or Italian American. Sometimes, though, Castro would be seen in the parking lot with them, drinking beer and smoking dope after work.

From a young age, he was openly prejudiced against African Americans and called them "niggers" or other slurs. When Castro was playing with a BB gun one day and shot a black kid from the neighborhood in the hand, nobody believed it was an accident.

Castro stayed in school at a time when many others were dropping out, graduating in 1979. A year later, when he was twenty, he met the woman who would in many ways become his first prisoner.

Ariel Castro noticed immediately when a pretty, dark-haired girl moved in across the street from his house on Buhrer Avenue, a few blocks from Seymour.

Grimilda Figueroa, a petite seventeen-year-old also from Yauco, hated her first name and told everyone to call her Nilda.

Their courtship was quick. One summer evening not long after they met, Castro took her on a date, and they spent hours parked on the shores of Lake Erie. When they returned home very late, Nilda's mother was furious that her daughter had spent all that time alone with a man. She told Castro that he was now responsible for Nilda: "Now you have to take her with you."

Nilda moved across the street to Castro's house. They didn't marry but considered themselves common-law spouses. After one miscarriage, their son, Ariel Anthony Castro, was born in 1981, when Nilda was just eighteen.

At first Nilda's younger sister Elida and the rest of her family thought Castro was fun, a talented bass guitar player who didn't drink too much and smoked weed only now and then. He owned a car and took Nilda's younger siblings on adventures. He got them a free McDonald's cheeseburger by bringing his half-eaten one back to the counter and lying about finding a hair in it. He kept that burger, too, saying he might as well give it to his dog.

But sometimes he also frightened the neighborhood kids, especially with an unnerving mannequin, a female torso with dark hair, that he had bought at a yard sale. He used to startle people by propping it up in the passenger seat of his car when he was driving around.

Castro also quickly became possessive about Nilda, ordering her to wear long skirts and forbidding her from wearing V-necks or anything even slightly revealing. If she wanted to dress in something that he thought was too provocative, he threatened her, saying, "You better not." Eventually he began buying all her clothes at thrift stores. He told her that her place was at home and hated when she went outside without him, even if just to go shopping.

"I can't believe this," she told her sister Elida. "I'm not doing anything wrong."

Castro worked in a series of low-paying jobs, first as a machinist at Les-Ner Products Co., a company that made tips for car antennas, then at a plastics company and a used-car dealership. In the evenings he played in several bands.

"Where were you?" Nilda asked him one night when he came home especially late. "Why do you always leave me here alone with the baby?"

"Don't worry about what I do. I do what I want," he told her and then slapped her hard across the face.

Not long afterward Elida came to visit her sister and was shocked to find Castro shoving her into a cardboard washing machine box, closing the flaps, and yelling: "You're not getting out of here until I tell you to get out!"

Elida, who was only twelve, was terrified and ran to get her mother from their apartment downstairs.

"What is going on here?" the mother demanded.

"Ah, nothing," Castro said, letting Nilda out. "We were just playing."

Everyone was growing concerned about Castro's increasingly violent behavior, but no one knew what to do. After their second child, Angie, arrived in 1983, and they were living on the top floor of a duplex on Riverside Avenue, he would lock the deadbolt from the outside and take the key so Nilda couldn't leave, telling her he was just trying to keep her safe.

"I feel like a prisoner," Nilda told Elida.

Even Elida could no longer freely visit, because she couldn't get past the bolted door. Castro didn't like Nilda visiting family or friends, or going anywhere, unless he accompanied her. One day in 1985, when Castro had left the door unlocked, Nilda walked to the grocery store.

When she returned, she was climbing the steep, wooden stairs to the second-floor apartment, carrying full bags in her arms, and Castro leaped out and shoved his mannequin toward her.

Nilda was so shocked that she fell backward down the stairs, smashing her skull when she landed at the bottom. She was rushed to the hospital and had emergency surgery. Nilda told her sister that Castro intentionally caused her fall because he was angry that she left the house alone.

Nilda confided in Elida that she wanted to leave Castro, but didn't see how she could. No one in her family had the means to support her and her children. Castro had threatened to harm her if she ever tried to take the kids away from him, and she wouldn't leave them alone with him. She had no job, no income, and nowhere to go.

The abusive behavior only became worse. Castro made wild accusations about Nilda having affairs. He hit her whenever she said or did something he didn't like. One day, in a rage, he broke her arm and her ribs, and punched her so hard that he broke her teeth, sending her to the hospital and requiring dental surgery.

After that beating, Nilda's family had had enough. Her father, brothers, and a few friends grabbed Castro in his yard, pummeled him, and warned him they'd kill him if he ever touched her again. Castro just smiled, never apologized, and left them with the impression that he was going to get even. When Nilda's father's garage later burned down, they suspected Castro.

On the evening of September 30, 1989, one of Castro's brothers came to the house to pick him up, and Nilda asked where they were going. "Don't worry about what I do. I do what I want," he yelled at her, furious that she had questioned him. He then slapped her and slammed her several times against a wall and the washing machine. Nilda ran to a neighbor's house and called the police. She told the officers who arrived that she had been assaulted by Castro several times before, and they advised her to file a formal complaint with the county prosecutor's office.

Nilda later told her sister that Castro threatened to kill her or take her kids if she pursued any charges against him, and he promised he wouldn't hurt her again. She didn't file a complaint.

There were good times between his violent rages. In February 1991, Castro was hired as a bus driver for the Cleveland Metropolitan School District. Angie Castro, who was then seven, recalled that her father was so proud on the day he got his bus driver's certificate that the family, now with four kids, had a big celebration.

In April 1992, Castro bought the house at 2207 Seymour Avenue for $12,000 from his uncle, Edwin Castro, and the family moved into the little two-story home.

Castro treated Angie and his other two daughters well, and Angie said it was fun when he would take the kids for rides in his school bus. When he was in a good mood he could be a good father. But on his worst days he continued to beat Nilda, and he began smacking around his son, Ariel Anthony, who was just ten. Nilda cried when she told her sister that he was forcing her to have sex when she didn't want to, and when the children could hear them.

Castro started nailing the windows shut, saying it wasn't a safe neighborhood. He would often act as if he were leaving, but then sneak back into the house and listen to Nilda's phone calls from an extension in the basement.

"What's that noise?" Elida asked Nilda one day when they were on the phone.

"Oh, I think that's Ariel listening on the other line."

Nilda told her sister that she wanted to take her kids and go far away, but she was afraid of what Castro might do.

"If you ever take my kids, I will kill you," he told her.

Nilda never felt well again after crashing down the stairs and suffered from chronic headaches and blood clots. In late 1993, eight years after the fall, doctors at the Cleveland Clinic discovered a tumor and operated to remove it. It was a meningioma, a type of tumor that is sometimes linked to injury or trauma to the brain, and the prognosis was not good.

"Ariel did this to me," she told Elida.

On the day after Christmas in 1993, about a month after Nilda's surgery, Castro got drunk and started hitting her, then left the house. She called 911 and told officers that Castro had beaten her, even though she had recently had brain surgery and was very weak.

While the police were searching the neighborhood for him, Castro returned to the house, banging on the door and screaming at Nilda to let him in. Angie, then ten, was upset that her father was outside in the cold and didn't realize he had just beaten her mother. She stood next to the Christmas tree in the living room and screamed: "Let Daddy in! Let Daddy in!"

Nilda relented, and when she unlocked the door he began beating her again. As the terrified children watched, she fell to the floor and he began to stomp on her head with his boot. When Castro realized that his son was running to call the police, he chased after him out the front door. Police officers saw Castro running away from the house, captured him, and took him to jail. Nilda, pushed past her limit, went to the police station the following day and gave a more detailed, formal statement. The case was referred to the county prosecutor, who decided there was enough evidence of domestic violence to present it to a grand jury.

A felony conviction could have put Castro behind bars, but on February 9, 1994, a grand jury declined to indict him. Because Nilda refused to testify, there was insufficient evidence. Castro had been staking out the entrance to the Justice Center courthouse and stopped her just before she entered to testify, offering her money and a car if she remained silent. He also threatened her, called her a bitch, and warned her: "You know what will happen to you if you do."

Nilda called her sister and said Castro threatened to kill her and their kids if she testified before the grand jury. Convinced that he was capable of fulfilling his threat, Nilda turned around and walked away from the courthouse.

Fernando Colon first saw Nilda Figueroa in the summer of 1995 in the emergency room of Grace Hospital near downtown Cleveland. She was bleeding, had a broken nose, a missing tooth, and bruises on her face.

Colon, a security guard at the hospital, had encountered her there several times with similar injuries and knew that she was being beaten. Recently divorced, he had just moved from New York to Cleveland, where he was hoping to start over. He wanted to be a police officer.

Hospital staff were suspicious about Nilda's injuries, but she insisted that she had fallen down the stairs, or made up some other story. She confided in Colon that the beatings would only get worse if she told doctors the truth.

When Nilda returned for a follow-up visit, Colon found her sitting on a chair in the hallway, looking frightened.

"You all right?" he asked her.

"Yeah, well," she replied, "for the moment I'm okay."

"Do you want to talk?"

Nilda then began recounting her years of abuse at Castro's hands, including the times he beat her with barbells. She was in constant pain, suffering from seizures, and was losing vision in her left eye.

Colon and Nilda stayed in touch, and during one of her hospital appointments he said to her, "If I help, will you leave? You can't go through this no more. That dude's going to kill you."

When Nilda said she wanted help but was afraid of Castro, he told her, "Don't worry about him. Let me worry about him."

Nilda started making plans to leave Castro, and one day in early 1996, nearly sixteen years after she moved in with him, Colon drove over and took her away from Seymour Avenue when Castro was not home. She packed three of her kids and some belongings in his car, and he brought her to her mother's house. Angie, who was twelve, insisted on staying with her father.

When he discovered what had happened, Castro tracked Colon down by phone and yelled: "You have my wife!"

"You're abusing this woman," Colon shot back. "I got copies of the medical records from the hospital. If you want trouble, I'm going to give you trouble. So you either back off or you're going to end up in jail."

Nilda and the children eventually moved in with Colon, and one day Castro followed one of his daughters home to see where Nilda was living.

"What you did was wrong," he screamed at Colon.

"No, what I did was right, 'cause you was gonna kill that woman."

"I'm not like that," Castro said.

In March 1996, Nilda filed a Juvenile Court petition seeking full custody of all their children. She told the court that Angie was living with her father and being "improperly cared for" and that she feared for her safety because of Castro's "record for long-term spousal abuse."

Nilda said that Castro had been "able to remove my children from school because of his position as a Cleveland Public School bus driver." At times she had gone to the bus stop to pick up her children after school only to find that Castro had already taken them.

The case dragged on for months, but in January 1997, Nilda was awarded sole custody of all four children, including Angie, who came to live with her.

For Lillian Roldan, it was love at first sight.

She met Ariel Castro in 2000, at a friend's house. He was sitting in the living room, playing his bass, well dressed and attractive.

Castro was forty, almost twice her age. He lived alone, had been separated from his ex for four years, and though the oldest of his kids was almost Lillian's age, she found him charming and funny, and they began going out almost immediately. She went to his gigs and brought him to her parents' house, and he charmed them, too.

She would occasionally spend the night at Castro's house on Seymour Avenue. They slept in the master bedroom upstairs, and the house seemed completely normal to Lillian, apart from the fact that he kept the basement door locked with a padlock. When she asked about it, he explained that he kept his cash in the cellar, so he wanted to make certain it was secure.

The relationship went well until one day in late 2002, when Lillian received a letter from Castro in which he said he loved her, but not enough to keep the relationship going. He told her to call him if she ever needed help, but that they were no longer a couple.

Castro later told police that he broke it off with Lillian several months after he kidnapped Michelle Knight in August 2002, explaining that he "couldn't juggle both of them." On the day he abducted Michelle, he chained her in the basement and then left to spend the night with Lillian at her home. He tried to find excuses to keep Lillian out of the Seymour house, but it was getting more and more difficult. One day when they were standing in the driveway, she noticed a TV on upstairs, and she asked why, since there was no one in the house.

"It was a close call," Castro later admitted to police. "My heart started beating."

When Lillian's mother died in Puerto Rico a few months later and she didn't have enough cash to fly there to take care of the arrangements, she went to Castro's house to borrow money. He made her wait in the driveway while he went inside and got her a thousand dollars.

By then Amanda Berry was also locked in Castro's house.

Lillian later repaid him, but never saw him again.

April 2, 2004: Family Friend

Gina

It's six thirty on a drizzly Friday morning. Time to get up.

My mom is drinking coffee downstairs at the dining-room table, and my two little nieces are up already, too. I open the cabinet, find the Pop-Tarts, and drop two in the toaster.

"We gotta go! Let's go," says my dad as the girls run all over the kitchen, giggling. Though it's still dark outside, the house is already noisy. It's always like that. Seven people live here: my parents, Nancy Ruiz and Felix DeJesus; my brother, Ricky; my sister, Mayra; her two daughters, Tatiana and Nancy; and me. It's a small home, and we all share one bathroom. My dad talks about building an addition, but it never seems to happen, because there's never enough money.

My mom stays home and takes care of all of us, and my dad works in a factory that makes blades for industrial saws. They're both from Puerto Rico and have huge families. We have big reunions with tons of relatives and close friends we call cousins but who are not actually related. On holidays it feels like our front door never stops opening.

Sometimes it's actually a little too crazy for me. I'm only fourteen and shyer than everybody else in the family. When we have big parties, I take the little kids upstairs away from the music and noise. We play games and laugh, and that's just fine by me. Everybody's always hugging, and I don't like being touched. I don't even like making eye contact with strangers. My mom's always trying to get me to look people in the eye. I know she's right, but it makes me uncomfortable. I love all the fun we have in our busy house, but I also love peace. I like things quiet.

It's getting late, so I hurry. I grab a few bites of a Pop-Tart and tell the girls they can eat the rest.

When it's cold outside, my dad and I have a morning routine: He goes out first and gets the car warm for me. We have an old white Nissan Sentra that my dad bought for $500 from my friend Arlene's dad, Ariel Castro. It's kind of junky, but at least we have a car. A lot of people in my neighborhood can't even afford one. And our car's heater works really well.

"Bye, Mom! Love you!" I yell as I grab my blue coat with white fur lining. "See ya later!"

"Bye, Gina. Love you," she says. "See you after school!"

We live on West 71st Street, two blocks from the railroad tracks. The trains race through our neighborhood in the middle of the night and are really loud, especially when they blow their horns. Lots of people cut across the tracks to get to Kmart and Big Lots on West 65th Street, but my mom never lets me do that. A few homeless people sleep by the tracks, and people sell drugs there. There's an empty warehouse on our street, and a couple of abandoned factories near the tracks.

My mom says this neighborhood isn't safe, so she lets me play in our front yard, but that's it. One day the cops were chasing a guy, and he threw baggies filled with dope into our bushes, then came back later to get them. After that my dad cut down all our bushes. Another time a lady right down the street got mugged in her own garage, so now she has a huge fence and padlocks everywhere. Mom says it looks like Fort Knox.

This is a neighborhood where families live for a while, then move farther west toward the suburbs when they get some money. Four years ago we moved out of an apartment over on Scranton Road and bought this house so we could have more space. I don't know how long we'll stay. I think my mom would leave now if we could.

As my dad and I drive away from my house, I turn the radio to 96.5 KISS FM and listen until they have a commercial, then switch to a different station. Dad says he is amazed at all the lyrics I know. It doesn't matter who comes on—Christina Aguilera, Gwen Stefani, Alicia Keys, Usher, Kanye West—I sing along with the radio the whole way to school, and my dad smiles.

He and Mom were understanding last week when I lost my glasses. I dropped them in the street and they were run over by a car. They were new prescription ones with gold wire rims. I need them because my left eye is weaker than my right, so I have an appointment in two weeks to get another pair.

My dad is quiet like me. We love to go out in the backyard at night, just the two of us, and stare up at the stars. He came to Cleveland from Puerto Rico when he was twelve, dropped out of high school, and started working in factories. When he was twenty-one he met my mom at a bar, and then they went to a party where a couple got into such a big fight that she started throwing all his clothes out the window. My dad couldn't stop laughing, and my mom fell for him right then.

He played softball and football with the guys from the neighborhood, but he also hung out with a tough crowd that got him into trouble with the cops. But that was before I was born. Now he is always telling me to be careful about who my friends are. I'm his baby, and he's my big teddy bear.

My mom was born in Cleveland in 1960, but when she was nine she moved with my grandparents back to Yauco, a coffee-growing town in Puerto Rico where many people in Cleveland had come from. Life was simple and healthy there. The family would "eat off the trees," with oranges and avocados and other fruits and vegetables they grew on their own land. They caught their own fish and walked everywhere. Mom lived there until she was seventeen, when my grandpa Benny moved the family back to Cleveland. She cried for days because she couldn't get used to it. She weighed a hundred fifteen pounds when she got here, then gained sixty pounds in a year. In Yauco, breakfast would be coffee with a little goat's milk and crackers— maybe toast once in a while. But in Cleveland, the kitchen was filled with gallons of milk, cereal, bread, and cans of spaghetti, and Mom ate like crazy.

Mom dropped out of high school on the day she turned eighteen and started working as a breakfast waitress at a pool hall called La Cue, which was owned by Cesi Castro, the great-uncle of my friend Arlene. It was at the corner of Seymour Avenue and West 25th Street, which was the heart of the Puerto Rican community back in those days. When they were dating, Mom and Dad met at the Seymour Café, right there on the same corner, which is maybe a mile from where we live.

Dad is hurrying down Lorain Avenue this morning because he has to be at work by seven thirty, the same time the doors open at Wilbur Wright Middle School. So again today I'm one of the first seventh-graders here, and I wait in the cold with a few other kids until they let us inside.

I've been in special-ed classes since a teacher in the first grade said I was a slow learner. That's why I go to Wilbur Wright, which is kind of far from my house. It's a huge school with all kinds of classes. I used to go to a different school, but they had one of those little buses to pick me up, and I would get teased about it. Everybody knew those "short buses" were for kids going to special classes. I hated when neighborhood kids made fun of me. They called me "slow," which really hurt. There's no way I'm going to take a school bus again, so my dad drives me in the morning, and I take the city bus or walk home. That makes my mom nervous, and she tells me to always try to walk with other kids who are going my way.

A few days ago I got great news. My teacher told me I was doing really well. Last quarter I had an A in science, a B in math, and C's in English and reading. Social studies was still a D, but it was a pretty good quarter. If I kept this up, my teacher said, I could move into regular classes, maybe even this year. She said that if I worked hard, there was no reason I couldn't go to college someday. College! My mom would be so proud. She and my dad didn't finish high school, and she's always telling me how important school is. So if I could get my high school diploma and then go to college, she would be crazy happy. Maybe I could go to Florida State University. My grandpa Benny—my mom's dad—lives in Florida, and I might be able to live with him. I would love to make my parents so proud and be the first person in our family to go to college. That would surprise everyone!

School today is the same old stuff: science, reading, math, social studies. Nothing special at lunch, just pizza and chocolate milk. I'm extra hungry, so I buy potato chips with some of the $1.50 in bus money my mom gave me. That means I won't have enough left for the bus later, so I guess I'm walking home. It's about two miles, but I don't mind.

At 2:30 the bell rings, and I climb the stairs to my locker on the third floor, talking with my friends Beverly, Marilyn, Anela, and Juan. It wasn't a bad day, but I'm a tiny bit bummed because I lost my lip gloss. My gym teacher made me hand it over last week because students aren't supposed to carry anything into the gym, and today when I remembered to pick it up, he said he couldn't find it. He says I should have come back sooner. Oh, well.

I'm laughing with my friends as I head out of school for the week-end. At the front door, I run into my friend Arlene Castro, who's in the same grade as me. I really like Arlene.

"Hey, let's go skating!" I say to her. "It's Friday!"

I like ice skating and I try to imagine myself as an Olympic skater on TV. Once when I was watching them, I pretended to do a triple axel in my kitchen and fell and split my chin open. My poor mom freaked out, and I still have the scar.

But I love roller skating even more. I spend every weekend at Cleveland's big roller rinks, gliding along the polished floors, skating to the music. I'd go every day if I could.

Arlene and I skate a lot, and I'm excited that maybe we can go tonight. But as we start walking together the four blocks down West 110th Street to Lorain Avenue, the main street with lots of restaurants and shops, I remember: I'm grounded. Three weeks ago my parents caught me smoking cigarettes in my room. I haven't been allowed out with friends since.

"But wait," I tell Arlene. "I think I can still have people over. Can you come to my house?"

"I think so. Let me call my mom."

We walk to the pay phone on Lorain at West 105th Street. A couple of kids at school have cell phones, but not too many. And we sure don't.

I give her two quarters from my bus money, and Arlene dials. I can tell by her face what the answer is.

"She says I gotta go home."

"Okay," I tell her. "I'll see you. Call me later."

We give each other a quick hug, and I start walking home. I'd better hurry. It's still drizzly, and it's about a forty-minute walk. If I'm late, my mom will worry.

I have walked only a block when a guy in a Jeep Grand Cherokee pulls up and rolls down the passenger window. I can't quite hear him, but he's talking to me.

I know him. He's Arlene's dad. He drives a school bus. My parents and I were hanging out with him a few months ago at the Christmas choir concert, where Arlene and I were both singing.

"Hey, have you seen Arlene?" he asks.

"Yeah," I say, pointing behind him. "She just went that way."

"Can you help me find her?"

I tell him she just left a second ago, so she can't be far.

"Okay," he says, "but can you help me?"

He really wants me to help. I don't know why. But okay.

I get in the Jeep and tell him to turn the car around. But he starts driving straight, in the wrong direction.

"Aren't you supposed to turn here?" I ask him.

"I need to go to my house for a minute to get some money," he says.

This is a little weird, but I tell myself to chill. My parents know him. He's Arlene's dad. If he needs to get money at home, what's the big deal?

He's talking a lot as he drives, mostly about Arlene and his other kids. We turn onto Seymour Avenue, the same street my aunt lives on just a couple of blocks down. She has great parties in the summer. Lots of people from Puerto Rico live in this neighborhood, and we have some friends who live around here.

He pulls into the driveway and stops behind the house.

"I'm going to get my money—I'll be right back," he says.

His front yard is neat, but as I wait in the car I see that the backyard is messy and filled with cars and motorcycles. The trash cans are overflowing with plastic garbage bags.

He's back in a minute and says, "I have a speaker I want to put in the car. Can you help me move it?"

"Okay," I reply. Why not? I walk over to the back door and step inside.

The door leads to a small room, then his kitchen. It's nasty, with cobwebs on the ceiling and grease stains on the walls.

"Sit there for a minute," he says, pointing at the kitchen table. "Take your coat off and get comfortable."

It's one of those fold-up tables, the kind you put up at a backyard party. One leg is busted, so he has propped it up against the wall. I sit on a folding chair with a pink cushion.

He's in the bathroom now, which is right off the kitchen. The door's open, and I can see him looking at himself in the mirror, trimming his eyebrows and fussing with himself like ladies do. Weird!

"You have to take me home now," I say loudly. "My mom is waiting for me."

He walks right up to me, so close. He tries to touch my breasts, and I freak out.

"What are you doing? Don't! I want to get out of here!" This is crazy!

"Okay," he tells me, like everything is normal, "but you can't go out the same way you came in."

He's leading me toward a door and says that we have to go downstairs to get back outside. I can't believe what's happening. As soon as we walk down a few steps I realize it's a mistake. The next thing I know I'm on my back on the cold concrete floor, and he's on top of me.

"Get off me! Get away from me!" I scream.

He puts a pillow over my head and yells, "Shut up!"

I keep screaming into the pillow. It's dirty and smelly.

There's a pipe on the floor beside us and he picks it up.

"Shut up or I'll hurt you with this!"

He's sitting on me. I'm kicking as hard as I can.

"Are you done?" he yells.

I keep kicking. I'm pretty strong, but I can't get free. He's so heavy and I'm so little. I give him one good kick, which makes him mad.

"Are you done?" he asks again, and when I still keep kicking, he says, "I'm going to chain you."

Chain me? What?

I have to think of something—do something—to get out of here.

Maybe if I pretend not to resist, I can trick him. So I stop kicking, hold out my arms flat on the floor, and say, "Go ahead; chain me."

He slides off me to get the chain, and I jump up and run. I don't even make it to the first step before he grabs me. As I try to get away I pull some boxes of junk down, and they crash all over the place.

"You should not have done that!" he shouts.

He pulls me back over to the pole and puts a chain around my neck, tight. Then he puts another one around my stomach. They hurt. The chains look brand-new.

He pushes me down. I'm sitting in front of the pole, chained to it. He pulls my hands behind my back, behind the pole, and ties them together.

"It's plastic rope," he says. "Don't move, or it will cut you."

He picks up a filthy gray rag from the floor, winds a piece of rope around it, and pushes it into my mouth, smashing my teeth against my lower lip until it's bleeding. Then he puts duct tape over my mouth. I'm trying to scream but I can't. It's hard to breathe. All I can do is cry.

"How am I supposed to take you home if your eyes are bloodshot?" he asks.

I'm so scared. I need to stop crying.

He pulls his pants down and starts rubbing himself. He is only inches away from me, and I try to turn my head and look away, but it's hard because of how tightly he has my neck chained. I'm so scared he's going to rape me. I'm praying over and over in my head: *Please, God, please don't let him do this to me.*

Then, when he's done, he pulls up his pants and without saying a word walks upstairs.

My head is pounding, and I can't concentrate on anything. I'm trying to think of ways to escape, but my mind is blank. I want my mom. I wish my dad would come save me. I just want to be home. I think he's going to kill me, and I can't stop crying.

It's terrifying down here, so much stuff and tons of empty bottles of laundry detergent and empty giant-size pop bottles. What is he keeping them for? He's got boxes filled with magazines—I can see a bunch of pornos. What is this place? Has he brought other girls down here?

In a few minutes he comes back down with a radio. My whole body freezes up when I see him. I look down at the ground.

He doesn't say anything but just plugs in the radio, starts blasting it, and leaves. My mouth aches from the rag and rope. My lips are still bleeding, and I can't move my tongue. The chains around my neck and stomach are so tight that it's hard to breathe. I didn't know I could cry this much.

It's completely dark and freezing. I wish I hadn't listened to him and taken my coat off. I'm so scared. I'm praying to God. I need Him now. Don't let this man kill me.

It must be morning, because a little sunlight comes in when he opens the door to the basement. He brings a little black-and-white TV and turns it up loud and then turns the radio up even louder.

He rips the duct tape off my face and yanks the rag out of my mouth, making me scream because it hurts so bad when the tape pulls at my face and hair.

"If you scream any more, this will go right back in your mouth," he warns me. "I'm going to put it here to remind you." He drops the rag on top of a pile of clothes, right where I can see it.

After all the screaming I did yesterday, I know nobody can hear me. What's wrong with the neighbors around here? I don't know what he wants with me, but he knows I can tell my parents who he is, so there's no way he'll let me go.

I'm shaking, but I stay quiet. The last thing I want to do is make him mad.

He takes the chain off my neck, and I can breathe better.

"Don't scream. Nobody will hear you."

He grabs my breasts and squeezes them. I worry that he is going to do more disgusting things, but then he just stops, turns off the overhead lightbulb, and leaves. I'm alone again, and it's dark except for the TV. It's on WB 55, all sitcoms, and I can't reach it to change channels. It's hard to follow anything on TV because of the blaring radio. It's like having two people screaming in my face about completely different things. My skull aches.

I have to go to the bathroom. The concrete floor is so cold.

Why is Arlene's dad doing this to me?

I wonder if he was planning this. I've seen him so many times in my neighborhood in the past year. He'd be sitting in his school bus, parked on Dearborn Avenue, right around the corner from my house, and would wave at me. Other times he would drive by me slowly, smiling and waving. I always waved back. I figured my neighborhood must have been on his bus route. Now I bet he was stalking me.

I've been here hours, and suddenly I hear his heavy black work boots on the wooden stairs.

Is this it? I start shaking.

"I brought you some food," he says, handing me a plate of rice and beans. "My mom made this—it's good."

I'm so hungry, but I won't touch it.

"I'm only eating *my* mom's cooking. I want to go home!"

My mom's food is famous. Before the holidays she spends days cooking and baking. She makes chicken and pork and Puerto Rican specialties, like *arroz con gandules*—rice and pigeon peas. I try to imagine the salty taste and rich smell of my mom's hot food, right off the stove.

I wish I could do a drive-by! That's what we call it when somebody has to work on a holiday and can't come for dinner at our house. They call ahead, pull up outside, honk the horn, and Mom runs out with a plate of whatever she made that day. It's making me sadder to think about home, and I can't stop crying.

"Okay, I don't care if you starve," he says and takes the food back upstairs.

How long will he leave me here? It feels like hours and I'm getting more and more scared as time passes. I'm crying so hard that it hurts, and my stomach aches because of the chain.

Now he's back, this time carrying a McDonald's bag.

"You must be hungry by now," he says. "You gotta eat."

I'm starving, so I can't help it. I eat the cheeseburger and fries in seconds.

"We're going upstairs—don't try anything."

He unlocks me, but it's hard to stand up since I've been sitting on the floor since yesterday. My legs wobble as I walk upstairs in front of him. When we get to the top, I ask if I can use the bathroom.

"Hurry up," he says, standing right beside the toilet until I'm done.

Then he takes me to the dining room, where he has a twin bed pushed up against the wall. On top of the bed is a box made out of wood lattice fencing, the kind you see around gardens, with blankets draped over the whole thing. It looks like a fort that a kid would build to play in.

He makes me stand at the edge of the bed and wraps a chain around my ankle, attaching the other end to the bed frame.

"Get in," he orders.

So I crawl into his weird box, and he follows me. There's barely enough space for both of us. I'm having trouble breathing, I'm so scared. His hands are all over me, and he grabs my breasts as I close my eyes and pray. Then he just falls asleep.

I lie there wide-awake. The police must be looking for me. I know my parents have called them by now.

Somebody has to find me.

April 2004: Searching for Gina

Nancy Ruiz was expecting Gina home by about three thirty at the latest.

She would have been home sooner if she had taken the RTA bus, but knowing Gina, Nancy figured that she had probably walked. Factoring in time to chat with friends and a stop at the corner store for Funyuns and a Pepsi, she usually walked in the door between three and three thirty.

Nancy was planning to take Gina to the Parmatown Mall for their monthly mother-daughter shopping trip. Because Nancy didn't drive, they usually caught the bus near their house and made an evening of it. When Gina didn't show up by four, Nancy walked to the corner store on Clark Avenue and asked if anybody had seen her.

She returned home and started calling her daughter's friends. Nobody knew anything. Now Nancy was scared. She raced down to the corner again, and when there was still no sign of Gina at five thirty, she called 911.

A police car came immediately, and Nancy gave the officer a photo of Gina.

"Oh, your daughter is at that age," the officer said. "She's probably with her boyfriend."

"She doesn't have a boyfriend," Nancy told him. "She's fourteen. I'm telling you, she would call me. Something happened to her."

Nancy asked the police to issue an Amber Alert, but the officer explained that they couldn't do that unless they were certain there had been an abduction, and they had at least some description of an abductor or a vehicle.

"Don't worry, she'll show up," the officer assured her before leaving.

Nancy did not feel reassured and ran outside to meet Felix when he returned home a few minutes later.

"Gina is missing!" she shouted. "She never made it home from school!"

Felix immediately drove off to check around the school and drive the route she would have taken home. Nancy continued to call Gina's friends while Gina's older brother, Ricky, went looking for her in his own car.

By seven thirty Gina's family was in a full-blown panic. They began searching the neighborhood on foot, walking along the railroad tracks, through vacant lots, and around the area's factories. Nancy stayed by the phone in case Gina called.

Nobody slept that night as the search continued. In alleys behind bars, several people, clearly drunk, came out at closing time and asked what they were doing. When they heard a young girl was missing, they pitched in and started picking through Dumpsters.

On Saturday afternoon Cleveland police lieutenant Marge Laskowski arrived at 2:30 for her shift. She was the shift supervisor that day, so the missing-persons report on Gina was referred to her for follow-up and she drove to Gina's house.

Laskowski, an eighteen-year veteran police officer, spent an hour with Nancy, sitting on Gina's bed, listening to the tearful, distraught mother describe their tight-knit family. Laskowski had responded to scores of missing-children reports, and most of them turned out to be nothing. But something about this one felt different, and she believed Nancy when she said that Gina would never run away.

Back at the station she told a detective, "This is bad. I think this one is real."

"Oh, don't worry, Lieutenant," he replied. "I guarantee you, she'll be home before midnight."

Laskowski was annoyed. She suspected that the detective's response would have been different had Gina lived in a wealthy suburb, but because she came from a poor urban neighborhood, he assumed she was just another runaway shacked up with her boyfriend.

She passed her concerns directly to District Commander Gary Gingell, who immediately assigned detectives to work the case.

When news of Gina's abduction reached Brian Heffernan late Saturday night, it hit him like a punch to the gut: *Oh, my God, it happened again.*

He immediately called Tim Kolonick at the FBI, with whom he had been investigating Amanda Berry's disappearance for the past year, beginning and ending every workday by going over the case. Heffernan wanted all the manpower he could muster on this new one, and on Sunday morning he and Kolonick went to interview Nancy and Felix. On the way there, Kolonick called FBI agent Phil Torsney, who was at home packing his car for the long drive to Quantico, Virginia, for firearms training. Torsney drove over to join them, his car fully loaded for the trip, thinking the case would be resolved quickly and he would be on his way.

Torsney, who had been an FBI agent for more than twenty years, specialized in finding people. In 2011 he would make news around the world for his pivotal role in locating and arresting James "Whitey" Bulger, the infamous Boston mobster who had been a fugitive for sixteen years.

Torsney was a wiry, old-school agent who enjoyed strapping on his body armor and kicking in bad guys' doors. Patient and methodical, he made ten peanut butter sandwiches every Sunday, putting two in his car for Monday and freezing the rest, removing two each morning the rest of the week so he didn't have to leave a stakeout to eat. He, too, had been working the Amanda Berry case, and had spent hours sitting in his car at Westown Square, watching, hoping that something would catch his eye—someone out of place, someone stalking young girls, anything unusual.

Torsney got a bad feeling when he heard the details of Gina's case. It was too soon to conclude that Amanda and Gina had been abducted by the same man, but there were too many similarities to ignore, and something dangerous was clearly happening in this part of Cleveland.

By noon, Gina's house was swarming with media interviewing Nancy, Felix, and the police. Gina's vanishing made the news within forty-eight hours, and reporters were raising the possibility that the two cases were related.

Using dogs and flashlights, police officers and FBI agents combed through the neighborhood, tracing Gina's two-mile walk home, picking their way through abandoned houses and empty factories. They interviewed Arlene Castro, the last person to see Gina, and her mother, Grimilda Figueroa—Ariel Castro's ex.

On Monday morning, several students at Wilbur Wright Middle School told police they had seen a suspicious white two-door car, driven by a Hispanic male, with a distinctive sticker on its back window: an image of a rainbow and a wolf. Police put out an alert for a vehicle of that description and began searching the Internet to try to identify the sticker, but could find nothing. They questioned every person who appeared on tapes recovered from a surveillance camera in the school's office, but a camera at the school's main door had been out of order that day. Had the camera been working, it would have recorded Ariel Castro entering the building. As school was letting out, Castro had walked in the school's front door, looking for Arlene, and asked a security guard, a man he had grown up with, if he had seen his daughter. Nothing about the exchange had seemed unusual to the security guard, and because Castro worked for the school system, he didn't think to mention the incident to the police.

Police also photographed a blue jacket, black pants, white hoodie, and blue-and-white sneakers that matched the outfit Gina had been wearing and put them on a "missing" flyer that they posted around the neighborhood.

On Monday evening, as Felix was helping post flyers along Lorain Avenue, a man walked out of an apartment near where Gina had disappeared and asked what he was doing. When Felix explained, the man said, "I'll be looking out for your daughter."

Felix thought there was something a little odd about him.

On Tuesday, police officers with a bloodhound searched the area around the pay phone on Lorain Avenue where Gina had last been seen. The dog picked up Gina's scent and followed it, but the trail went cold around the corner of 104th Street, near McKenna's Irish Pub—almost the exact spot where the man had asked Felix about Gina the night before.

That didn't seem like a coincidence to Felix and his brother, Fernando. Without informing the police, they and some friends forced their way into the man's apartment, roughing him up and demanding to know if he had had anything to do with Gina's disappearance. He hadn't, and Brian Heffernan soon got an angry call from the building's owner, complaining that a door had been broken down. Heffernan explained that Felix was a distraught father looking for his missing daughter, and the man eventually calmed down and did not press charges, but Felix did have to pay him $900 in restitution, a huge sum for the family.

April 2004: Early Days

Gina

After I spent a few freezing days on the concrete in the basement, he finally gave me an old twin mattress to sit on and a thin, pink blanket to pull around me, but I'm still cold.

Days and days are passing, all the same.

He leaves me alone in the basement until he comes to take me to sleep with him in the strange covered bed upstairs. He gropes me, then falls asleep for the entire night.

The chains are digging into me, my whole body aches, and I'm always hungry.

I used to think time moved slowly in social studies class, but it's nothing like how it drags by now. I sit and wait, jittery, for the next horrible thing to happen. I hate how he strokes my hair, how he wants me to sit on the couch with him and watch TV. It's like he thinks we are friends. I'm terrified of him.

I see myself on the news! There's a story about how the police are looking for me and another girl, Amanda Berry, who disappeared a year before me, near where I did. I've never heard of her, but I have never watched the news before now.

I see my mom and dad on TV, and all I can think of is them. I imagine my dad running down the stairs, ripping open these chains, picking me up, and carrying me home. I picture myself hugging my mom and never letting her go.

It makes me feel better to see that so many people are trying to find me, but I bet they have no idea where I am.

Lots of people know him, but no one gets how messed up he is. He goes to work every day, talks to his kids, acts normal—he even played in the high school band with my mom. Will anyone ever figure out that he is the perv who took me?

I start thinking about when he used to wave to me from his bus.

"Were you following me all those times?" I ask him.

"Yeah, I was," he says. "You turned me on. I liked your cleavage. I liked it when you wore a black V-neck shirt and a jeans skirt. That was my favorite."

I wonder if at the Christmas concert, when he was talking to my parents, he was already planning to kidnap me.

He takes me upstairs for dinner: Tonight it's doughnuts, the grocery-store kind in a white box with a mix of powdered sugar, cinnamon, and chocolate. He gives me so little food that when he does, I'll eat anything.

I have been asking him to let me write a letter to my family so I can tell them I'm alive, and one night in the kitchen he hands me a pen and piece of notebook paper. "Don't say where you are, or who you're with," he warns. "But you can say you're okay and you'll be home soon."

I don't really think he will give my letter to them, but I want to believe he will, so I start writing.

> *Dear Everybody,*
>   *How are you? I am okay. I love you.*
>   *Mom and Dad, I love you. Don't give up hope. I am not dead.*
>   *I want to come home now. People from my school who like me, and people who don't like me, were on TV participating in my vigil. I want to say thank you to them.*
>   *Tell Chrissy not to go skating without me.*
>   *When I go home I want my family and friends over and we can cry together and have fun.*

I tell my brother, Ricky, that he is funny sometimes, and that I miss him, and I tell my sister, Mayra, that I love her. And then I write: *P.S. I want mom to know I cut my hair.*

My hair had grown all the way down my back, and I used to like it that way. But I just chopped it off with the little kiddie scissors I use to cut pictures out of newspapers, because it makes me crazy how he keeps touching it. I hope he hates it short, and that he'll now leave me alone. I put my ponytail in a plastic bag, and I'm going to give it to my mom when I get out.

Before I give the letter to him, I draw hearts at the top of the page and write in the margins, "Miss you a lot," and on the envelope, "I love you" five times. I imagine them getting the letter and realizing I'm alive.

He takes me into the dining room and chains me up to the weird bed. When he leaves, I try for the millionth time to break free.

I keep staring at the padlock and then have an idea. I grab a pencil near the bed and push the tip of it into the lock. Maybe I can pick it. I fiddle with it, like they do on TV, but the pencil snaps, and the tip gets stuck in the keyhole. I lean back and start crying.

He laughs at me when he comes back into the room and points at the lock. He must have been watching me.

"I told you not to try anything. If I can't trust you, I'm not sending your letter."

He hands it back to me, and I hold it close to me and cry.

Every morning when he goes to work, I have to go back to the basement, where I feel like I'm in a dark hole. I can't stand being with him upstairs, but I also hate being below ground with no light. So I wait until he seems to be in a good mood, and I work up my courage to ask him to move me.

"Do you have other rooms? Somewhere else I can stay in the day?"

"Yeah," he replies. "I got rooms upstairs."

"Well, can you put me up there? I can't stand the basement anymore."

"The other rooms are not fixed up. I'll have to clean them."

He actually seems to be considering the idea. I pray that he does.

Two days later he announces cheerily: "Okay. Your room is ready!"

He takes me to the second floor, where I have never been, and pushes open one of the closed doors. The room looks like a prison cell, with dirty yellow walls, a big bed with no sheets, and an old dresser and a TV. There is a thick chain with one end tied to a big steam radiator. He picks it up and says the other end is for me, and wraps it around my ankle.

At least I'm not underground anymore.

* * *

They keep showing Amanda Berry's picture on the news, and there is something familiar about her. Then I realize: she looks just like the picture of a blond girl taped to the mirror in my new room.

I point to the photo and ask him who she is.

"Oh, that's my ex-girlfriend."

But I get a sick feeling. I'm sure it's Amanda Berry. Why would her photo be in his house? What if he kidnapped her, too? Oh, my God, I bet he killed her.

"Did you take her?" I ask him.

"No."

I don't believe him.

We sit there for a long time watching TV, then I ask him a few more questions about Amanda Berry. The more I think about it, the more scared I am. She's been missing for a year. If he did kill her, he's probably going to kill me.

He can see how terrified I am and finally admits that he has her.

"Come on, I'll show you."

He unlocks me and takes me into the hallway outside my bedroom.

"You can look in, but pull your head back fast so she doesn't see you," he says.

He opens the door to the room right across the hall from mine, and I see a girl with blond hair sitting on the bed with her back to the door, watching TV.

He closes the door quickly and then, almost bragging, says, "I have another one, too."

Oh, my God! There are two other girls in here!

I'm too shocked to respond, but I finally ask: "What's her name?"

"Michelle."

He leads me to another door in the hallway, opens it, and I look quickly and see a girl with dark hair lying on a bed, also watching TV. She doesn't see me.

Who is this Michelle?

April 2004: Hiding Something

April 4

Amanda

I'm watching the news, and there's another girl missing: Gina DeJesus, a seventh-grader at Wilbur Wright who disappeared at Lorain and West 105th. That's so close to where I got taken! You can see the Burger King where I worked from there.

It sounds just like what happened to me, so I wonder if he had anything to do with it. But I haven't heard anybody else in the house.

I do know that the other girl is still here. He told me her name is Michelle. She's in the room right next to me, and she's aggravating. I hate the head-banger music that she plays and sings along with.

"You should be more like her; she doesn't cry at all," he says.

He keeps telling me that she's happy. He says her family is screwed up, and they are paying him to give her a place to live. He says he's doing them a favor, and that her life here is better than the one she had before.

I've never talked to her to find out what is really going on, because he keeps us apart. Every once in a while we're both downstairs at the same time, and we say hello, but I've seen her only briefly, and maybe ten times this whole year. Once when we were in the kitchen together and he went into the other room for a minute, I whispered to her, "My name is Amanda Berry."

"I know who you are," she said. "I've seen you on the news."

But then he came back in, and we couldn't talk anymore.

Now he's in my room yelling at me again: "Stop it! Stop it now!"

"She says you're making noise," he says. "What are you doing?"

One of his big rules is that we have to be quiet. The only noise allowed is from the TV and radio.

"I'm sitting here watching TV," I say. "What noise could I be making? When I stand up to pee, maybe she hears my chain. Does she have her ear to my wall?"

I'm not making noise. Why is she telling him lies about me?

April 7

"I only took your freedom," he tells me.

He's actually suggesting I should be grateful to him because he didn't kill me. I want to kill him. His sick strategy is to take everything from me, then make me feel lucky and appreciative when he gives me a sandwich or lets me take a shower.

"It's really hard to lose everything," I tell him. "It's so hard to sit here, stuck in this house. Everybody else is going on with their life outside, and you have me chained to a wall."

"Don't think like that," he says.

He talks as if I have no right to be upset, as if all he has done is inconvenience me. *Oops, I didn't mean to burn your toast, sorry.* That's his tone. He acts as if it's his right to do whatever he wants to me.

He's not God. He can't decide my life for me.

It would be so much easier if I just died, but I can't think like that.

I can't let him win.

April 10

I'm on *America's Most Wanted*! They are showing pictures of me and Gina DeJesus together, because we both disappeared in the same neighborhood.

I've watched that show so many times, never once imagining I would be on it. They said Gina and I would be on next Saturday, too. Maybe somebody saw him with me, and this TV show will jog their memory.

April 10: I Feel Like She's Close

Louwana had lost about thirty pounds in the year since Amanda had disappeared, and Beth could feel her mother was breaking. All the rage, sadness, and drinking were taking their toll. Louwana had not been able to go back to work and was now surviving on welfare checks.

She often felt guilty about the little arguments she'd had with Amanda before she disappeared. She knew Amanda was thinking of skipping work on the day she went missing, and she wished she let her. Regret ate at her.

Beth decided that she needed to be a positive force, because that was the most important thing she could do for her mother and her sister.

"I'm not going to eat today," Louwana would say. "What if Mandy didn't get to eat today?"

"It won't do Mandy any good if you get sick," Beth would reply.

She kept her mother busy putting up "missing" flyers and yellow ribbons around town, and she made sure her daughters kept their grandmother company. The kids sat and watched movies with her and often spent the night.

Louwana and Beth were constantly calling reporters and asking for coverage of Amanda, appealing to them on holidays like Mother's Day or Christmas, or with any other hook they could think of. Sometimes the reporters came to interview them, but mostly not. Louwana yelled at them when they ignored her, but Beth reminded her that some coverage was better than none.

Beth hated public speaking, so to get over her fright she imagined that when she was looking into the lens of the TV camera, she was talking directly to Amanda and telling her everything would be okay.

One day a producer from *America's Most Wanted* called and said that John Walsh, the show's host, wanted to give Amanda's case national exposure. A crew came to film in Cleveland, and Beth took the lead in the interviews: "We love you, Mandy. We want you home. We're always going to be looking for you. We'll never give up."

Beth knew the odds were not good that Amanda would be found alive, but her instincts were telling her something different.

"My heart doesn't feel empty like it would if she was gone," she told her mother after the camera crew left. "I feel like she's close."

April 16

Amanda

He takes me downstairs to have a shower, the first one in days. As we're walking through the dining room I see something strange. He sleeps down here a lot on a bed pushed over by the wall but now he has a strange, boxy contraption on top of it, like something kids would build. He pretends to not even notice it as we walk by. He seems like he's hiding something.

Oh, my God, I bet Gina DeJesus is in there.

He must have taken her, too.

April 20

I'm in a new room now. He just moved me across the hallway into a smaller bedroom that's painted blue. He didn't say why, but I wonder if it's because he put Gina in my old room. I still haven't seen or heard her, but I sense something different in the house. I think she's here.

I hate this room. It's not like I loved the other one, but I had gotten used to it after almost a year. Change here usually means trouble.

He has a mirror set up on one wall of my room so he can stand in the hallway and see what I'm watching on TV. He put another mirror downstairs over the sink in the kitchen, so when he's standing there he can keep an eye on what's happening behind him. It's awful to be watched every second. I've been crying all the time since he moved me.

"A baby doesn't even cry that much," he tells me.

I hate him.

"Did you take that girl, Gina?" I ask.

"No, of course not," he says.

"I don't believe you. I think she's here."

"Stay out of my business," he snaps.

I smile to myself because I hit a nerve. So she *is* in this house!

"You told me if you ever got another girl, I could go home. So now that Gina is here, I should be home. Unless that was just another lie."

That makes him really mad, and his voice gets deeper and meaner.

"You better shut up," he says. "I've gone this far, I don't know what I'm capable of now."

He claims he moved me so he could sleep in my old room. Why does he lie? Does he think he can hide another girl in this little house, and I won't find out?

He keeps the door to my old room shut and locked. Why lock it if nobody's in there? The radio is blasting in the hallway, so I can't hear if anybody's moving around in there.

Maybe the police looking for Gina will find this house and rescue me and Michelle, too. I have to believe that every time he kidnaps another girl he is more likely to get caught.

April 21

"You think you are a victim, but I am a victim, too," he says.

"What are you talking about?"

He tells me that when he was a boy in Puerto Rico, he was sexually abused by a boy who was a few years older.

"That doesn't give you the right to do this to me."

"Shut up!" he says, looking furious.

Does he really want me to feel sorry for him? Because someone hurt him, he thinks he can hurt other people? I don't even know whether to believe him.

It's been exactly a year since he took me and there's been a lot about my case on TV today. I guess he's decided to tell me now about his childhood because the news reports are talking about how sad my story is, and he's so selfish that he doesn't like me getting all the sympathy. On the eleven o'clock news I see my mom and Beth crying, and they're showing Gina's sister bringing flowers to my house. If Gina really is here, it's great that our two families are together. Maybe someday when this is over we can all be friends.

A few weeks ago I saw my mom on the news, and she was burning a candle for me. I asked him to get me one just like it, and he did. It's in a tall, red glass container with a picture of Jesus that he got at Marc's discount store. I lit it today and I'm going to light it on all my important anniversaries and family birthdays. It makes my room feel a little warmer.

I think for a second about setting the room on fire. I have the candle and a cigarette lighter he gave me. Somebody might see the smoke and call the Fire Department, and they'd find us here. But the neighbors seem so clueless that they might not even call, and I could be dead by the time the firefighters got here. I guess he knows I would never risk it.

It makes me lonelier to see my family on TV, but it's also a gift. At least one day a year, on the anniversary of my kidnapping, I know they will appear on the news, and I'll be able to see if they look healthy, what they are wearing, if they've changed their hair, how my nieces are growing up.

April 21 is My Day.

April 22

It's my eighteenth birthday, and he comes into my room like he's Santa Claus or something.

"Happy birthday! Can I get you a cake?"

He doesn't seem to understand how much I hate him. Who chains someone up and then offers to get them a birthday cake?

"No," I tell him in a dead, cold voice. "I don't want anything."

But really, there's a lot I do want for my birthday.

I want to be able to take back my stupid mistake of getting into his van. I want to take back every mean thing I ever said to my mom. I want to be a normal eighteen-year-old, having fun and saving up to go to college. I want my own room back and my clean, pressed clothes. I want to wash and cut my hair. I want to take a shower, twice a day, like I used to. I want to talk on the phone, walk outside, go shopping. I so, so, so want a Dr Pepper.

I don't want to need counseling for the rest of my life.

I don't want to always be scared of everyone I ever meet.

I want this to be over.

April 2004: Get Away from Me!

On the afternoon of Friday, April 16, Ariel Castro's daughter Angie and her husband, Sam Gregg, came home to find the message light blinking on their answering machine. They had just moved and had a new landline number. They assumed the message was from either Angie's mother or her father, as they were the only two people who knew the new number.

When they listened to the message, at first they heard only muffled sounds, like the caller's phone was in a purse or a pocket—as if someone had inadvertently "pocket dialed" them. Then they heard the voice of a young woman, sounding terrified, screaming, "Get away from me!"

Angie and Sam were so shaken that they called the police. When officers came to their house and listened to the message, they said it was probably a prank call.

"Didn't a girl come up missing around here?" Angie asked them.

Gina DeJesus's disappearance two weeks earlier had been covered extensively by the local news, and Angie's sister Arlene had been the last person to see Gina. Angie wondered if Gina, or someone holding her, had called her.

"Does Gina DeJesus know your phone number?" the officer asked.

"No," she said.

"Why would she be calling you?" the officer asked.

"I don't know," Angie said.

The officers called a detective to come out and listen to the tape. After making a recording of it, he asked Angie if Gina had ever been to her house. Angie said she didn't know Gina, and that Gina would have had no way of knowing her phone number.

Brian Heffernan passed the one-minute, forty-nine-second tape on to the FBI, and Tim Kolonick brought it to Nancy's house and played it for her. Nancy thought it was Gina's voice.

The FBI checked Angie's phone records and traced the call to a cell phone belonging to a woman, who had lent it to her boyfriend, Richard Rogers. They interviewed Rogers, a local roofer, and he said that he had been at a family party at the time with many young teens, including his two kids, who had been fooling around, dialing random numbers. They didn't remember who they called or what they said.*

April 2004: Suspects and Leads

Early in their investigation of Gina's case the FBI focused on Fernando Colon, Arlene Castro's stepfather, as a suspect.

When the two girls said their good-byes at the phone booth on the day Gina disappeared, Arlene crossed the street and walked directly to Westown Square, where Colon worked as a security guard, and he gave her a ride to their house on West 106th Street, only a few blocks away. The FBI figured that Colon would have needed no more than five minutes to drop Arlene off and then go back for Gina. Colon raised red flags for the FBI because he knew Gina, he carried a gun, and he had opportunity.

Five days after Gina had gone missing, the FBI picked up Colon for questioning. The FBI was familiar with Colon, as they had recently given him an award for helping them solve a bank robbery at Westown Square. While he was being questioned downtown, agents searched his car and his office, using Luminol to look for traces of blood, but they found nothing. Colon agreed to a lie-detector test, which he passed.

Colon and the FBI have starkly different memories of one aspect of his interrogation that day. Colon insists he told the agents that they were talking to the wrong man, and that they should turn their attention instead to Arlene's biological father, Ariel Castro. He claims he informed them that Castro not only knew Gina but was a violent man who had

---

*After Ariel Castro was arrested, Nancy Ruiz and Angie Gregg both remembered the phone call and couldn't believe that it was just a coincidence.

To Angie, it had sounded so desperate and real that she still hears it in her head, and she can't dismiss the possibility that it might have been her father accidentally dialing her while he held Amanda and Gina captive.

Nancy wondered if there had been some mistake in the trace of the call, and it was actually from Castro's cell phone. In early 2015, the FBI played the tape for Gina, who said the sound quality of the recording was so poor that she couldn't tell whose voice it was.

been abusive to Arlene's mother, Grimilda Figueroa. Kolonick and Torsney insist that Colon never mentioned Ariel Castro.

The FBI pulled police and court records listing sex offenders, parolees, and people with outstanding arrest warrants who lived in Gina's and Amanda's neighborhoods. Courts are often so backlogged that police can't keep up with warrants issued for everything from assaults to traffic violations and Torsney started serving these outstanding warrants to get access to hundreds of homes to check for any signs of the missing girls. Sex offenders, those convicted of possessing child pornography, forcible rape or other crime involving a sex act, were a particular focus. Required by law to register their address, dozens were living in Amanda's 44111 zip code and the FBI paid special attention to them, because sex offenders often repeat their crimes and are frequently linked to missing-children cases.

When the kids at Wilbur Wright reported seeing a suspicious Hispanic man driving a white car, it immediately reminded police of Amanda's boyfriend, DJ Diaz. They had been keeping a close eye on DJ for the past year, but had never found any evidence linking him to Amanda's case.

On Saturday, eight days after Gina's disappearance, police spotted him driving a stolen car, arrested him, and got a search warrant for his house. They found plenty of marijuana but nothing to suggest that he was abducting girls.

Three weeks after Gina went missing, the FBI brought Arlene Castro in to be hypnotized.

Arlene, distraught about her friend's disappearance, was eager to help police in any way she could. Investigators wanted to see if hypnosis could help her remember any detail—a car, a person, anything that she hadn't already mentioned.

Heffernan and Kolonick sat with Arlene's mother, Nilda Figueroa, during the session, which was conducted by a psychologist hired by the FBI. Arlene, who was thirteen, recounted events exactly as she had told police in her statement. There was nothing more.

In early May 2004, Torsney stood on Lorain Avenue near where Gina was taken and where Amanda had disappeared the year before and wondered if a serial killer was at work on this stretch of road. He and Kolonick feared that a careful killer had taken the two girls, then dropped their bodies in some Dumpster that had been carted off to a landfill.

Both men knew that the odds were against Amanda still being alive a year after her disappearance. But it was possible, they kept telling themselves. They spent a lot of time with Gina's and Amanda's families and they badly wanted to solve their cases.

One May afternoon, Torsney stared up at the apartment windows overlooking Lorain and had an idea. He climbed the stairs of one of the buildings on the street and knocked on a door. The man who answered was clearly drunk, but his apartment had a perfect panoramic view of Lorain Avenue.

Torsney proposed a deal: The FBI would set up video surveillance gear in the man's apartment for a few weeks, and they would pay him for his trouble. He happily agreed.

FBI technicians positioned thousands of dollars' worth of video cameras in the space, which recorded every person and car that passed on Lorain. Agents pored over the hours of footage but didn't find anything useful.

The surveillance continued for several weeks. Then one day when an FBI agent came to put in a new set of blank tapes, he discovered that all the expensive gear was gone. The man who lived there said it had been stolen by burglars.

May 2004: Friends

Gina

It's May 7. I know that because they mentioned the date on TV, and that means I've been here a month and five days. I'm on the news all the time and I keep waiting for the cops to break down the door and rescue me. Where are they?

He keeps asking if I'm a virgin.

"Of course I am. I'm only fourteen."

"When we have sex," he tells me, "I'm going to get, like, a hundred points, because you're a virgin."

When we have sex. His words ring in my ears, and I'm scared he's going to rape me. A hundred points? What is he talking about?

I start talking about my mom and dad, hoping he'll feel guilty because he knows them.

"If I knew you were Felix's daughter, I would have left you alone," he replies.

Why is he claiming that he didn't know who I was? When he was stalking me, he saw me walk into my house. He knew I was Arlene's friend and saw me with her just before he took me. Does he just like to lie?

We watch TV for a while until he says, "Let's go talk in the living room."

I never know what he's thinking. Why do we have to talk in the living room? But I do what he says because I have no choice. He says he'll put me back in the basement if I don't obey him.

I sit down on the couch.

He stands in front of me and starts to take off his clothes.

"What are you doing?" I ask, terrified.

"Just shut up and take your clothes off."

"No!" I shout, but he's on top of me in a second, tugging at the sweatpants and T-shirt he makes me wear. And then he rapes me.

He's so much bigger than I am and hurts me horribly as he slams against me. He seems angry, like he wants to hurt me as much as he can. I'm screaming and crying and beating him back, but it's useless.

I'm crying and bleeding. I've been terrified he would do this. But having this old pig on top of me was even more horrible than I'd imagined. He just took something I'll never get back. I want to die. I try to cover myself with my clothes.

"We gotta celebrate!" he says, standing up and pulling his pants back on. "That was your first time!"

He goes to the kitchen and returns with a bottle of red wine and two glasses, then pours one for each of us.

"Now you'll never forget me," he says. "I was your first, and you never forget your first."

I can't look at him.

He makes me take a drink. I have never had wine before, and it tastes awful.

Now that he's started raping me, he can't stop.

It's three or four times every day.

Day after day it's the same: He comes in, takes off his clothes, and climbs on me. He's so hairy everywhere, even his butt. He's the most disgusting man I can imagine.

He makes me look at him and tell him all this ridiculous stuff. *"I love it." "I want it." "You're so sexy."* If I don't say it, he yells at me and makes it hurt more.

He doesn't even unchain me.

"Do you want a friend?" he asks one day.

He knows I do. I'm desperately lonely and I have nobody to talk to but him. I've told him how much I miss my parents, my brother and sister, my cousins and friends. I have been here for over a month.

"I can go kidnap your friend Chrissy to keep you company," he says.

"No!" I scream. I told him once that I missed Chrissy, and I should never have mentioned her name.

"Well, if you help me clean up, I'll bring one of the other girls here to talk to you," he says. "But only if you do what I tell you to."

I'm almost always alone. He knows how sad I am, so he's started giving me cigarettes, a lot of them. It feels weird to smoke so much, since I got grounded for sneaking just one cigarette at home. Now I'm going through a pack every other day because I have nothing else to do.

He gives me alcohol, too. I can't stand the taste of wine or beer, but Mike's Hard Lemonade is okay.

I wonder how the other girls are dealing with him. He says Amanda doesn't like to talk to anyone and keeps to herself. A couple of times Michelle and I have both been downstairs together, but he didn't let us talk, except to say hello.

Now he tells me that he's going to take me over to Michelle's room. But he has rules, like always. "You can talk to her, but you can't tell her your real name," he says. "Tell her you're Arlene."

"I look older than Arlene," I remind him. "She's only thirteen, and I'm fourteen. I'll say I'm your daughter Emily."

I don't want to do every little thing he says. If he is going to make me pretend I'm somebody else, at least I can pick who it is.

"All right, I don't care," he says.

He unlocks me from the radiator but leaves the chain around my stomach, then walks me to Michelle's room down the hallway. She is sitting on her bed, but I can see her chain sticking out from under the blanket.

"My daughter wants to say hi," he tells her.

"I'm Emily," I say.

She looks at me curiously and says, "I'm Michelle Knight."

That's the first time I've heard her full name. I'm dying to talk to her more. I wonder how she got here. I wonder if he treats her as badly as he treats me.

But he's standing right there, so we talk about nothing much, just TV and music.

"I like to do people's hair," I say. "I could do yours sometime if you want."

"That would be nice," she says, smiling.

We try to talk more but he cuts us off, snapping, "That's enough."

"Nice talking to you," I tell her.

A couple of days later, he tells me I can come downstairs and fix Michelle's hair.

"You can use the bathroom. There's a mirror in there."

I'm happy to have something to do. I am learning to read his moods and right now, thank God, he seems to be in a good one. He's not yelling that I'm "good for nothing" and calling me mean names. When that happens I know not to talk to him, or even look at him. But when he's in a good mood, I can get favors, like the other day when I asked for an empty cardboard box to draw on.

"I need some rubber bands," I tell him as we go into the bathroom. He must have some in all his piles of junk. He doesn't throw anything away. There are rows of big plastic pop bottles filled with water sitting in the closets and the hall. He says they'll be handy if there's ever a fire. That makes me wonder: What would happen to us if the house caught fire and we were locked in our rooms?

I don't want to push my luck, but I also ask: "I see you have some hair gel. Can I use a little bit?"

"Sure," he says.

Why is he being nice today?

I bring a kitchen chair into the bathroom, and Michelle sits down. I ask her how she'd like her hair.

"I'm going to be right here in the kitchen," he warns us, "and I can hear everything."

I start styling her hair, and we talk about music and clothes. He ducks in, says Michelle's hair looks good, and then goes into the living room. I lean over and whisper in her ear, "I'm not really Emily. I'm Gina DeJesus."

"I know who you are," she whispers back. "I've seen you on TV."

He walks back into the kitchen, and we go back to talking about hair.

May 23, 2004: *America's Most Wanted*

Gina

"You want to see your family on TV?"

"Of course I do!" I tell him.

"Amanda recorded *America's Most Wanted*, and your family is on it. Let's go watch."

The guy who kidnapped me wants me to watch a TV show about my kidnapping! He unchains me, and we walk into Amanda's room, directly across the hallway. I have seen her a couple of times, but we haven't talked. One time our doors were open at the same time, and we waved to each other, but that was it.

We all sit on her bed, and she only says "hi," so I try to make conversation.

"I like your nails," I tell her, noticing that he must have bought her polish. "And your rings are really pretty."

"Thanks," she responds, though she's not smiling, and it's pretty clear she doesn't want to talk. She seems tough. On TV they say she has been missing for a year. A whole year—how has she been able to stand it? I would love to ask her.

The show starts with my mom crying and talking about the day I disappeared. Then Arlene comes on, describing how we said good-bye at the pay phone. She says my last words to her were: "Well, okay. I'll talk to you later." I remember that, too. I wish she knew what happened next. It's crazy that they're showing pictures of me and Arlene being happy together while her father is keeping me prisoner.

Now they're showing pictures of Amanda, her mom and sister, and people walking near the Burger King with signs that read WE LOVE YOU, MANDY. They say the police aren't sure if our two cases are related.

It's intense sitting here, all of us on Amanda's little bed, watching this. I think he likes it. He keeps smiling, especially when Arlene is talking. He doesn't seem worried that millions of people are watching this show all over the country. Doesn't he care that people are looking for us and our kidnapper?

As soon as the show is over, he tells me I have to go back to my room. Amanda is crying, and I start, too. I was so happy to see my parents, but now that the TV is off, I feel worse, like my mom and dad have been taken from me again.

I haven't cried this hard since the first couple of weeks, and that seems to annoy him.

"I guess I shouldn't have let you watch it," he says.

May 2004: Poinciana

Nancy Ruiz was afraid that if she left her house, even for a minute, she might miss a call from Gina, or that Gina might actually walk in. So for a long time she stayed in her kitchen, barely stepping outside. When for the first time in weeks she finally did go out, the neighborhood seemed entirely different. Every person she saw looked suspicious, and houses that had been familiar now frightened her. When reporters showed up, she would freeze in front of the cameras and let Felix do the talking.

Felix, meanwhile, continued to organize searches in every alleyway in the city. Nancy had fixated on one house a couple of blocks away that had broken windows covered with Christmas wrapping paper. One night she noticed a bright light inside, as if someone was trying to make an abandoned home look occupied. When she walked by again at three in the morning and saw the light still on, she called Phil Torsney, who found an old, mentally ill man living there, but no sign of Gina.

Nancy told Torsney about a suspicious house in her neighborhood where the curtains were always drawn, so he knocked on the door. When the owner gave him permission to go inside, the stench was so overpowering from the large number of dogs who lived there and had defecated everywhere that one officer had to step out to vomit.

Nancy kept passing on leads to police and even investigated some herself. She searched around Gina's school and in nearby neighborhoods, always hoping she would see a poinciana blossom. Gina loved to draw the red tropical flower, and Nancy thought she might have drawn one where she was being held, a signal that only her mother would understand.

May 2004: Ariel Castro, Interviewer

One afternoon in May 2004, Castro's son, who was named Ariel after his father, knocked on the door of Gina DeJesus's house on West 71st Street.

The young Ariel, who was twenty-two, had been studying journalism at

Bowling Green State University and wanted to write a story about Gina's disappearance for the *Plain Press*, a community newspaper on the west side of Cleveland. He said he was very sorry about what had happened.

Nancy had met him with his father when he was a young boy, and because she was eager for any publicity about the case, she invited him in. For the next few hours she recounted everything she knew about Gina's disappearance, and he listened politely.

His story appeared the following month:

Since April 2, 2004, the day 14-year-old Gina DeJesus was last seen on her way home from Wilbur Wright Middle School, neighborhood residents have been taken by an overwhelming need for caution. Parents are more strictly enforcing curfews, encouraging their children to walk in groups, or driving them to and from school when they had previously walked alone.

"You can tell the difference," DeJesus' mother, Nancy Ruiz said. "People are watching out for each other's kids. It's a shame that a tragedy had to happen for me to really know my neighbors. Bless their hearts, they've been great."

On Cleveland 's west side, it is difficult to go any length of time without seeing Gina's picture on telephone poles, in windows, or on cars along the busy streets.

"People are really looking out for my daughter," Ruiz said.

For seven weeks, Gina's family has been organizing searches, holding prayer vigils, posting flyers and calling press conferences. Despite the many tips and rumors that have been circulating in the neighborhood, there has been no sign of her.

One thing is for certain, however. Almost everyone feels a connection with the family, and Gina's disappearance has the whole area talking.

July 21, 2004: Chains

Amanda

At night, the heavy chain around my stomach makes it hard to sleep, and during the day it makes it impossible to forget where I am.

My chain is actually a few different chains linked by padlocks, and it stretches five feet from the radiator to my stomach. So five feet has become the size of my whole world.

I shift the chain around so the padlock rests on my belly, then on my side, and finally on my back. But nothing feels better. I am covered with bruises and calluses. Just looking at the chain makes me cry. It's like a snake in the bed with me, threatening to squeeze me to death.

"I can't take this anymore! Can you at least move it to my ankle?"

He thinks about it for a minute and says, "Okay."

I'm surprised.

"Which ankle?" he asks.

I try to figure out which one will give me more room.

"Right," I tell him, holding it out.

"There," he says, as he winds it around my ankle several times. "Try that."

I take a few steps and feel lighter, freer, without the extra pounds around my stomach. I lie down on the bed and roll from side to side.

After he leaves, I am happier for a moment, then suddenly scared. There was absolutely no way to get that chain off my waist, but my ankle is so skinny. Maybe I can slip it off. Could this be my chance to escape? Would I have the nerve to try? I feel like he knows what I'm thinking and he's testing me, so I try to think about something else.

"I need to know I can trust you," he always says. "You know what I can do to you."

I never know when he is watching me or even when he is home. I think he just went downstairs, but I'm not sure because of the noise from the radio. What if he's just outside the door and looking at me through the hole where the doorknob should be? I decide to not fiddle with the chain. If he saw me trying to take it off, he might move it back to my waist, and I couldn't take that.

An hour passes. I slowly flex my ankle back and forth and feel the painful new sensation of heavy metal there. I think again how I might be able to slide the chain off. It's tempting and terrifying.

I hear his footsteps on the stairs, and then they stop outside my room. He must be watching me. I keep my eyes on the TV and don't even look at the chain.

Finally he unlocks the door, hands me a bag of Wendy's, and takes a long look at my ankle to see if I tried anything. I knew it.

August 2004: One Bullet

Gina

He seems to treat me better than the other girls. I have the nicer room, and he brings me downstairs more often than them. He lets me eat first, so when he brings home a pizza that has ten slices, I can take four, and the other two get three each. I feel guilty about having more, but I'm hungry all the time, and it's hard to wait for hours and hours to eat. I wonder if he's kinder to me because I'm the new girl, and I wonder what happens when I'm not new anymore.

I want to go back to before this all happened, to when I could just walk to the refrigerator if I was thirsty or hungry, to when I had fun doing cartwheels with my friends and playing pranks on my mom. I remember once sneaking up to our big front window when she was sitting on the couch watching TV with her back to me. I smacked the window hard, and she jumped straight up. It was the funniest thing ever, and she laughed when she saw it was me.

I'm daydreaming about all that when he comes into the living room with a gun.

Michelle starts freaking out, but he's not pointing it at us and he seems to be in a good mood.

"Let's play a game," he says.

He opens the gun to show us that it is loaded with one bullet. He takes it out, puts it back, and spins the chamber around.

Michelle is scared and moves as far away as she can. But I just keep staring at the gun. When he brought me here, he told me he had a revolver and would kill me if I tried to escape. He brought it from the kitchen, so he must keep it hidden on top of the refrigerator or in one of the high cupboards. He's always telling us we are short and can't reach anything. I'm the tallest and I'm not quite five-foot-two.

He explains the game: If I'm willing to take the risk, he will put the gun to my head and pull the trigger. If I live, he'll give me a chance to put the gun to his head.

"Come on," he says. "Want to play?"

"Okay," I tell him. "I'll play with you."

He seems surprised. Michelle looks shocked and says it's a bad idea.

"What do I have to lose?" I say. "I'll play."

"You understand I'm going to pull the trigger, right?" he asks.

I'm getting more nervous as I have time to think about it. But I can't stand what's happening in this house anymore, so I say a prayer to God and then to my parents to forgive me.

"I'm ready," I tell him.

He puts the gun to my temple and pulls the trigger.

I hear a click and then open my eyes. My heart is beating fast. I don't know what I feel, but he seems excited.

"Let's keep playing," he says. "Will you pull the trigger on me? If you do, it means you hate me. And if you can't, it means you don't hate me."

Is he serious? Doesn't he know how much I hate him?

"Think about it," he says.

He gets on his knees and says he needs a minute to pray. He bows his head and closes his eyes. Then he looks up and tells me again: "If you pull the trigger, it means you hate me." He's been drinking beer, and maybe he's had more than I realize, because it should be obvious to him by now that I'd love to blow his head off.

He hands me the gun and I don't waste a second. I put it right to his head and pull the trigger.

Click.

I was hoping he'd be dead on the floor, and I would run out of the house, and we'd all be free. Now I'm afraid that I might be in big trouble, but he stands up and doesn't say a word. He doesn't seem mad. It's like he doesn't care at all.

August 2004: Summer

Gina

I can't take being here anymore. It's been four months. I can't stand what he's doing to me. I'm scared every time the door opens.

"I want to kill myself," I tell him.

"Okay, he says. "Let me help you."

He leaves and returns in a minute with a rope. He ties it into a noose and hands it to me. "If you really want to die, take this. I'll watch."

When he first kidnapped me, all I cared about was staying alive because I was sure he was going to kill me. I kicked and clawed and screamed. But now I feel hollowed out. I have nothing left, no strength.

I desperately want to go home, but I don't see how this will ever end.

I put the rope around my neck.

He stands there watching me. He doesn't seem to care if I die.

I start thinking about what he will do with my dead body, so I ask him.

"I'll bury you in the backyard," he says. "Nobody will ever know."

I think about my parents and start crying. They'll never know Arlene's dad did this to me. I don't want him to get away with this.

I lift the rope off.

"I'll keep this in your closet in case you need it later," he says.

I don't even bother to turn on the TV anymore. I spend all day lying down, staring at the ceiling, trying to forget where I am. Sometimes I stay like this for days at a time, barely moving.

Every few hours back. Even after he leaves the room, I can still feel his hands on me.

I tried to shoot him and I've looked in the kitchen for knives to stab him. I daydream about shoving him down the stairs and running out of the house, or finding a window he hasn't boarded up and climbing out onto the roof. But it's no use because of these chains, and I'm losing strength. Instead of trying to kill him, I'm now just trying to push him out of my head.

"I can bring a friend into your room," he says one day. "This is a big bed. You can share it." He says Michelle can stay in this room with me. I would like to have someone to talk to, but I don't want to share a bed, so I don't answer him.

He leaves and comes back with Michelle, orders her to sit on my bed, and chains her ankle to the radiator. I guess he made up his mind: I'm going to have a roommate. He leaves and locks the door.

Neither of us says anything for a while, then Michelle tells me he's worried that I'm going to set the room on fire with my cigarettes. The other day, I emptied my ashtray into a cardboard box we use for trash, and it started smoking. He pretended that he was concerned that I was depressed, but I guess the real reason that he brought me a roommate was so that I don't burn down his house.

I'm glad I have Michelle here, but then he ruins everything. He comes in and starts taking his clothes off. He climbs on Michelle, and I roll away and try not to watch. I can't stop crying.

Then it's my turn.

Michelle and I have been talking for days, telling each other everything. She's been here for two years, since she was twenty-one. He got her into his car by saying that he had puppies at his house and that she could have one.

She knows his daughter Emily, so of course she didn't believe it when I said I was Emily. I can't believe we're both friends with his kids.

She says her family is messed up. She has a son, but somebody else had been taking care of him even before she got here, and she has no idea where he is now. She's never been on the news, so she thinks her family didn't even report her missing.

She knows everything about my family and Amanda's because she sees them on TV all the time. She and Amanda were in this house together for a whole year before I got here, but he's kept them separate so they've never talked—just said hi a few times.

It's like he's collecting girls. I wonder if he's going to kidnap any more.

We've actually been laughing a little and trying to cheer each other up. We sing to the radio and do silly stuff like throw spitballs. We can't move around much because we're chained, but I'm happy to have somebody to help me pass the time.

Then he's back, and it starts all over again.

We've been watching the Olympics in Athens almost every night. He gets so excited at the sight of these gymnasts. I don't get it. These girls are so small and young.

"Wow, look at her," he says.

I don't want to, but he makes me.

Then he rapes me.

I used to love to watch the Olympics, but now I'll never watch them again.

August 2004: New Strategy

Amanda

Those two girls in the next room make it even harder to be here. They bug me, laughing and talking all the time. I can hear them through the door, and they actually joke with him, like everything's okay. They sing constantly with their radio up loud. I feel like I'm the only sane person here, but I guess everybody has their own way of coping with being kidnapped.

He tells me that they're nice to him, and that they say I'm stuck up and won't talk to them when we are all together downstairs. We're all in the same mess, but it feels like it's me against them. He does treat them better. Lots of nights he takes them downstairs to watch movies, and I can hear them having fun. Sometimes he asks me to join them, but I think that's messed up. I can't feed his fantasy that we're a big happy family.

But I am starting to wonder if I'm handling this wrong. Being mad at him all the time is getting me nothing but more abuse. I had a bad headache tonight, and he wouldn't give me any aspirin. I'm still hungry all the time, and he feeds them first. Last night I didn't get Chicken McNuggets until two a.m., which is when their movie ended, I guess.

Maybe those girls have the right idea. Maybe I should try being nicer to him. I might as well try anything to get better treatment. I can pretend to like him. That's going to be my new strategy.

August 30
He can't wait to tell me his news.

"I saw your mom at Value City!" he says. "I was walking out, and she was walking in with two other ladies I didn't recognize."

"Was she okay? Did she look healthy?" I ask him as I start to cry.

"Yeah, she looked good," he says, like it's no big deal.

What are the chances that he and my mom would come face-to-face? I wonder if she felt anything when she was close to him. She has strong intuition, so could she have sensed me, even for a second, as she passed him? I hope so. I would give anything to feel her close to me.

My new plan seems to be working. I've been laughing a little more and crying a little less. I've been talking to him and acting less miserable, and he likes it. He's been nicer to me. He got me six goldfish, which I'm calling Ry, Riss, Chica, Blanca, Harley, and Shady, and he got me an Eminem picture in a frame. He even let me shave my legs for the first time since I got here almost a year and a half ago. It's good to have my legs as smooth as they used to be.

I've been going downstairs with him to watch TV, which means I get a little time without my chain. The other night he rented *The Passion of the Christ,* the Mel Gibson movie that he really wanted to see. It was weird to sit beside such an evil man and watch the story of Jesus.

October 8

He thinks I don't notice that he treats Gina and Michelle better. I see him going into their room and I'll bet he's bringing them things he's not giving to me. He treats them like friends but uses me for sex.

As hard as this is to admit, I want him to talk to me, just not about sex. I need someone to talk to. I haven't had a real conversation with anyone in eighteen months. When I try to talk to him, I'm careful not to mention family or anything that's bothering me. He always wants to talk about sex, but I try to get him to talk about music or anything else. He plays his bass in the house, and he's actually good. He sings, too, and thinks he's great, but his voice is terrible.

"Why can't you talk normally to me?" I ask him. He doesn't reply.

I'm having a terrible day—even the last of my fish died. I've been crying since I woke up.

"What's wrong?" he asks, sitting on the edge of my bed.

"Can I have a hug?" I say. "I just really need a hug."

I can't believe I said that. I know it's not right. It's strange. But just now I do need a hug. It's hard to be so filled with anger and hate all the time. He puts his arms around me and holds me.

"Don't worry," he says, "everything is going to be okay. I'm going to take you home one day, and you'll be back together with your family."

"When?" I ask.

"I don't know—soon," he says.

I'm so tired of waiting that I begin sobbing into his shirt.

"It's okay, it's normal to cry," he says. "I want to tell you something."

"What?" I ask, wiping my tears.

"I have feelings for you."

That's crazy. How can he say that? He treats me like garbage. He has ruined my life. And he has "feelings" for me?

I'm so confused. I decided to be nicer to him so he would treat me better. But I don't want to be his girlfriend. Why did I ask for a hug from this monster? Is this what prison does to you?

October 11

He is doing laundry and says that we all have to help, so I go to the basement with him, Gina, and Michelle.

We're looking at one another awkwardly. We've been together as a group only a few times but have never had a real conversation. Gina and Michelle live in the same room, so they talk all the time, but I'm by myself.

He stays there with us as we fold and hang clothes, so we really can't talk about anything other than TV shows and movies. Gina and Michelle actually seem nice and it feels good to talk. We even laugh a little. There is so much I'd like to ask them. How did they get here? Do they know any way out?

I think about escaping all the time. I have fantasies about prying open a window and jumping.

I never thought I could hurt anybody, but now I find myself day-dreaming about whether I could actually kill him. I picture trying to stick a knife in his back when we're in the kitchen, but he has only two or three sharp ones, and he knows exactly where they are all the time. I could hit him over the head with a beer bottle. But what if I only wounded him? If he ever thought I was trying to kill him, he'd kill me first.

He has a handgun—I saw him put it in a closet near the basement steps. He says he found it at his father's car dealership after his father died last January. He took it out to show me once. I can't get it out of my head because I know he would use it.

He weighs 180 pounds—he talks about his weight all the time—and we're all tiny. Gina's about my size, and Michelle is even smaller, not even five feet tall, so if we attacked him it would be like three puppies trying to kill a grizzly bear. I wonder if that's why he picked us. The only thing we have in common is that we're all petite, and we all have big breasts. I guess that's his type.

November 16, 2004: Psychic

Amanda

This is huge! Mom's going to be on *The Montel Williams Show*.

I just saw a promo on TV, which said she's going to be on tomorrow with Sylvia Browne, that cool psychic. I love her. This is amazing! Mom and I used to watch *Montel* all the time and we loved it when Sylvia was on. She made some amazing predictions.

I've been praying that Montel saw me on *America's Most Wanted* and that he would have Mom on with Sylvia. Now it's happening. I hope Sylvia can see that I'm kidnapped and that I'm right here, so close to home. I want my mom to know I'm alive. Sylvia has to tell her!

November 17

There she is! My mom's on TV, sitting right there with Montel and Sylvia. And they show Beth sitting in the audience. They must have flown to New York for the show. This is so exciting!

Sylvia is asking Mom about a "Cuban-looking" guy who is short and stocky. It's him! He's Puerto Rican, not Cuban, but it's close.

"Can you tell me if they'll ever find her?" Mom asks. "Is she out there?"

Then Sylvia says: "I hate this when they're in water. I just hate this. She's not alive, honey."

What? Why did she say that?

Mom's face just drops. I start crying and shouting at the TV. I'm not dead! I'm alive and I'm right here!

Now Sylvia's describing how the Cuban guy wears his pants really low. What is she talking about? I can't believe this.

My mom sounds desperate: "So you don't think I'll ever get to see her again?"

"Yeah," Sylvia tells her. "In heaven, on the other side."

This is awful. When I get out of here, I'm going to have a few words with Sylvia Browne. She is a fraud. Now my poor mother is going to be convinced I'm dead, because she trusts Sylvia. This is going to crush her.

She has to ignore what she was told and keep believing I'm alive and fighting to bring me home. If she doesn't, how can I keep hoping?

They cut to a commercial, and my mom is gone.

November 21

"I wrote a letter to my mom," I say, handing it to him. "Please let me send it."

As he takes it from me and starts reading, I tell him, "I don't say anything about you. I just tell her not to listen to Sylvia Browne, and that I'm alive. It breaks my heart that she thinks I'm dead."

"It says you're being held hostage," he says.

"Well, what do you call this?" I snap back. "I am being held hostage. Please, I don't mention anything about you. I just say that I want to come home, but I can't."

I'm crying now. I didn't mean to sass him, because that makes him mad. But I'm so upset I can't help it. I can't sleep, I can't eat. I'm sick to my stomach worrying about my mom.

"You shouldn't believe in psychics anyway," he says. "It's stupid."

"I know, but I just want her to know I'm alive."

"You can't send this," he says and then tears the letter up and hands the pieces back to me.

December 5

My mom has been on the news a lot and she seems different, sadder. She says she took down the yellow ribbons at our house, washed them, and left them in my room.

He brought me the *Plain Dealer* because there's a story about me, and it says my mom took down the posters in my room and gave away my computer. She says she's not even buying me a Christmas present this year because she's not sure anymore that I'm alive.

All because of Sylvia Browne, that fake. She put a knife right in my mom's heart because it made for good TV ratings. The article says my mom is 98 percent sure that what Sylvia told her is true, that I'm dead. She said she "lost it" after that show.

I write down what she told the reporter Stephen Hudak: "Please don't misunderstand me. I still don't want to believe it. I want to have hope but after a year and a half what else is there?"

I am crying so hard that I'm shaking. I wish God would show her some sort of sign that I'm alive. I get my strength from knowing that my mom is fighting for me. If she gives up, I'll feel like I don't exist.

December: Psychic Fallout

On the drive back to the airport after her appearance on Montel Williams's show, Louwana stared out the window in silence. She and Beth talked a little about 9/11 as they drove near Ground Zero, but Louwana didn't mention Sylvia or Amanda. When they returned home Louwana, who had been so angry for so long, now seemed only sad. Beth tried to cheer her up, but nothing seemed to get through.

On the first Christmas that Amanda had been gone, Louwana had bought her an Eminem poster and a gold bracelet, little things she thought Amanda would like. But this year there was no talk of gifts. Instead Louwana would lie silently on Amanda's bed and listen to her radio for hours, smoking and drinking and alone.

April 2, 2005: Vigils

For a year after Gina went missing, Nancy and Felix held candlelight vigils every Friday on the corner where she was last seen. The crowds eventually waned, and they held the gatherings less often, but more than fifty people turned out on the cold, windy night of the first-year anniversary of her disappearance, standing in a circle at Lorain and West 105th Street, holding hands and praying. They then marched five blocks to Wilbur Wright Middle School, chanting Gina's and Amanda's names, along with the name of another girl who had been missing from the neighborhood for a decade, Christina Adkins. Beth marched with them.

Over the past year Nancy and Felix had become aware of what seemed to be an epidemic of missing children in America, and they felt an obligation to talk about not just Gina, but all of them. Nancy began making calls to groups that supported the cause, educating herself on the issue. She discovered that thousands of children disappear in America every year, and was struck by how little she had known about them. It seemed to her that no one was paying enough attention to the issue.

Nancy only learned about Christina Adkins after her own daughter never came home from school. She started to tell everyone she could: "People are taking our children, and we've got to stop it!"

She was determined to become a public advocate, a voice for the missing kids, but she was often crippled by sadness. One night when she thought she couldn't take the pain any longer, she prayed, "Please take this burden off of me because I cannot carry it." She felt immediate relief and a shot of new energy and kept praying, "Please, God, open your arms and wrap them around Gina."

She remained certain that Gina was alive and that God would watch over her. In a quiet act of faith, Nancy opened a bank account for Gina and deposited twenty or thirty dollars in it every month.

August 2005: Testimony

On August 30, 2005, Fernando Colon stood trial on charges that he had molested Nilda and Ariel Castro's daughters, Emily, age sixteen, and Arlene, age thirteen. The previous September, at a time when Castro was holding Amanda, Gina, and Michelle captive, he had taken his two daughters to a police station to file a complaint that Colon had touched them inappropriately while they slept.

Colon insisted that the charges were false and had been instigated by Castro, who he said had coached them into making the allegations. Nilda defended Colon in court, corroborating Colon's testimony that Castro had persuaded the girls to make false charges in exchange for money and gifts.

"If anything inappropriate had occurred, my daughters would have been quick to tell me," Nilda said in an affidavit filed in the case. She explained that Arlene told her that she'd had a dream that Colon had touched her, and that dream had become "an exaggerated story."

Five days before Colon's trial, Nilda reported to police that Castro was pressuring Emily, who was then living in Fort Wayne, Indiana, to return to Cleveland to testify against Colon. Nilda said Castro told her he was going to "bring Emily back and beat your ass in front of her."

Nilda sought a restraining order in domestic relations court barring Castro from coming near her or her children, telling the court about years of violence by Castro and that he had threatened to kill her and her kids. Even though Castro had no visitation rights, she said he "frequently abducts his daughters and keeps them from [her]."

The court issued a temporary restraining order that required Castro to complete "batterer counseling" and banned him from drinking alcohol, using illegal drugs, or possessing a deadly weapon. No home visit was ordered. The temporary restraining order raised no red flags at the school system where Castro was a bus driver. A prosecutor said there were so many domestic violence cases that it was virtually impossible to check them against all school and city employees. The court then scheduled a hearing to determine whether to make that restraining order permanent. On the day of the hearing, Castro and his lawyer appeared before the magistrate, as did Nilda, but her lawyer, Robert A. Ferreri, failed to show up because he had a hearing at the same time in juvenile court.

The magistrate would not proceed without Nilda's lawyer present, and he gave her two weeks to file for a new hearing. Because she did not, her case was dismissed and Castro was free of any legal constraints. Nilda later told Elida that after her lawyer failed to appear, she lost her nerve to pursue the case.

But Colon's case went to trial and provided dramatic courtroom testimony about Ariel Castro's long history of violence against Nilda.

The defense's central argument was that Ariel Castro was a violent, vindictive, and controlling man who was fully capable of using his own daughters as a means to settle a grudge against a man who was now living with his ex-wife.

"What did take place here is not exactly a love triangle," Ferreri told the judge. "It's kind of a power triangle. It's kind of a control triangle. Mr. Castro is obsessed with power and control over Nilda."

Just after lunch on Wednesday, September 1, Castro took the witness stand.

Prosecutor John Kosko asked for his address, and Castro told him 2207 Seymour Avenue, where at that moment he was holding Amanda, Gina, and Michelle.

"Does anyone live there with you?" Kosko asked.

"No," Castro replied.

Under questioning, Castro acknowledged that his relationship with Nilda had been violent at times, but that she provoked it.

"We were always arguing, you know. She always—she always waited until I would come home, like especially on the holidays or something. She always waited for me to have a beer or two before she would start stuff, and I never understood that. Why? When I was okay, there was no fights, but for some reason, when I would have a beer or two, she always started fighting. So I couldn't understand why."

When asked if their confrontations had ever gotten physical, Castro replied, "There was times that she did get physical with me. She would throw herself on me, striking me. One time, yes, we struggled together, and we fell and she fell and hit . . . her head on the doorjamb."

Castro denied more than twenty times that he had ever laid a hand on Nilda.

Nilda took the stand the following day, describing publicly for the first time what Castro had done to her over the course of many years.

"Did Mr. Castro ever physically assault you?" Ferreri asked.

"Yes."

"Did he do that more than once?"

"Yes."

"Did Mr. Castro ever strike you in such a way that you required medical attention?"

"Yes."

"Did he ever do that more than once?"

"Yes."

"Did Mr. Castro ever cause you to get medical attention at a hospital?"

"Yes."

"Did you ever receive any cuts or any bruises from Mr. Castro?"

"Yes."

"Did you ever have any dislocated limbs from Mr. Castro?"

"Yes."

"Did you ever have any problems with your eyesight or your nerves in your face as a result of Mr. Castro?"

"Yes."

"Did you ever have any problems with your brain or the inner workings of your brain?"

"Yes."

"Thanks to Mr. Castro?"

"Yes."

Nilda recounted the first time Castro beat her, when a small disagreement escalated and he punched her in the face, grabbed her by the head, and threw her onto the concrete floor. She said Castro had punched her so many times in the face over the years that she required two reconstructive surgeries on her nose, as well as dental surgery.

She recalled that one time when she was pregnant, he demanded that she wash the dishes.

"I told him I was tired and to wait, and I yelled a little, but I don't usually yell, but I was too tired, so he just punched me in the mouth and took my teeth out. . . . He dislocated my shoulders about twice by just throwing me around, most of the time pulling my arm to the back. He felt that it was some kind of punishment that I needed."

"Did he always just hit you with his hand, or did he sometimes use other objects?"

"He used whatever he can get his hands on. Once he used a metal pipe."

"And what did he do with the pipe?"

"He beat me over the head with it. It was always on the head. Most of the time."

"And did the hospital do any surgical procedures on you at that time when he hit you with the metal piece?"

"Yes. I had maybe about twenty-five, forty stitches on my head at that time."

"Did Mr. Castro ever hit you in the head again?"

"Yes."

"Did he use his hand or did he use an object?"

"Then next time after that it was with a hand bar, weight."

"An exercise weight?"

"Yes. I was nine months pregnant with Emily. . . . He hit me over the head with it, beat me."

Nilda testified that Castro had punched her so hard in the eye that her sight was severely damaged, and it left one of her eyes permanently "squinty." She said Castro repeatedly referred to her as "his property."

"He says it all the time, repeats that to me all the time. . . . I'm scared of him."

Asked about the prognosis for the tumor that had been discovered, she testified: "I have none. I mean, there's nothing they can do for the tumor. They tried. But they couldn't do anything."

"Would it be fair to say that the prognosis is, in medical terms, terminal?"

"Yes."

Emily and Arlene had testified at the start of the trial that Colon had touched them inappropriately many times. But Nilda asserted in her own testimony that she believed Castro had manipulated the girls into making up the allegations against Colon. She said both girls had emotional and behavioral problems, and Arlene's had become much worse since her close friend Gina DeJesus had disappeared the previous year:

"I took her, Arlene, to a psychologist and he evaluated her with posttraumatic stress disorder. She was Gina's best friend, and she was with her when she disappeared, shortly before that, so it traumatized Arlene because Arlene felt responsible for her disappearance."

Gina's vanishing had affected the entire family. Arlene had to change schools and repeat seventh grade and ultimately was expelled from her new school for poor attendance and disruptive behavior.

Ferreri pressed Nilda about why she hadn't sought more help from the police over the years of beatings she endured.

"Because I always thought that he was gonna change."

"In your culture, is it likely—or in your family, if there's something that goes on, do you run to the police, or do you try to fix it up among yourselves?"

"Yes [we try to fix it among ourselves]."

"Do you consider it an intrusion on your family to bring the police into anything?"

"Yes."

"And when Mr. Castro said, 'I won't hit you anymore,' did you believe him?"

"Yes."

"Did you want to believe him?"

"I wanted—yes, I wanted to believe him because I thought that maybe he would change."

"Did you hope and pray that he would change?"

"Yes, I did."

"Do you believe he's ever capable of change?"

"No."

Colon was convicted of "gross sexual imposition," a felony, and sentenced to three years' probation, but was acquitted of the more serious charges of rape and being a "sexually violent predator." Without any physical evidence or witnesses, the only evidence against Colon was the testimony of the two girls. John Kosko, the prosecutor, said that because the case was in the end a matter of "he-said, she-said," the judge delivered a compromise verdict, which Kosko believed was fair. In the end Kosko didn't believe the theory that Castro had orchestrated the entire affair, saying that the girls' testimony was "pretty convincing."

Nilda and Colon ultimately split up.

August 23, 2005: Back to the Basement

Amanda

"Pack up everything. I want it all out of here," he says.

"What are you talking about?" I ask.

"My kids have been asking a lot of questions. They want to know why they can't go upstairs and see their old bedrooms."

I've always wondered why his mother has never been here, and why his brothers and kids don't think it's suspicious that he never lets them past the kitchen. He tells them he doesn't want them to see upstairs because it's such a mess. But I guess now they're insisting, and his daughter Emily is coming for a visit from Indiana. She's going to stay here for a couple of days, he tells me, "So I'm putting you in the basement."

I can't believe he's going to take the risk of having his daughter sleeping in this house, and I hate the idea of going back to the basement. But what can I do?

He unchains my ankle and hands me a plastic laundry basket, and I start filling it with my stuff. I gather my pens, crayons, paper, my picture of Jesus and my mom's photos and stack them neatly in the basket. I fold up the few clothes he has given me and I put them on top. I slip my diary to the bottom so he won't see it, because I'm afraid if he reads it he might rip it up.

He walks with me down to the basement, where I leave the basket. We go back up to the room and he watches as I pick up my sheets and trash-can toilet and carry them downstairs, too. Then he helps me carry out the mattress and the TV.

Every trace of me is gone from the bedroom, except for the chains. They run through a hole in the wall and are attached to something in the next room. He pulls the chains through, then moves the dresser in front of the hole to hide it.

I pray that his kids notice something is not right. We've cleaned the room up pretty well, but maybe they'll wonder why there's wood covering the windows behind the curtains.

He takes me back to the basement, where this all started more than two years ago, and then goes back upstairs. I sit on the mattress on the floor, wondering how long I'll be down here. I look around to see if there might be a way to escape, but the door to the backyard is bolted and padlocked.

After a while he comes down with Gina and Michelle. They're carrying their own things and look scared. We're all wondering what he really has in mind down here.

"I need more privacy," I tell him. "I don't want to go to the bathroom in front of them. It's embarrassing."

I can see his mind working. He always thinks that he can rig up some gizmo and find the answer to any problem somewhere in his piles of junk. And sure enough, he sees a dirty old wooden dresser and drags it to the middle of the room, like a divider.

Now when I'm sitting on my mattress, I don't have to see them. I just wish I didn't have to hear them.

Gina

I don't want to be back down here. He kept me here for two weeks after he kidnapped me. This time I'm chained to Michelle and the pole.

Amanda's ignoring us on the other side of the dresser. She's trying to pretend that we're not even here. He's told us that she doesn't like us, but I don't know why.

"You know the rules," he warns all of us. "You know what you're not supposed to talk about."

He loves rules. He has rules about which size spatula to use, which direction to flip an egg, what songs I can listen to. When I cook I have to keep the pan exactly in the center of the burner, or he calls me "retard" or "dumbass." But his biggest rule is that we're not allowed to talk about anything he says or does with us.

He must really be freaked out about his kids coming over if he's putting us all together like this.

Amanda

I'm watching my TV, and they're just a few feet away on the other side of the dresser, watching theirs. It's a little hard to concentrate with two TVs playing different channels, but I try to tune out their shows.

We've been down here for a couple of hours, and we haven't said anything to one another. I'm trying to keep to myself. But I am getting more and more curious. What is he so worried about? If he doesn't want us talking, that seems like a good reason to do it.

Why the hell not?

I slide over and look around the dresser at them.

"Hey," I say.

They both turn to look at me, surprised.

I'm whispering so that they understand that I'm trying to make sure he doesn't hear us. It's quiet upstairs now, so maybe he's out. But for all we know, he could be hiding at the top of the stairs, testing us to see if we're talking.

"What are you guys watching?" I ask.

"Just stupid stuff," Gina says.

I move my chain so I can sit on their side of the dresser, and we start talking a little. It's awkward at first, but we discuss music and TV shows. I mention that I like Eminem, and Gina says she's into Christina Aguilera. She says she misses her family and her mom's cooking.

I tell them about him driving by my sister's house and telling me that he saw her girls outside wearing matching clothes. That really scared me, I tell them, because I knew it was a threat. He meant he could kidnap them if I didn't do what he said.

"He did the same thing to me!" Gina says. "He told me that if I wanted company he would kidnap my friend Chrissy."

The more we talk, the more I like them. Gina is nicer than I thought, and I think our families have a lot in common. We have seen them together on TV, so we make jokes about Tennessee hillbillies and Cleveland Puerto Ricans hanging out, and we actually laugh.

"Our families are better friends than we are," Gina says.

A Will Smith movie is playing on their TV.

"He's so cute," I say.

"Oh, yeah, he's cute," Gina agrees.

"Does he tell you not to watch TV shows with black people?" I ask.

"Yes!" they both say.

We talk about what a horrible racist he is, and I tell them how he took my radio, opened it up, and stuck a little piece of a plastic spoon from Wendy's inside, so I couldn't turn the dial to the station that plays mostly rap music.

We make fun of how cheap he is. He insists that I water down the dishwashing liquid because he says a small bottle needs to last for at least two months. If I need more, I have to ask him, and he puts a little pea-size drop on the sponge. He has a fit if I use too much.

It feels good to talk, and to know that we're all feeling the same things.

Gina

Amanda isn't stuck-up at all, like I thought. She listens and cares when I tell her about all the sick stuff he does to me and Michelle, like how he rapes me and her while we're chained together. It's as horrible watching it happen to someone else as it is having it happen to you.

Amanda's crying now as I tell her.

"I'm so sorry," she says. "I didn't know he was doing that to you."

She says that he told her that he was not having sex with me and Michelle, so she thought it was easier for us.

"He says he has me for sex, but you two are here to be his maids. I always figured he was lying, because why would you go to all the trouble of kidnapping two girls just to have them clean your house?"

We talk about how he says he has a "sexual problem," and he calls his thing Charlie.

"He told me it's not his fault," I say. "He blames Charlie. He's always saying, 'What Charlie wants, Charlie gets.'"

Amanda

I realize now what he's been doing. He lies to them about me, and he lies to me about them. That's his way of dividing us and making sure we don't trust one another. Screw him. We're on to his mind games.

Conan O'Brien's show comes on TV, and there's a funny skit about a bear in a diaper that runs around being really obscene. It's so silly that we all crack up. It feels great to laugh after we've been talking for hours and crying.

It's late, and I'm about to fall asleep. But I feel like we need to get something straight first.

"Anything we talk about, we have to trust each other not to say anything to him," I tell them. "Otherwise we're going to get each other in trouble. We have to stick together."

August 24

Amanda

I've barely gotten to sleep when I feel him next to me. He has his clothes off, and he's pulling at my sweatpants. It's humiliating. Gina and Michelle are on the other side of the dresser, and I know they're just pretending to be asleep.

"They're right there," I whisper through my tears. "Stop it."

He's mad, but he gets up and unchains me. "Come upstairs," he orders, loud enough for everybody to hear. "I need you to help me clean the kitchen."

I walk upstairs with him and he takes me to the living room, where he finishes what he started downstairs.

When he's done with me, he leads me back to the basement. It's so hot in the house that I can feel his sweat all over me. I smell like him, and it sickens me. He twists the chain around my ankle again and snaps the padlock shut.

August 25

Gina

We've been down here all day, watching TV and playing with a PlayStation. We've been talking about how he kidnapped us—it was almost the same experience for Amanda and me. He tricked us into his car by talking about one of his kids.

We hear his footsteps across the kitchen floor, and as the basement door opens Amanda hurries back over to her side of the dresser.

"My daughter Rosie is coming over," he says.

Oh, my God. That's my friend Arlene. Rosie is her middle name, and a lot of people call her that. I haven't seen her since that day I was taken, except when she was on *America's Most Wanted,* crying about missing me.

"Don't make a sound," he warns us. "Don't talk. Don't get up to use the bathroom. Shut the TVs off. I better not hear any sound from down here."

He turns off the light and leaves.

"She's my friend," I whisper as we sit in the dark. "We go to school together, and she was with me right before he kidnapped me."

Amanda says he was dropping Arlene off at her mom's house right before he kidnapped her. Poor Arlene. What will she think if she ever finds out?

We have other connections to his kids, too. Amanda tells us she went to school with Angie, his older daughter, and that she's met his son, Anthony. Michelle says she knows his daughter Emily.

I hope the police notice all the connections we have to him and his kids.

We hear the back door open, then footsteps and voices in the kitchen.

Arlene is ten feet over my head.

Amanda

We can't make out what they're saying, but Gina can tell it's Arlene's voice. There's somebody else up there, too. Maybe a friend of Arlene's? They walk through the kitchen and up the stairs to the second floor. We're too scared to make a sound.

Arlene lived in this house until she was about five or six, and he told me her bedroom was the one where he kept Michelle for a long time. So I guess she wants to see her old room.

After a few minutes we hear them coming back down, and then the living room TV comes on. It sounds like they are watching videos and having a good time.

"They're up there laughing, and look where we are," I whisper.

We're all mad, but we can't help being a little goofy, cupping our ears with our hands, as if that will help us hear them better. Of course it doesn't work, but we're giggling. It's hard to stay completely quiet, especially when you know you have to.

"What if we scream?" Gina asks.

We've all been thinking the same thing, but I've been too afraid to speak it out loud.

"I don't think so," I say. It's too risky. He's smart, and Arlene is only fourteen. I'm sure he could come up with some story. He could tell her, "Oh, my girlfriend is downstairs with her friends, and they're just messing around." He could think of some lie that Arlene would believe. He's that clever. I've seen it.

And what would he do to us?

He doesn't make mistakes. I'm so worried the police and FBI will never figure it out. He seems like a nice, normal, middle-aged, friendly guy. He doesn't look crazy.

That's how he gets away with this. He hides in plain sight. He says he can get away with anything, including killing us. If his daughter found out about us, how do we know he wouldn't do something terrible to her to protect himself?

I tell Gina and Michelle all this, but I don't say what else I'm thinking: I'm still not completely sure I can trust them. We have become closer down here in the past few days, but maybe they are so afraid of him they would betray me. If we screamed for help, they could claim it was all my idea, and he might kill only me.

"I think we should just keep quiet," I say. "It's too dangerous."

Gina

Amanda is right. We don't know what he might do if we screamed.

I once told him my father was looking for me and asked him what he would do if my dad found us: "Would you shoot him?"

"I'm not going to talk about that," he answered.

I do think he would kill my dad. He doesn't care about anybody but himself.

After Arlene has been up there for about an hour, we hear them get up and walk out the back door. He comes down the basement stairs in a good mood.

"They're gone," he says. "You can watch TV now if you want."

He's talking a lot, which usually means he's happy.

"Rosie wanted to see the basement, but I made up a lie," he says. "I told her I couldn't find the key, and it was a mess down there anyway."

He's so proud of himself.

He keeps talking about what a great time he had with Arlene, and how they were laughing as they watched old family videos.

August 27, 2005: Chained in the Van

Gina

We've been down in the cellar for four days. Between visits from his kids, he's come down here a bunch of times to take Michelle upstairs to help with the "cleaning." Yeah, right. We know what he's really doing with her, and she tells us anyway. So why does he try to hide it? I don't get it.

He takes Amanda upstairs, too, and she's crying each time she comes back, but he hasn't bothered me. I don't know why. Maybe seeing Arlene has made him feel guilty. It's so rare that I get this much time away from his disgusting body.

Late at night we're all watching TV when we hear him come down the stairs.

"Okay," he says. "Time to go."

Thank God. It's so damp and smelly down here.

"Emily is coming to stay overnight for a couple of days. I have to get you out of here. You're going to the garage."

The garage? Oh, no. Maybe Arlene or his other kids figured out there was something weird going on here, so he has to get rid of us.

He unlocks the chain tying me and Michelle to the pole and makes us stand up. We're still chained together at the ankles. He tells us to pick up our pillows and sheets and follow him out the basement door up the steps and into the darkness of the backyard, like prison inmates in leg chains.

"Be quiet out here," he orders. "No noise!"

"Are you going to kill us?" I ask him.

"If I were going to kill you, I would have done that already," he says, laughing.

As we make our way across the backyard in the dark I realize it's the first time I've been outside in a year and a half. I smell freshly cut grass and feel a breeze. We see lights in the neighbors' houses on both sides, but I'm too scared to make a sound. The garage door is open, and I can see his van inside, facing out.

"Keep your heads down and walk straight to the garage," he says.

We shuffle along the side of the van, looking at the ground. The side door is open, and he tells us to get in. The two seats in the back are folded all the way down, and he makes us lie down there, chaining us to the seats.

"I'll be right back," he says. "Remember—no noise."

We lie in the dark, afraid to say a word, and he returns a couple of minutes later with Amanda. She has a chain around her ankle and she's carrying her pillow. He has a small mattress that he wedges through the van door, and Amanda climbs in and sits on it. He locks her chains to the seats, too.

He brings out Amanda's TV and a tiny fan, sets them between the front seats, and plugs them into the garage wall. He gives us a little blue bucket for a toilet and hands us some chips and a couple of old pop bottles filled with water.

"I'll be back in a little while," he says, locking the van doors.

It must be a hundred degrees in here. The little fan is swinging slowly from side to side, pushing around the hot, wet air.

August 28

Amanda

This van. It's the one. It's the same maroon van that drove me away from my life. I see that day happening all over again: He pulls up alongside me, and I get into that passenger seat. So stupid.

I'm lost enough in my thoughts that at first I don't hear Michelle speaking.

"I always thought that you didn't like me," she says.

"What?" I ask.

"I wanted to be your friend at the beginning," she says, "but I thought you didn't like me."

I'm too hot for this conversation. Sweat is pouring off me, and it stinks in here. The bucket is on the floor right next to my mattress and everybody has used it. I'm in a rotten mood and I snap back at her, "Don't be stupid. I don't need friends."

I don't know why I say that. I'm not trying to be mean, but I just gave her my super-bitch attitude. I think I'm just fed up with everything.

Michelle doesn't say anything, but Gina speaks up: "Oooh, you are so cool!" she says to me sarcastically.

We look at one another for a second, and then all crack up. Gina totally called me out, and it was exactly the right thing to lighten the mood. It was like she popped a balloon, and all the built-up tension rushed out.

Amanda

Since we were taken to the basement five days ago the news on our little TV has been nothing but Hurricane Katrina. New Orleans is underwater, and it looks like a war zone. We feel bad for all those poor people who lost their homes. Rain is falling hard on the roof of the garage, and the news says our storm in Ohio is what's left of Katrina, moving north.

The garage door opens, and he comes in carrying a Georgio's pizza and a bag of candy. When he opens the van door he cringes from the smell and takes the bucket, dumps it out in the yard, then brings it back. It still stinks because he didn't bother to rinse it out. Even with the fan there's no circulation, and we're all feeling sick, so we ask him for some air. He cracks open one of the little sliding windows.

"Keep your heads down," he says.

He opens the garage door for a few minutes while he putters around near the front of the van. He's obsessed with making the house look normal so the neighbors don't suspect anything. The people on one side are from Puerto Rico, and he's always speaking Spanish with them. Usually on summer days he's out in the yard or the garage working, so he says they might think something is strange if the garage door stays closed for days at a time. He doesn't miss a detail.

He tells us Emily just arrived at the house.

Gina

I'm lying here, hot and sweaty, trying to think about anything but the heat.

Whomp!

What the hell? Somebody just smacked me with a pillow.

"Michelle!" I shout.

"I didn't do anything!" she says. "That was Amanda!"

I look at Amanda, and she's cracking up.

"Okay, girl!" I say, and I swing my pillow right back at her.

Whomp! Whomp! Whomp!

It's a full-on pillow fight now. All three of us are slamming one another with our pillows and laughing like crazy.

"We better be quiet," I warn.

But it's no use. This is too much fun. I can't remember the last time I had fun.

Whomp!

I hope he doesn't hear us.

August 29

Amanda

I wake to the sound of the garage door. He opens it just enough to duck under and then pulls it shut again. I pretend to be asleep. I can't tell if Gina and Michelle are sleeping or not, but they don't move.

When the door was open I could see light, so it must be morning. He slips into the van quietly, crawls up next to me, and says, "Take your clothes off."

"Please, they're right there," I say, nodding toward Gina and Michelle. "Please, no."

"Just shut up and do it."

He yanks at my sweats and is on top of me. It's such a small space, and I know Gina and Michelle have to be hearing this.

I think of his daughter. She's now sleeping comfortably in the house while he attacks me fifty feet away.

When he's done, he'll probably go inside and cook her breakfast.

We're watching afternoon TV when the garage door opens again.

I guess it's time for the daily show for the neighbors.

But instead he unplugs our TV and fan from the garage wall, gets into the driver's seat, and puts the key in the ignition. What's he up to?

"Okay, I'm going to take the van out of the garage for a couple of minutes," he says. "Get under your covers. Don't get up. Don't move. Don't do nothing."

He starts the engine and pulls the van ahead just a few feet until it's completely out of the garage. It's so bright out that after all the darkness my eyes hurt.

He gets out of the van and leaves the engine running.

I peek out and see him go into the garage. Was the van blocking something he couldn't reach?

Then I have an idea.

Gina

Amanda whispers that she thinks she can reach the gas pedal.

Her chain is too short, so she can't actually sit in the driver's seat, but she thinks she could probably press the gas pedal with her hand and ram the van through the gate across the driveway and out into the street.

Somebody would have to notice that!

"Do you think we should?" I whisper.

She's never driven a car. I wonder if she even knows how to do it.

This is terrifying. We've been fantasizing in the garage about how we could escape. He has a lawn mower, a snow blower, and some tools there. We've been talking about how we could attack him with the lawn mower or hit him with a shovel.

But it's just talk. We couldn't reach anything because of the chains. And what if we hit him on the head with a shovel and didn't kill him? Then he'd be so mad that he'd kill us.

But Amanda looks serious. She's staring at that gas pedal.

"That's crazy," I say.

Amanda

I can do this. But I have to move, now.

I have to stretch myself into the front-seat area, put the car in drive, and push that gas pedal. I think the chain is long enough. If I can make a big enough crash, somebody will come to see what's going on.

But what if nobody does?

I'm trying to get my courage up. *I can do this. I have to do this.* I'm breathing harder. All I can see is that gas pedal. Gotta go now!

Just then the driver's side door opens, and he hops in and reverses the van back into the garage.

"Good job keeping quiet," he tells us.

I feel my whole body deflate. Did I just miss our best chance of escaping? Maybe our only chance?

He plugs in the TV and the fan, locks the van, and closes the garage door. We were outside for maybe five minutes. Now we're back in the dark.

Why did I hesitate? I keep replaying it in my mind, again and again and again.

August 30

Amanda

He's back. It's dark outside, and he's in one of those nasty moods where you have to be extra careful.

"Emily's gone, so you're going back inside," he says.

He unchains us, and we pick up our pillows. The only sound is the clinking of the chains as we walk across the yard. When we're back in the house he tells us to fill the laundry baskets with our stuff. We're all moving to new rooms.

I'm going back to the big room with the yellow walls that Gina and Michelle have been in together for a while. And they're being put into the tiny room next to it, which is not much bigger than a closet. The only way into their room is through my room, which has the only entrance to the hallway. So by bolting my door, he has all three of us trapped inside. It's simpler for him.

I don't know why he put the two of them in the smaller room, and me by myself in the big one. Just when things are getting a little better between us, I'm afraid this is going to make Gina and Michelle resent me. When we have so little, it's easy to get jealous over even the smallest things.

When we walk in, we see the chains waiting for us. He locks my ankle with one fixed to the big steam radiator. He links Gina and Michelle together by the ankles, and they sit down on one mattress.

I hope they keep their promise and don't tell him anything that we talked about.

September 6

Amanda

Everyone in this house is a liar.

He just yelled at me for telling Gina and Michelle that he forces me to have sex, and he's furious that I was thinking about trying to escape in the van.

I'm scared about what he's going to do to me. Sometimes he hits me across the face. Sometimes he won't feed me, or gives me only the worst leftovers. Other times he unplugs everything for days: my TV, my radio, my fan.

How could they have told him those things?

Maybe they didn't. Maybe he was spying on us.

I go to their door and ask them why they talked. They claim they didn't. They say he knows things about them that I must have told him, so they're mad at me.

I don't know what to believe, so I don't believe anyone. I'm done trusting anybody in this house. The only person I can rely on is me.

Gina

I don't know what Amanda is so angry about. I didn't say anything to him.

He told us that she thinks we're stupid, and that she's helping him watch us. I can't believe that's true. She seemed so nice in the van, but I don't know what the truth is anymore.

I'm so annoyed that he moved me and Michelle into this tiny room. It's completely unfair. I guess I'm not the new girl anymore.

"Why does she have the big room, and the two of us are stuck in this shoebox?" I ask him.

"She has more stuff than you," he says.

"You're putting us in a shoebox!" I say, but he doesn't care.

I just want to go home. I already missed my fifteenth birthday. I want out of here.

Christmas Day, 2005: Broken Heart

Amanda

My third Christmas here.

I wake up chained next to him, just as he's leaving to go to a family Christmas party. At least I have my tree. It's a little plastic green one from the dollar store that he bought for me. It's about two feet tall, and it came in a box with some ornaments and a string of different-colored lights. I set it up on my dresser in early November to add a little cheer to this dull room.

I try to go back to sleep because at least when I'm asleep I don't feel lonely.

When I wake up hours later it's quiet in the house, so he must still be out. I plug in the tape I've been making of all the newscasts about me. My TV has a built-in VCR, so I can use it to tape over old movies. I record everything I can about my family on the news, so I can see them whenever I want.

I start writing in my diary, and note the time: 2:57 p.m.

Hi Mom! How are you? Are you having a good day? I hope you all are! I'm sitting here crying. I miss my life! We're so close! I'm so lucky for that. I always had someone to talk to. Just the little things now are such big things—saying good night or good morning or I love you.

He comes in from his party. I think he's been drinking.

"Merry Christmas," he says.

"It doesn't feel like Christmas. I'm in prison."

I'm usually careful not to talk back. But I can't help myself today.

"It's not a prison," he barks. "You have it good."

"It's worse than prison," I tell him. "If I were in a regular prison my family would know that I am alive and they could come visit. Prisoners get to go outside for an hour a day. I can't do anything. I can't even feel sunshine on my face."

I'm making him mad.

"You have TV! You have food!" he shouts. "If you were home you would be slumming. You would be still working at Burger King."

He storms out, slamming the door, and bolts it from the outside.

I'm going to forget him and focus on happier things, like what's happening at my house right now. It's almost dinnertime, so I imagine my mom roasting a turkey and making ham and mashed potatoes. I bet she has music on. I wonder if Beth let Ry and Rissa open one present on Christmas Eve like we used to.

I start writing again:

This has taught me a lot—like NEVER take life or anything for granted! Sitting down and eating dinner with your family or watching TV with them and talking and laughing!

At six o'clock I turn on the television, and there is breaking news: my mom is in the hospital. She has some kind of pancreatic illness. She's lost a lot of weight and is in bad shape. Here I am feeling bad for myself, and suddenly everything is worse! Maybe I should be grateful for what I have, like he says.

Please Lord, make her better. Don't let her pass. Especially while I'm here. I need to see her. She's my everything. She's gotten me this far. If something happens to her, I don't know what I'll do.

I cry for hours, flipping around the channels for more news of her, but there is nothing.

I light my candle for Mom.

I put her picture on my bed and lie down next to it. It's the only way I have to be close to her.

December 26

I've been up all night crying and watching the candle burn.

I'm wearing my glow-in-the-dark plastic rosary. He had been keeping it in the bathroom as a kind of night light, and a few months ago I asked him if I could have it.

He's not really religious anyway, so he doesn't care. He goes to church sometimes, usually St. Michael's, which has Mass in Spanish. But I think he goes mainly to get the free food they give away. He says his mother joined the Jehovah's Witnesses and doesn't celebrate Christmas anymore.

This is all my fault. If I hadn't gotten in that van and been kidnapped, my mom would be healthy. I'm sorry for everything I put her through.

I keep having this dream: I'm free, I get to my house and run up the stairs and open the door, and my mom is sitting there watching TV, and I run to her and hug her so tightly.

December 29

Finally, on Channel 3 at six, Mom is back on the news. She has an infection called *C. diff* because some doctor didn't wash his hands before doing surgery. They don't say why she had the surgery, or when, but she had to have another operation today to stop the internal bleeding. I can't believe what I'm hearing.

"If my mom dies, will you let me go to the funeral?" I ask him.

"Sure," he says.

Maybe he'd let me go in a disguise or come up with some other plan so that I could go out and he wouldn't get arrested.

Hours pass until I hear another news update. It's worse. Now they're saying she's in critical condition! There's Beth at the hospital. She has a baby boy! I didn't even know she was pregnant. I wonder when he was born. I have my candle burning for you, Mom. Hang in there, and when I get home I will take care of you.

December 30

On the news I hear that my mother went in for yet another surgery today. That's two surgeries in two days.

I've heard her tell TV reporters that not knowing what happened to me is the hardest part. I understand exactly how she feels, because it's terrible not knowing how she is doing.

December 31

It's New Year's Eve.

I have a little tape recorder he gave me, and I'm making a tape of Aerosmith songs Mom likes so I can listen to them and think of her.

All of a sudden the flame on my candle just got a lot stronger. I hope that's a sign. Maybe it means she's doing better. I keep watching the news, but they don't have anything about her.

I miss my sister and can't wait to hold her new baby. I don't know his name, so I call him "Little Man." I wish we could all be together on New Year's, eating great food. We always have Tennessee Pride sausage, the roll that you slice into patties. Just thinking about it is making me hungry.

It's almost midnight. Ten . . . nine . . . eight. Everyone on TV in Times Square looks so excited, but I am crying harder and harder. There goes the ball. This is the third New Year's in a row that I'm not with my mom, locked up by myself in this room.

Now it's 2006. Maybe this year will be better.

January 25

It's been a month since there has been any news about my mom. Maybe she's better and went home from the hospital.

He unplugged my lamp, my TV, and my radio because he was mad at me. So I just sit here in the dark, though I can still write in my diary, because I have the light from Mom's candle to help me.

But now he comes in and he's being a jerk and I can't take it anymore, so I call him an asshole.

"Take it back," he demands.

Take it back? What is he, six years old?

"You call me names all the time, and *you* never take it back," I tell him.

"Apologize!" he says, more angry now.

When I tell him I won't, he takes a needle and digs it into my toe until blood starts pouring out, and I scream.

March 2

His alarm goes off before six. I'm sleeping downstairs in the dining room with him. He's been making me do that a lot. It's Thursday, so he has to go to work. I still can't believe they let him drive kids on a school bus.

He gets the key from the kitchen and unlocks the chain around my ankle. I don't want to wake up but he walks me upstairs. He always stays so close behind me whenever I'm not chained that I can feel his breath. Like I'm going to run. Where would I go? I don't need him hitting me or taking away my TV, and I do need sleep. I lie down on my bed, and he chains my ankle. I think I'm going to have scars for life from these chains.

I flip on the six a.m. news to see if there's anything about my mom. They're talking about the weather. It's freezing rain outside: thirty-two degrees, with a wind chill of twenty-one.

Breaking news: LOUWANA MILLER, MOTHER OF AMANDA BERRY, HAS PASSED AWAY FROM A MASSIVE HEART ATTACK.

I can barely breathe. I stare at the TV. I'm numb. I don't know what else to do. I pick up a pen and start writing:

> *March 2, 2006. 6:27 a.m.,*
> *Thursday.*
>
> *Hi Mommy. How are you? I know you're doing better because you're with the Lord now, in a better place. At least, I know you're not in pain anymore. You were in the hospital for almost three months! I'm so sorry I wasn't by your side. I didn't get to hug or kiss you, and I never will be able to again.*
>
> *Is this my fault? You were fine when I was there. I always pictured when I got to return I'd run into your arms and squeeze you and see your beautiful smile, your beautiful face. But now I never will. I know you'll always be looking down over me and will always know where I am.*
>
> *I hope Beth saves everything because I need to have your scent and your stuff close to me. God must have needed an angel. There's no other reason he would have taken you. You're so young.*

Why did God do this? I won't be able to even go to your funeral or
touch you one last time. I love you, I love you, I love you. Thank you
for never giving up on me and everything you've done for me.
 R.I.P.
 God bless you.
     Love,
     Me.

I watch the news all day. It's the top story. People on TV are saying my mom was never the same after I disappeared and that she died of a broken heart.

Gina opens the door.

"Did you see the news?" she asks me.

"Yeah," I say.

"I'm sorry about your mother."

That's kind of her. I know she's being nice, but I don't want to talk to her about this. I just want to be left alone. I want my mom.

He's gone all day until he comes back with bags of Wendy's for dinner. He's standing in the doorway between our rooms when I hear Gina ask him, "Did you see the news?"

"What news?" he asks.

He acts like he doesn't know. Maybe he doesn't.

"My mom passed," I say. I'm still crying.

He doesn't say anything but just hands me a bag. I shake my head; I'm not hungry.

"I want a cigarette," I tell him.

"You should quit," he says. He's been trying to get us all to quit, so I haven't had a cigarette in weeks.

"My mom is dead and I really need a cigarette, please."

"Okay, okay," he says.

He goes out and returns a few minutes later with a pack of Marlboros. I light the first one and keep flipping the channels to find more news.

I watch all night, not getting any sleep, but it's just the same stuff over and over. Nothing new.

It's already morning when he pushes the door open.

That look in his eyes. I know what he wants. My mom just died, and this is what he wants from me?

"You can't do this," I say.

I can't stop him.

March 5

Eminem's movie, *8 Mile*, is on TV when he brings me a copy of the *Plain Dealer*. There's a story about Mom on the front page of Metro. It makes me smile to see what Regina Brett wrote about her:

> She didn't act the way moms of missing children do on TV, delicately wiping tears with folded tissues while whispering pleas for help. Louwana was angry. She chain-smoked Marlboros. She didn't trust the police, so she put her own phone number on the flyers. She would cuss out the very people who tried to help her, then she would apologize and sob like a baby, tears rolling down her big, puffy cheeks.

That sounds just like her!

I also learned from the article that she named me for a Conway Twitty country-western song called "Amanda" that starts, *"Amanda light of my life."* She used to sing it to me, but I didn't know that's where she got my name.

I hope Beth saves all her stuff. I want to keep her toothbrush, soap, shampoo, her cigarettes and lighter. Everything she touched. The clothes, hairbrush, pillows. I want to sleep in her bed.

"You told me if somebody close to me dies, like my mom or dad, you would let me go to the funeral," I remind him.

"I never said that," he says.

"Yes, you did!" I shout.

Now he's mad.

"No!" he says.

"I want to go to her funeral. Please let me go."

He walks out.

March 7

The news shows clips from the funeral, and I see Beth carrying her new baby, and Teddy and Aunt Theresa. I can't see anybody else, because they're filming it from the back of the church. I wonder if Daddy is there.

I see the casket. It's white. That's what I hoped they'd get. It has gold trim and pink flowers on top.

At least Mom doesn't have to be in pain anymore because from heaven she knows where I am, and that I'm alive.

I don't know where she's buried, but when I get free I'm going to visit her grave all the time.

I wish I had a cigarette or some weed for my nerves, but he has cut me off. He says it's too expensive.

April 2

He tells me he saw a storage truck in front of my family's house. I don't know why he drives by there, but I'm glad to hear that Beth is saving Mom's stuff.

Mom died a month ago today. I made her a butterfly with hearts on it. I saw on TV that she made a "missing" poster for me with butterflies, so they are going to be our special thing.

I'm so sad and lonely, I can barely eat.

I want to die so I can be with her.

April 22

Happy birthday to me. I'm twenty. I have a secret. I think I'm pregnant. I missed my period, and I'm throwing up all the time.

I think this has something to do with Mom. It's crazy. All this time and I've never gotten pregnant. But then she dies, and now I'm pretty sure I am.

I think my mom sent this baby. It's her way of giving me an angel. Someone to help pull me through, give me a reason to fight.

I think she is sending me a miracle.

May 2006: First Trimester

Amanda

Yuck, Fritos. When I was in high school, I ate them by the bag. Now all it takes is one whiff, and I'm puking my guts out. He has been leaving bowls of Fritos out in case he doesn't get home by dinnertime, and I can't escape the smell. I try to move the trash-can toilet as far from my bed as I can, but I need to keep it close enough that I can retch into it. I had no idea that's what pregnancy does to you.

I worry about what he's going to do when he figures out that I'm having a baby. He's already begun to notice that the only thing I can keep down is milk and cereal. For every meal I ask for the same thing: Peanut Butter Captain Crunch or Cinnamon Toast Crunch cereal. I've been telling him I have the flu, but this is getting to be the world's longest illness. I feel dizzy and faint, too, and I think my blood sugar is out of whack.

I weighed about a hundred twenty pounds when he kidnapped me, and I'm probably ninety-five pounds now. I wish he had a scale, because I still seem to keep losing weight.

Last year, when he put us all in the basement and the van, Michelle told me that he beat her to make her miscarry. I once saw him slam Michelle into a wall. He said they were "play fighting," just messing around, but Michelle said later that it was because he was trying to force her to have a miscarriage.

If he didn't let her carry that baby, will he let me?

He gets home from work and brings Burger King food to Gina and Michelle, and then comes into my room with a burger and fries.

"No thanks," I tell him. "I'm still too sick. I can't keep anything down but cereal."

He looks at me suspiciously. "Are you pregnant?"

I feel the breath sucked right out of my lungs.

"I think so. I missed my period."

He doesn't say anything. I'm trying to read the expression on his face. Is he furious? Happy? Worried? He stays silent, but his eyes are saying, *Oh, shit.*

I can tell he's thinking. I've seen this before. Whenever he has a problem, his mind starts turning as he figures out how to solve it. I'm frozen with fear as I watch him deciding how to solve this "problem."

Finally he says: "We could always bring it to a church right after it's born, and leave it on the steps. Somebody would take care of it."

"Please," I say softly. "I want to keep the baby."

He doesn't answer but only looks confused.

Gina

I hate summer in this house. It's the worst time of year. It must be a hundred degrees in my room, sometimes hotter. I sweat so much that I soak my sheets. Sometimes it feels good to roll over into the puddle of sweat, because it's a little cooler.

It doesn't help that Amanda is puking constantly. The smell from her room is horrible. She lies, too. She's been telling us she isn't pregnant, but then he tells us she is. I make fake puking sounds just to bug her and to let her know that I know she's pregnant.

He gives her special treatment. She has the bigger bedroom to herself and she has the nicer TV. I have to scrub the floor on my hands and knees, and she never does. He says she doesn't want to because it will mess up her nails. He always tells us that we have to have sex with him because she doesn't want to. She gets first choice of the food that he brings home. I used to be the favorite one, but those days are over. Now it's Amanda for sure. I think he actually likes her. And weirdest of all, when he's with me now, it's like he's trying to hide it from her.

"Let's go downstairs to clean," he tells me, loud enough that everybody can hear. Then we go to the living room, where he forces himself on me. It's almost like he thinks Amanda would be jealous. Maybe she would be, because things are just getting stranger here.

I know it's mean but it's fun to get on her nerves. She told me she hates the sound of people chewing with their mouth open, so when he gets me gum I make sure to chew it really loudly. She comes to the door between our rooms and gives me a dirty look. It's so funny. I do it with bananas and hamburgers and fries, too, so it sounds like a cow, and Amanda goes crazy.

She also hates the hip-hop song "Laffy Taffy," so whenever it comes on the radio, I turn up the volume. She screams at us to turn it down, and Michelle and I can't stop laughing and we sing as loud as we can: "Shake that Laffy Taffy!"

I don't know why I think it's so funny. I just do.

July: Second Trimester

Amanda

I just watched the July 4 fireworks on Channel 3. He went to a barbecue at his mother's house and now he's back with leftovers. For the first time in over two months, food smells good. In fact, it smells delicious. He brought us back ribs, salad, rice and beans. I can't stop eating.

"Wow, you were hungry," he says, sounding like he actually cares.

I'm startled because I remember all those times when I was hungry and begged him for food, and he said no. But now he's being kinder. I hope this lasts.

It's been a month since I told him I was pregnant. I don't feel nauseous anymore, but I keep fainting. Even though I'm finally eating real food I know I'm still not eating right. I wish I had vitamins, but he says I don't need them.

One day I passed out and fell down on the floor of my room. He picked me up, put me on the bed, and made me ramen noodle soup. But another time I fainted in the hall upstairs, and he just left me lying there. He was with me when it happened and decided that while I was passed out he would go into Gina and Michelle's room and get what he always wants. I must have been lying there for fifteen minutes, if not more, and when I came to I saw him zipping up his pants and leaving their room.

I don't know how he can treat me this way. I'm having a baby. What if there was seriously something wrong with me or the baby? Doesn't he care? I'm hurt and angry that he's still having sex with them, but I don't understand why I feel this way. He tells me that he's not and he's always calling Gina his "cousin" and saying he wouldn't touch her. But it's obvious that he is. I hate it that he sneaks around and lies. I want to kill him, but I also want to be with him. God, what's wrong with me?

September 22: Digging for Gina

Gina

"Hey, you're on TV!" he shouts, waking me out of a dead sleep. It's about noon, and I was up all night, like I usually am.

I jump up and turn on my TV and see lots of cops at some house I don't recognize. The reporters say the police got a tip that some guy named Matthew Hurayt buried my body under his garage, so they're ripping the place apart with big machines.

He comes to sit on the end of my bed, watching with me.

"They ain't gonna find you," he says.

"Yeah," I tell him. "No kidding."

"What a waste of taxpayers' money." He thinks it's funny that the cops are looking in the wrong place.

It's bad for me because it means they have no idea where I actually am. They're so close! The house is on West 50th Street. I could easily walk there in maybe ten minutes.

I watch the live news coverage all day long. Hundreds of people are on the street watching. They say Hurayt served time for molesting two little boys. The concrete floor in his garage is new, so the reporters are saying they think maybe he put it in to hide my body. They're even digging up under a doghouse.

What if they do find a body under there? Maybe they'll tell my parents it's me, just to keep them quiet. If they say it's me, then they won't have to look for me anymore, and it'll get my mom off their backs. No more vigils, no more explaining why the police haven't found me yet. I think they could do that.

At about eight o'clock the police announce they didn't find a body.

My mom is on the TV again and she's crying. "I know deep in my heart that my baby's still out there," she says. "I just want whoever has her to let her go. Just let her go so she can come home."

October: Third Trimester

Amanda

"My ears are ringing," he says, like it's a national tragedy.

I'm six months pregnant, my breasts and legs are sore, I can't sleep because of the chains, I'm getting more and more scared about delivering a baby alone in this house, and he thinks I care that his ears are ringing?

"So why don't you go to a doctor?" I tell him. "Maybe you should take *me* to the doctor, too. Pregnant women are supposed to go to the doctor."

That came out a little sassy, but I'm so miserable that I don't care.

He ignores me, thank goodness, and says, "I'm going to the library."

An hour later he's back with a thick medical encyclopedia and starts reading all the reasons that his ears might be ringing. We're sitting in the living room, and I wait until I think he might be done worrying about himself.

"Can I look at that?" I ask.

"Sure," he says. "But only down here. You can't take it upstairs."

"Why not?"

"Just do it."

I know exactly why he won't let me take it upstairs. Somehow he figured out my plan to leave "Help me!" notes in his library books. I dreamed of doing that when I first saw that he was borrowing books. I thought about writing on a page inside, "This is Amanda Berry. Please call the

Amanda Berry (left) was kidnapped on April 21, 2003, one day before her seventeenth birthday. Gina DeJesus (below) was only fourteen when she disappeared nearly a year later, on April 2, 2004.

2207 Seymour Avenue, the house in Cleveland where Ariel Castro kept three women imprisoned for about a decade.

After their abductions, Amanda and Gina were each initially held in the cluttered Seymour house basement, where they were chained to a post.

A few weeks after she was taken, Gina wrote a letter to her parents to reassure them that she alive, but Castro never allowed her to send it.

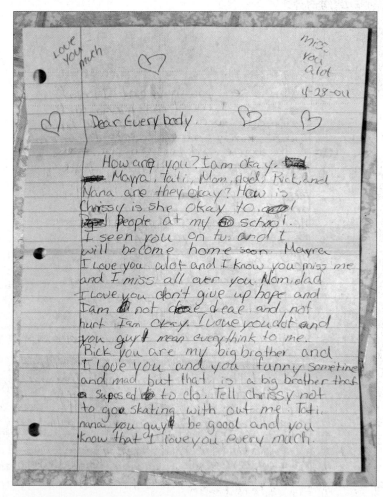

Louwana Miller appeared often in the media pleading for the return of her daughter. She died in 2006 without ever learning what happened to Amanda.

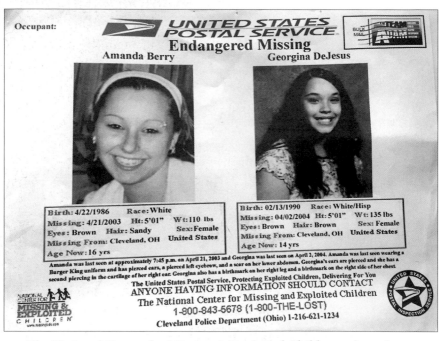

Gina's parents, Felix DeJesus and Nancy Ruiz, became impassioned advocates on behalf of missing children during the search for their daughter. Here Felix looks at photos of the missing.

Occupant:

UNITED STATES POSTAL SERVICE

Endangered Missing

Amanda Berry   Georgina DeJesus

Birth: 4/22/1986   Race: White
Missing: 4/21/2003   Ht: 5'01"   Wt: 110 lbs
Eyes: Brown   Hair: Sandy   Sex: Female
Missing From: Cleveland, OH   United States
Age Now: 16 yrs

Birth: 02/13/1990   Race: White/Hisp
Missing: 04/02/2004   Ht: 5'01"   Wt: 135 lbs
Eyes: Brown   Hair: Brown   Sex: Female
Missing From: Cleveland, OH   United States
Age Now: 14 yrs

Amanda was last seen at approximately 7:45 p.m. on April 21, 2003 and Georgina was last seen on April 2, 2004. Amanda was last seen wearing a Burger King uniform and has pierced ears, a pierced left eyebrow, and a scar on her lower abdomen. Georgina's ears are pierced and she has a second piercing in the cartilage of her right ear. Georgina also has a birthmark on her right leg and a birthmark on the right side of her chest.

The United States Postal Service, Protecting Exploited Children, Delivering For You

ANYONE HAVING INFORMATION SHOULD CONTACT
The National Center for Missing and Exploited Children
1-800-843-5678 (1-800-THE-LOST)
Cleveland Police Department (Ohio) 1-216-621-1234

The National Center for Missing & Exploited Children released a "missing" poster of Amanda and Gina that was widely distributed by the U.S. Postal Service.

The FBI later created a scale model of the Seymour house (above). An overhead shot (right) shows the second-floor rooms where the girls were held. For most of their captivity, Amanda lived in bedroom (I), while Gina and Michelle Knight lived in the adjacent room (J).

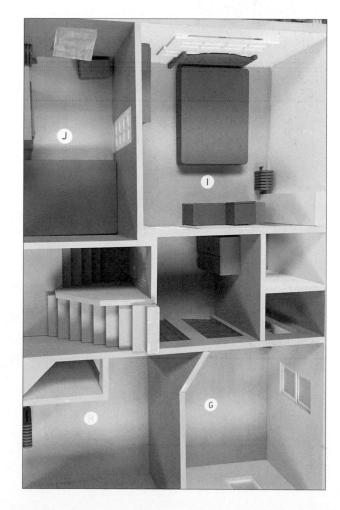

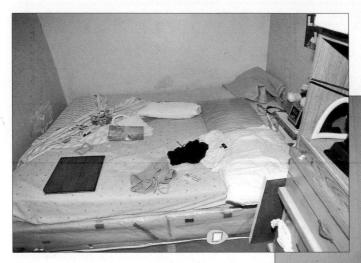

Chained in their rooms each day when Castro left for his job, the young women attempted to make their captivity as comfortable as possible by adding personal touches. Gina and Michelle, who were forced to share a bed (above and right), decorated a small refrigerator in their room (below).

In her bedroom (left), Amanda put a colorful cloth over the two doors that Castro nailed up to cover the windows behind the bed.

Castro often slept in the first-floor dining room (below), which he turned into a bedroom filled with his clothes and the junk he collected.

Castro used heavy chains to restrain the girls, first around their waists and then around their ankles.

The kitchen of 2207 Seymour, where Castro enforced strict housekeeping rules for each of his captives.

One day in May 2012, when Nancy Ruiz was handing out "missing" flyers of Gina, Castro asked for one. An hour later he gave it to Gina, who decorated it with hearts and glitter and the foods that she craved.

Amanda gave birth to a daughter, Jocelyn, on Christmas Day 2006, and took extraordinary steps to give her child as normal a life as possible, including turning their bedroom into a classroom (above) and creating a play area in an empty upstairs bedroom (below).

Amanda decorated the walls of her room with posters, Jocelyn's artwork, and worksheets from their home-schooling classes.

Amanda and Jocelyn had a dresser, closet, a clothesline to hang laundry, and a small refrigerator with a picture of Amanda's late mother.

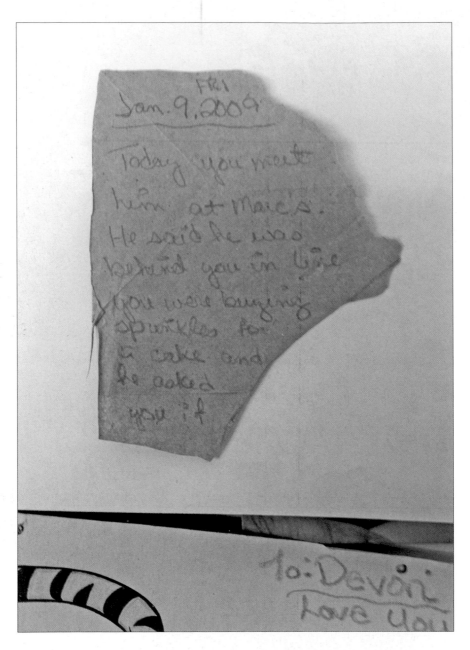

For years Amanda kept a diary charting Castro's abuse of her and vowing to be strong enough to survive the experience. Her diary was written in small notebooks that Castro gave her but she also wrote hundreds of entries on any scrap of paper she could find. In this entry from January 2009 she records Castro's telling her that he had just seen her sister, Beth Serrano, at a local store.

On May 6, 2013, after realizing that Castro had left the house and forgotten to lock her bedroom door for the first time in ten years, Amanda kicked her way through the front storm door of the Seymour house and used a neighbor's phone to call 911.

That evening Amanda was reunited with her sister Beth at the hospital where the freed girls were taken. This photo was taken moments after Beth met Jocelyn for the first time.

Nancy Ruiz shared her gratitude for the safe return of her daughter at a press conference. Felix Ruiz is at far right.

News of the girls' escape made headlines around the world, and people from all over the United States sent letters and gifts to celebrate their freedom.

Less than an hour after the girls' escape, Ariel Castro was arrested. He ultimately pled guilty to 937 criminal counts and was sentenced to life in prison without the possibility of parole plus 1,000 years. One month into his sentence, Castro committed suicide by hanging himself in his prison cell.

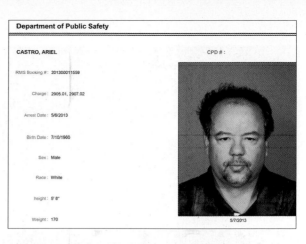

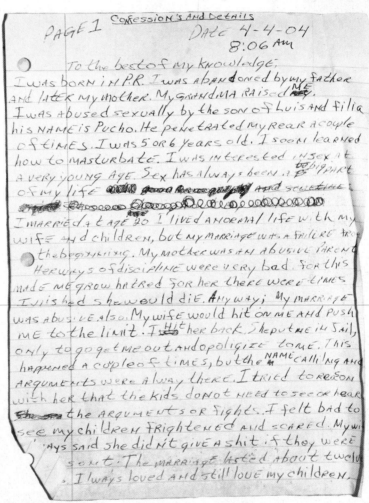

PAGE 1   CONFESSION'S AND DETAILS
DATE 4-4-04
8:06 AM

To the best of my knowledge;
I was born in P.R. I was abandoned by my father
and later my mother. My grandma raised ME.
I was abused sexually by the son of Luis and filia
his name is Pucho. He penetrated my rear a couple
of times. I was 5 or 6 years old. I soon learned
how to masturbate. I was interested in sex at
a very young age. Sex has always been a to big part
of my life
I married at age 20 I lived a normal life with my
wife and children, but my marriage was a failure from
the beginning. My mother was an abusive parent
Her ways of discipline were very bad. for this
made me grow hatred for her there were times
I wished she would die. Anyway; My marriage
was abusive also. My wife would hit on me and push
me to the limit. I hit her back. She put me in Jail,
only to go get me out and apologize to me. This
happened a couple of times, but the NAME calling and
arguments were always there. I tried to reason
with her that the kids do not need to see or hear
the arguments or fights. I felt bad to
see my children frightened and scared. My wi
ays said she didn't give a shit if they were
sout. The marriage lasted about twelv
I lways loved and still love my children.

Police searching the Seymour Avenue house the day after the escape found a four-page handwritten note dated April 4, 2004—two days after Gina's abduction. In it, Castro called himself a "sexual predator" and traced his behavior to being sexually abused as a boy in Puerto Rico. The note was part confession, part suicide note, and part rambling fatherly advice to his children.

On May 6, 2014, Amanda and Gina, along with Beth Serrano, Nancy Ruiz, and Felix DeJesus, met with President Barack Obama and Vice President Joseph Biden at the White House.

Gina and Amanda.

police. I am being held hostage by Ariel Castro at 2207 Seymour Avenue." Then I would wait until the next person checked out the book and found the note. I imagined the cops bursting through the door to rescue us, saying they got my message.

But he thought of that, too, and now makes a big point of showing me how he checks every page of a library book before he returns it. He does the same thing with the movies he borrows, giving us the disc but always keeping the case. He doesn't want us to slip a note inside the cover.

I take the medical encyclopedia and look up pregnancy. It says that at six months the baby is already more than a foot long. Amazing.

I'd love to know if I am having a girl or a boy. I'd love to have a sonogram. I'd love to hear my baby's heartbeat, and have a doctor tell me everything is going to be okay.

I keep thinking about Beth being in labor for eighteen hours with her first baby. She was in so much pain, but she was in the hospital. What will it be like for me in here? Is he going to help me deliver the baby? Do I have to ask Gina or Michelle?

One good thing is that he seems interested in the baby. I still can't tell what he's planning to do when it's born, but for now he's less mean to me. I told him yesterday I was craving butter pecan ice cream, so he went out and bought some. That's something.

"I think you're going to have this baby on Christmas," he says. "It will be like a Christmas miracle."

December 19

Until today I haven't written a word about being pregnant in my diary. I've been too scared. If I write down that I'm having a baby and then he takes the baby away, somehow I think it will be sadder. I want this child.

Hi Mommy! I guess I should tell you—I'm pregnant! Like 8 months or 9! I should be having the baby anytime. He says I can't keep it—because of "the situation." I'm not really ready, but I don't want the baby out in this cruel world without me.

I keep writing to my mom. It's like talking to her. I tell her that this baby is part of me, living and growing inside me, not him. I used to worry that if I had the baby it would remind me of him for the rest of my life. But I don't anymore. This is my baby.

I'm so close now. I am still pretty small, maybe a hundred fifteen pounds, less than when I arrived here, but my stomach looks huge to me. I already feel more like "we" than "I." Whenever I'm sadder or more depressed than usual, or when he does something especially mean and my hope starts slipping away, I rub my belly and talk to my baby.

Christmas Day 2006: New Life

Amanda

The pains started a few hours ago and they're getting stronger. I wish I was in a hospital. I've been trying to get myself mentally ready for weeks, but I'm still so worried.

It's 12:30—after midnight, so it's now officially Christmas. I've been watching TV while he's asleep next to me in his bed in the dining room. Lately I've been sleeping down here most nights. He wants me to, and it's easier just to do what he wants. Sometimes it's even comforting to sleep beside him because it makes me feel less alone and less scared about being pregnant in this house.

The bathroom is right next door, which is an even bigger deal now that I'm pregnant and have to pee all the time. But most nights he still makes me go in a bucket so he doesn't have to get up to unchain me.

"Wake up, I have to use the bathroom," I tell him. "I'm in a lot of pain." He grunts, sits up, and goes to the kitchen and reaches into the red Pringles can on the table where he keeps the keys to my chains. He unlocks the padlock on my ankle. The chain seems even heavier these days, and it drops to the floor with a thud.

The heat is on, but because there's no radiator in the kitchen, it's freezing all winter. I hurry through it and into the bathroom. He's standing there half-asleep, leaning against the sink, waiting. He looks worried. He's already had four kids and he thinks I could be in labor.

"Do you think you're having the baby?" he asks.

"I don't know," I say.

Then I hear something go "pop." It startles me. He heard it, too, and I show him that there's a little blood.

"I think your water just broke," he says.

"But I didn't feel any gush."

I'm starting to get more scared. What will I do if everything doesn't go just right? He won't take me to a hospital. I don't want to die here.

I have to stay calm.

"I don't know what's going on, but you might be having the baby," he says. "Let's go upstairs."

He wants me to have the baby in my room because the windows are so well covered there. It would be hard for anybody to hear me screaming while I'm in labor, or to hear a baby crying.

He walks with me up the stairs, slowly. I sit on my bed as he opens the door to Gina and Michelle's room.

"I think Amanda's water broke," he tells Michelle.

Michelle and I haven't been getting along and I don't want her near me, but I don't think I can do this without help. He has no idea what to do. But Michelle had a baby before she was kidnapped, so she knows what to expect. And she said that she also helped deliver a baby for somebody in her family. Besides, he told her she had to help me, so she has no choice.

He keeps Gina locked in the room.

He runs upstairs to the attic and comes back with a plastic wading pool that he sets on the bed. It's white, with blue lines and a whole bunch of colorful fish, and nearly covers the whole queen-size bed.

"Okay," he says. "Get in here."

This is his idea for how to avoid making a huge mess because he doesn't want me to ruin his mattress. It's weird and uncomfortable, but I'm in pain and not arguing.

I take off everything but my T-shirt. It's cold, especially with my bare skin against the plastic. I'm shivering and feel helpless and exposed.

"Can I have a sweater, please?" I ask.

He goes into another room and comes back with a warm black sweater.

The contractions have really started now, and the pains are sharper.

"You're not breathing right," Michelle tells me.

"I don't know how to do it," I say, wishing I had a nurse to show me.

It really hurts, and Michelle takes my hand.

"You've got to calm down," she says gently. "You've got to breathe like this."

She's shows me how—*puff, puff, puff*—and is being really nice.

"It's going to be okay," she says.

These pains are freaking me out and I start squeezing her hand so hard that she yells "Ouch!" She's just teasing and trying to make me smile. It goes on like this for what seems like hours.

He sits down in an old rocking chair that he brought into the room and is reading a medical book—the chapters about pregnancy and birth.

I scream as the contractions come faster.

"Be quiet!" he shouts. "Don't be so loud!" Handing me a shirt he tells me, "Bite on this."

I ball it up and put it into my mouth to muffle the sound. It's harder to breathe.

The cloth is drying out my mouth, and I tell him, "I'm thirsty."

He says he read that ice chips are best, so he hurries down to the kitchen to get some.

He's barely out of the room when I push, and the baby slips out.

The next few moments are a blur. I think I passed out.

Gina

I'm in my room listening and I hear Amanda scream, "The baby's not breathing! The baby's not breathing! Do something!"

For a minute there's no sound, and I'm so scared.

Then I hear a baby crying.

Amanda

He comes back into the room, sees the baby. "It's a girl," he says, smiling. "Wow!"

He seems so excited to be a father again. His eyes are wide as he gently takes her from Michelle and cradles her in his arms.

"Let me hold her," I say.

He and Michelle wrap her in a towel, and he hands her to me.

I hold my baby on my chest and touch her for the first time. I can't believe her little face. Her eyes are wide open. She's so cute. And so quiet. In the movies, new babies are always crying. She's just lying here with me, so calm. I'm amazed.

I stare into her eyes. She's all I can see.

"Cut the cord," he tells me.

He's handing me my stubby little school scissors, the ones I use to cut pictures out of magazines.

"No. I'm scared," I tell him. I'm worried that I'll do it wrong and hurt her.

"No," he insists. "You should do it."

Finally he sees that there's no way I'm going to do it, so he takes the little scissors and snips the cord. Soon after that I push out the placenta.

He says we should go downstairs and get everybody cleaned up. He turns up the radio in case the baby cries. It's Christmas music.

He carries the baby as we walk down to the bathroom. I'm sore and still sort of in shock. He wants me and the baby to get into the tub with him. It's tight, but we figure out how to cross our legs so we all fit. He's washing her tiny body.

"She's so small," he says. "You have to be really careful with her because she's so fragile."

The look in his eyes is amazing. He's so in love with this little girl already. He's always telling me that his kids are the most important thing in the world. They are older now, and it's been a long time since he's had a little kid who depends on him for everything.

There's not a lot of good in his life. It's his own fault, but sometimes I think he's as stuck in this house as we are. He and Nilda split years ago, he hates his job, and he's going to prison forever if the police find out what he's done to us. Now he's sitting here holding this beautiful baby who is nothing but pure goodness, and he's happy. I think she gives him new meaning in his life.

He gives me a pair of his one-piece red long johns to wear, and they're soft and comfortable. It's almost morning, and we're all hungry, so we step into the kitchen. It's so cold that Michelle holds the baby with a towel over her face to keep her warm.

He starts frying eggs and sausages while I make toast. He tells me that it's unbelievable that I'm standing up cooking breakfast just hours after giving birth, with no drugs or anything.

I take the baby from Michelle, and she gets some food for her and Gina, and we all walk upstairs. He goes into their room and chains Michelle again.

I crawl into bed with my new baby. As he fastens the chain around my ankle, I think about my daughter being born into this prison, and who her father is. But I try to focus on happier thoughts: She seems healthy and she's beautiful. I am going to protect her, and the rest we will figure out as we go.

He finds a brown cardboard box to use as a bassinet. We put some towels and a little pillow in it and set it on the bed, and he lies down next to it. He is smiling. I can't remember ever seeing him this happy.

"Oh, my God," he says, a little awed. "I can't believe I'm a dad again."

A couple of weeks ago, we had been watching *The Polar Express* on TV when the baby started kicking like crazy. I reached for his hand and placed it on my stomach, wanting him to feel connected to the baby. I knew my baby would be safer, and would have a better chance of staying with me, if he was excited about being a new father. I think it worked, because he seemed thrilled to feel the kicking in my belly.

Then, one night when I was trying to sleep on my stomach because the padlock was hurting me, he told me, "You can't sleep on your stomach because you'll hurt the baby."

I guess he had been starting to care, but I don't think he had ever been completely sure, right up to today, that he'd let me keep this baby.

Now he can't stop looking at his daughter.

* * *

I wake up a few hours later when I hear the baby crying. I try to get her to breastfeed, but no matter how hard I try, it's not working.

"Can you please go to the store and get some formula?" I ask him.

"No," he tells me. "You can feed her yourself."

He says he doesn't want anyone to see him or risk that a store camera might film him buying baby things. We don't have a blanket, or diapers, or formula—nothing.

He tells me to watch a breastfeeding video. He didn't have to get one for me, because he already had one in his porn stash. He is so obsessed by breasts that it even turns him on to watch breastfeeding.

Hours pass, and the baby is not latching on, and she's still crying but takes a few drops of water from a little spoon. What will I do if she gets sick in here? I'm just a few blocks from a big hospital, but I might as well be shipwrecked on a desert island, since I have no chance of getting her to a doctor.

"She needs diapers," I tell him.

He leaves the room and comes back a few minutes later with scissors and a handful of old white athletic socks. He trims the top off and then cuts two little holes in the toe for her legs. We slip her into it, and that's her first diaper.

Then he takes another sock and cuts a bigger hole in the toe for her head, and two little holes for her arms. We slip it over her head, and it's like a little dress.

It's her first outfit.

I want to call her Priscilla, but he hates that name. I don't know why I care what he thinks about the name, but I do. I need him to feel like he's a part of her life. I want him to feel invested in her, because I think that will keep her safe.

I can't think of too many other girls' names that I like, so he gets a phone book, and we start going through it. He suggests some that I hate, mainly Spanish ones, and I like some others that he rejects. Finally I think, *Jocelyn*. When I was little I had a friend called Jocelyn, and I always loved that name. He's not crazy about it, but he says okay.

I want to give her a middle name to honor my mom. But there is no way I am calling her Jocelyn Louwana, because Mom never liked her name.

But Mom loved Aerosmith, and one of the songs she always sang to me was called "Jaded." So I decide: Jocelyn Jade.

Jocelyn Jade Berry.

Jocelyn is three days old and has not eaten anything yet. All she's had is water, and she has been crying a lot.

I tell him I'm doing my best, but she's a baby—she cries. He walks around with her to try to get her to quiet down. He goes kind of crazy when she wails, so he turns the radio up even louder. The neighbors won't hear Jocelyn crying, but the loud music makes it harder for her to sleep.

I have given up asking for formula. He says it's expensive, and it never goes on sale. I keep trying to get her to breastfeed. C'mon, baby. We can do this. I start praying that my mom makes my little baby a fighter.

After hours and hours she finally latches on and doesn't let go. She's drinking, and I know she's going to make it.

Someday I'm going to have a lot to explain to her.

Part Three

February 2007: Moving

Less than a month after Louwana Miller died, new tenants moved into the second-floor apartment she had shared with Amanda. For Beth and Teddy, it became simply too sad having strangers living upstairs, so, just less than a year later, they moved to a new house on West 129th Street. They put up photos of Louwana and Amanda and hung "missing" posters on the porch.

Beth had not been well and was dropping weight. She had been diagnosed with Crohn's disease when she was seventeen, and it had recently been flaring up. She was unable to work, and she and Teddy were struggling to pay the rent and raise their three kids. Still, nearly four years after her sister vanished, they continued passing out flyers about Amanda in every store they visited, hoping to keep her disappearance in the news. Beth believed that Amanda was alive and just might be watching TV. She was grateful that her new friends, Nancy Ruiz and Felix De-Jesus, were spreading the word even more widely. They were as certain that Gina was still alive as she was about Amanda, and they seemed inexhaustible.

June 2007: Finding a Voice

Wealthier families who had missing children often drew media attention to their cause by offering huge rewards, but because Gina's family had little money, Nancy found other ways to keep her daughter's case in the public eye. She sewed a big banner that read THE MISSING and set up a booth at events like Cleveland's annual Night Out Against Crime, where hundreds of people gathered. She traveled to missing-children events in Akron and Columbus and marched down busy Cleveland streets with the Guardian Angels, once coming within a block of Ariel Castro's house, chanting, "Who do we want? Gina! When do we want her? Now!"

She learned from a friend about the work of Dennis Bair, a former Minor League Baseball pitcher who had started BairFind, an organization dedicated to bringing home missing children. Bair had been featuring Gina's photo and description in one of his poster campaigns in Minor League ball parks. When Nancy called to thank him, the two struck up a friendship and started working together. Nancy handed out flyers with pictures of Gina and other missing kids at ball parks around Ohio and Pennsylvania, even throwing out a couple of ceremonial first pitches—anything to keep people looking for Gina.

On June 14, 2007, the Cleveland Cavaliers featured Gina's and Amanda's pictures on their giant display screen during Game 4 of the NBA finals. With LeBron James trying to keep the San Antonio Spurs from sweeping the series, the girls' photos were seen by a huge national TV audience. Nancy stood outside the arena and gave interviews to local TV stations. No longer terrified of the microphone, she was committed to the cause of missing children.

Spring 2007: Digging a Grave

Gina

"Come downstairs," he orders.

"Why?"

"Just come downstairs!"

It always makes me nervous when he tells me that, because it usually ends the same way. But I have no choice. This time, though, when we get to the kitchen, he surprises me.

"I need you to help me bury my dog," he says.

Poor Kashla. She was a big brown pit bull that he kept chained outside in the driveway, and last week he backed over her accidentally with his car. "The stupid dog saw me coming and didn't move," he said. Typical. It was the dog's fault.

Kashla lived for a few days afterward, but then she stopped eating and died. He threw her body in the garbage can outside, where it's been since yesterday. I bet he's worried, because you're not supposed to put dead animals in the trash, and the garbage men might report him.

"I have to disguise you," he tells me, handing me a jacket, a black wig, sunglasses, a white surgical mask, and a cowboy hat. The getup is so completely over the top that it'll probably attract more attention than just dressing normally. Who knows? Maybe I'll get lucky, and somebody will see me and think it's so weird that they call the cops.

It's about noon when we start digging with two shovels he got from the garage. I think he picked me to help him because I'm the strongest, and he knows I love dogs. It's more like a used car lot than a yard out here, and the ground is hard and packed down from all the cars that have driven over it. It's cold and drizzly, and we chip away at it for hours.

He drags the garbage can over and dumps Kashla's body into the hole. We start shoveling the dirt on top of her, and I quietly tell her that I'm sorry. She deserved better than to die in this awful place.

June 2007: Seamstress

Gina

I really like the T-shirt he bought me at a thrift shop that says YOUNG AND ANGRY across the front. It used to fit me, but I've lost a lot of weight, and now it's too big. So I cut out the words, glue them on construction paper, and tape the piece to my wall. That's me! I'm young and I am angry.

I have a hole in my jogging pants, so I ask him for a needle and thread and start sewing. When I'm done he says I did a good job, and he never says anything nice.

"Can you sew these buttons back on?" he asks, handing me a shirt and the popped buttons.

I do that quickly and then stitch a ripped blanket, too. I like sewing. I taught myself in here, and it's fun and makes time move faster. I suddenly think of a million more things I can fix, and what I can do with the secondhand shirts and dresses he has bought us. They will look a lot better if they're not four sizes too big. He says he'll get me more thread, and I hope he hurries up about it.

October 2007: A Place to Crawl

Amanda

Finally, after almost ten months, he brings in a piece of burgundy carpet to cover my floor. I wish it was softer, not the cheap industrial kind for offices, but at least it's brand-new and smells good. I hold Jocelyn while he and Gina move the bed and lay down the carpet that will widen Jocelyn's world.

Joce is ten months old and needs space to crawl. Since she was born, I've been keeping her on the bed because I don't want her on the dirty floor. He's in and out of here all the time with his muddy boots, and I'm worried about Joce picking up germs.

He nailed a purple foam exercise mat over my door to the hallway to muffle any sound in case he had people downstairs. Then he screwed two wooden doors over my bedroom windows so nobody outside could hear Jocelyn crying. I covered the doors with a shower curtain that has cute green frogs on it, and I pasted hearts, triangles, and other shapes on the foam so it looks like a classroom. I don't want my daughter to know she is growing up in prison.

I read that babies are supposed to start eating solid food when they are six months old, but he says baby food is too expensive. I tried to give her watermelon and mushed-up beans, but she spit them out. Thank God she keeps taking breast milk.

He rapes me less since she was born, but he hasn't stopped. He just waits until Jocelyn falls asleep, then he climbs in the bed. It makes me sick that he does this to me with my daughter lying next to me. I am only safe when she's awake.

I can see he's fallen in love with her. He calls her "Pretty." He shifted my furniture around so that even with the chain I can sit in the rocking chair. The seat is busted, so I put a pillow on top of it, rocking and feeding Joce for hours. He comes home from work almost every afternoon on his lunch break, sits in the rocker, and holds her, making sweet baby talk and sometimes singing her to sleep.

"She's my life now," he says.

He made a little mobile out of string and plastic Easter eggs and hung it from the ceiling over the bed where Joce and I sleep. He even broke down and bought her some baby supplies. He came back from Unique with two blankets and a little bouncy chair. He shops at the thrift shop on Monday when everything is half off, so the cheap stuff is even cheaper.

I just found a strange-looking bag in the freezer and asked what it was, and he told me it was my placenta! I couldn't believe it. He keeps everything. He said he was afraid that if he threw it away, the garbage men might see it and get suspicious.

Joce loves crawling on the new carpet, but now I have new challenges. Because my chain only reaches so far, if she strays too far from the bed, I can't reach her and need to coax her to crawl back to me. And I need to keep her away from the plastic toilet—it's so gross.

Gina

I pick up the little cooler filled with Jocelyn's dirty diapers and bring it downstairs. Amanda has the baby, and he and Michelle are always fighting, so I do most of the laundry and cleaning in the house; it's like I'm the maid. But most of the time I don't mind because it gives me something to do and it's better than watching TV all day.

I hand-wash the diapers and baby clothes in the bathroom sink. Jocelyn is too big now for using socks as diapers, so he cuts up old towels and gives Amanda a couple of safety pins. He also put a little plastic cooler in her room, big enough for a six-pack, to store the dirty ones and help with the smell. When the clothes are washed I bring them upstairs, and Amanda helps me hang them on clotheslines he has strung across her room.

I like helping out with Jocelyn and playing with her. She's so cute with her dark brown eyes and long, beautiful eyelashes. I make her laugh, and she makes me forget where I am. Amanda and I have been talking more since I've been helping with the baby, and she is nicer to me. He's in a better mood these days, too, and that's good for all of us.

Life is better with Jocelyn here.

Castro's Story: Neighborly

Ariel Castro's shabby two-story house stood on a short block of Seymour Avenue that connects two major thoroughfares, West 25th Street and Scranton Road, an unremarkable stretch of urban neglect, more shortcut than destination. The neighborhood butts up against trendy comeback areas, where young professionals restore historic homes and cafés sell $12-a-glass pinot noirs.

The white wooden house, built in 1890, was valued at $36,000 in 2012, and was one of the tidier ones on the street. Police paid more attention to the *bandos*, abandoned houses that the desperate would break into and steal wire and copper pipe from to get quick cash for crack or heroin. The house at 2207 Seymour Avenue was flanked on one side by a house where four men, including a restaurant dishwasher named Charles Ramsey, each paid $75 a week to rent a room, and on the other side by a home that became a *bando* when a Puerto Rican family moved out around 2009. A century-old redbrick apartment building, the Vera, sat derelict across the street.

Horst Hoyer had been pastor at the Immanuel Lutheran Church, four doors down from the Castro house, for fifty-seven years before he retired in 2013. He recalled that German immigrants dominated the neighborhood when he arrived in the 1950s, and his church still offers Sunday services in German. But the neighborhood is now a mix of races and ethnicities after successive waves of newcomers settled there from the American South, as well as Hispanics from Puerto Rico and the Dominican Republic. Hoyer said it is not as cohesive as it was when a single immigrant group dominated. The block still has a handful of longtime residents, but today it is mostly home to itinerant, low-income people.

Castro moved onto Seymour in 1992 and was well-known on the block. Several neighbors remembered the days when he would walk down to the corner of West 25th Street with his young children to buy candy at his uncle's Caribe Grocery. In addition to family photos, the market's walls were covered with photos of political figures, including one of Bill and Hillary Clinton, with a handwritten note from Bill Clinton thanking Cesi for donating to his presidential campaign. Many people hung out there and remember talking to Castro.

After Castro and Nilda split in 1996, neighbors said they didn't see him as much, although they often saw his big yellow school bus parked on the street around lunchtime.

Castro became increasingly private, and his house was almost always dark at night. From the outside it did not look boarded up but simply as if the drapes had been drawn, because he had hung curtains over the windows before he nailed wood over them from the inside.

Aurora Marti, who lived across the street from Castro for more than twenty years, was touched when he stopped by to offer condolences after her husband died. Henrietta Bell, a neighbor for thirteen years who lived in a house built by the nonprofit group Habitat for Humanity, saw Castro outside talking to neighbors now and then and doing yard work on summer evenings. It was a nuisance when he parked his school bus in front of her house, but not enough to complain. Bell was more concerned about the addicts breaking into the Vera apartment building, which was next door to her home, and police came to the street several times in response to her calls.

Shortly after Charles Ramsey moved in next door to Castro in October 2012, Castro came knocking at two in the morning to complain about Ramsey playing loud music. "Hey, I know you just moved in," Castro told him. "But I have to get up early to drive a school bus."

Not long afterward he told Ramsey that a lightbulb was missing from his front porch, and he suspected that someone was stealing from him. "I need you to watch my property," he told Ramsey.

Castro was friendly enough with Ramsey but made it clear that no one was welcome on his property. He would occasionally barbecue in his backyard and bring a plate to Ramsey, but never invited him over.

Castro played regularly in bands at Belinda's Night Club at West 96th Street and Madison Avenue. That building is a symbol of the changing face of Cleveland's immigrant communities. For decades it had housed the West Side Irish American Club, but as the Irish migrated to the suburbs, Spanish-speaking immigrants moved in and the music turned from Celtic ceilidhs to salsa and merengue. William Perez, owner of Belinda's, thought it was unusual that Castro would buy huge amounts of food from the club to take home at three in the morning after a gig. He struck Perez as odd and a little hard to work with, but otherwise unremarkable.

Altagracia Tejeda, an immigrant from the Dominican Republic who lived directly across from Castro, recalled that Castro once invited her entire family to see his band play at Belinda's.

She said Castro liked her homemade popsicles and bought them when she set up a stand on her front porch on hot summer days. One day Tejeda saw a woman behind Castro's house. She had long hair and big, dark sunglasses, and Tejeda assumed that Castro finally had a girl-friend after all these years.

March 23, 2008: Easter

Amanda

"What have you got there, Pretty?" he asks Jocelyn from behind the video camera. "Is that candy? Tell Daddy what you have."

He is sitting on the floor of our room recording her. I had begged him to take photos of her so that someday she would have pictures of herself growing up, but he said he couldn't risk developing them in a store. What if someone asked who she was?

"Get a Polaroid, and you don't have to worry about that," I told him.

He soon found a Polaroid camera at a yard sale but then had trouble finding film for it, so he settled for an old video camera and started recording his little girl taking her first steps and, today, enjoying her first Easter basket.

He let me look through the piles of things scattered all over this house, and I found a purple plastic Easter basket that one of his kids must have had. I made a butterfly out of purple felt and black pipe cleaners and attached it to the handle. Butterflies still remind me of my mom, and I want her to be part of this holiday.

Joce looks so adorable in the pink dress, white shoes, and white lace socks he bought her. I gathered the wisps of her hair on top of her head into a scrunchie, so she looked like Pebbles Flintstone. She yanks it out while he's filming, and he and I both laugh.

"Where are your eyes?" he asks her, and she covers them with her little hands.

She sits down to examine her basket and the colorful plastic eggs and candy in it, and takes out a big Hershey's bar and tries to eat it with the wrapper on. I help her open it, and he starts singing, *"La la, la-la-la-la-la."*

"Pretty, sing!" he says. *"La la, la-la-la-la-la!"*

She smiles. It's a peaceful, happy moment for us all.

April 22, 2008: Milestones

Amanda

I know they call them the terrible twos, but it's more like the exhausting twos. Joce has so much energy that it's overwhelming and hard to keep her occupied every minute in such a confined space. We play games, color, draw, read books, and when I need a break, watch cartoons. He took a piece of an old crib and made a gate and rigged up a plastic kiddie swing in the doorway between our room and Gina and Michelle's. She loves the swing, and Gina pushes her on it, too.

I'm always thinking of ways to keep her busy, to pass the hours and days in this room, and usually when she takes a nap, I crash, too, physically and mentally exhausted. I dream of going outside, pushing her in a stroller around a park or a mall and watching her play with other toddlers. Joce has never even been outdoors yet.

I'm trying to get her on a schedule, but it's tough. We have no natural light in the room, so there's little difference between morning and night. That makes it harder to get up and go to sleep at the same time every day.

She has started saying a few words—"Mama" and "Dada" and "nose." She loves to touch her nose.

I mark down her milestones in my diary:

Dec. 13: She Took Her First Step Holding onto the Bed!
Feb. 2: She started walking by herself!
Feb. 15: She had her first high fever. This was the first time she was really sick, but she took some medicine, and the fever broke the next day.

He's been better to me. He still comes for me when she's asleep. It's not exactly like it used to be, since I have learned to accept it. I still consider it rape, because what else do you call sex with a prisoner on a chain? But it's not like it was before, not so rough and angry and hateful. He tries to make it easier for me.

I know it's wrong, but I feel closer to him. I appreciate that he treats Jocelyn well and buys her clothes and toys—she loves Daisy, the big doll he just brought her. He's even giving us better food and put a microwave on my dresser so I can warm up her mashed potatoes, beans, and rice. We all sit and watch kid movies together, and it almost feels normal, or at least a lot better than it used to.

I desperately want Jocelyn to have a normal life. And on the days that he helps me do that, I actually feel some affection for him. He tells me that we have a special relationship because of her. He says he only wants to be with me, not the other girls, but I don't believe that. Just when I start thinking there is good in him, he reminds me of how cruel he can be. Yesterday he called me a "nigger-loving bitch" because I wouldn't call black people the *n*-word like he does. He actually took my radio away as punishment for catching me listening to rap, which he calls "that black music." I hate it when he treats me like a child and calls me names. I'm so confused. How can he be so good one minute and so mean the next?

Today is my twenty-second birthday. I've been here five years, and I'm spending the day trying not to let Jocelyn see my tears.

June 12, 2008: Pulled Over

A little after eight thirty p.m. Cleveland police officer Jim Simone was sitting in traffic on Pearl Road, about a mile from Seymour Avenue, when a motorcycle whizzed by on his right, cut across traffic, and pulled into a gas station.

Simone noticed that the motorcycle's license plate wasn't attached correctly and was hanging sideways, which is illegal. He followed the rider into the Shell station and pulled up behind him, with his dashboard camera running.

The rider, wearing a white tank top and baggy shorts, stepped off his bike at the pumps and noticed the police car behind him.

"Let me see your driver's license," Simone said.

"Excuse me?" Ariel Castro asked.

"Let me see your driver's license, please."

"What's wrong?"

"First off, your plate's improperly displayed. It has to be displayed left to right, not upside down or sideways."

Castro produced his driver's license, and Simone saw that he wasn't licensed to operate a motorcycle. He recognized Castro's name; he'd been a Cleveland cop since 1973 and remembered having written up Castro's brothers for traffic violations over the years. He had also driven down Seymour Avenue thousands of times.

Simone noticed that Castro's license plate was registered to a Harley-Davidson, not the Yamaha he was riding. Castro wasn't wearing eye protection, which was also illegal.

Simone told him that all his violations could add up to serious trouble, warning him, "You subject yourself to being arrested. Is that what you want?"

"No, sir," Castro replied. "I don't want that."

"These plates don't belong to this bike, do they? What year Yamaha is this?"

"This is 2000."

"Where's the Harley?"

"Oh, the Harley. I sold it and I traded it in for this one."

"Well, Ariel," Simone said, "you keep getting deeper and deeper and deeper."

"I know," Castro replied, "but I just got off work. I'm a school bus driver." The school year had, in fact, ended the week before.

Simone was known as one of the toughest cops in Cleveland because he had shot and killed five people, and been shot twice himself, over the course of his long career. He could have arrested Castro, but Castro was being polite and compliant, and Simone knew that an arrest could cost him his job as a bus driver. So he decided to cut him a break and wrote him two tickets, one for the improperly attached plate and one for driving without a motorcycle license. He told Castro to push the motorcycle the mile home to Seymour Avenue and wondered if Castro would wait until he was out of sight to hop back on the bike. But about twenty minutes later, Simone spotted him well up Pearl Road, still pushing.

June 2008: New Names

Amanda

"You have to pick different names," he says. "Jocelyn can't know your real names."

All three of us are in the kitchen, washing dishes. Jocelyn is watching cartoons in the living room. He says now that Jocelyn can talk, he doesn't want her to repeat our names. He says he might want to take her outside at some point, and he's afraid that she might mention "Amanda" or "Gina" and make someone suspicious.

"What do you want to be called?" he asks.

When none of us has any ideas he suggests to Gina, "How about Hazel?"

"No," she says, making a face. "I'm not going to be Hazel. I'll be Chelsea."

We've been watching *Days of Our Lives* a lot, and there's a character on that show named Chelsea. Michelle picks "Juju."

He's been referring to me as "Nandy" for years, ever since he listened to the voice messages on my cell phone just after he kidnapped me and heard Mariyah calling me that. So he decides that I'm now officially Nandy.

It's going to be hard to get in the habit of calling Gina and Michelle by their new names, and I don't want Jocelyn or me to get in trouble, so I start practicing "Chelsea" and "Juju" over and over in my head.

September 2008: Night Terrors

Amanda

I jolt awake. Jocelyn is howling again. She jumps out of bed and starts running around the room, screaming like she's on fire.

She's been doing this a lot lately in the middle of the night. I don't know what's going on. I try to catch her, but sometimes I can't reach her because of my chain.

"Baby, what's wrong? Come here, Joce," I keep saying. "It's all right."

It's hard to calm her down, and he comes charging up the stairs and unlocks our door.

"Keep her quiet!"

"I'm trying!"

I know he's afraid that the neighbors are going to hear her, and he picks her up, saying softly, "It's okay, my love."

When she keeps screaming and squirms away he unlocks my chain so I can help, and we take Jocelyn into Gina and Michelle's room. They are wide-awake and used to this by now. Their room is the farthest away from any neighbors, and he has already nailed up more plastic and blankets over their window to muffle Jocelyn's night screams.

He turns the radio up even louder, which is not going to soothe her, but it might mask her shouting. We're both trying to calm Joce, stroking her hair and telling her everything is okay. It takes half an hour, but she finally quiets down, and we dry her tears. I lie back down on the bed with her in my arms.

I don't know what's giving Jocelyn these night terrors. He's alone with her sometimes, but I don't believe he would harm her in any way. He loves her so much. I know she's afraid of the closet, which has no door, because she thinks it's dark and spooky. Even though I try to shield her from what's going on in this house, I'm worried that she can sense the misery here.

November 4, 2008: President

Amanda

We have a new president: Barack Obama. I never thought a black man would be elected. It's so exciting! It's history! I wish I could have voted.

He sat with me to watch the election returns in the living room tonight, and we waited for Obama to come out and give his acceptance speech in Chicago. I'm afraid to say out loud that I'm happy that Obama won. He has been grumbling about so many black people moving into this neighborhood.

"I voted for Obama," he says.

"Really?" I ask, trying to not show my surprise.

"Yeah, I voted for him because the other guy is worse."

I never know what he's going to do. He forbids me and Gina and Michelle from watching TV shows with black actors, but then votes for a black president. I don't get him.

January 9, 2009: Encounter

Amanda

"I talked to Beth today," he says.

"You did?" I ask him, shocked. "Where?"

"We were at Marc's. She was in line in front of me, buying sprinkles to put on a cake. I asked her if she wanted a water, since I was putting one back, and she said, 'No, thank you, honey.'"

Honey? Beth called him "honey"? That makes me sick. I know he spoke to her just for the thrill, just so he could tell me that he did it.

"She had a little pin with your picture stuck to her purse," he says, taunting me.

He loves feeling like he's getting away with this, that nobody has any clue.

February 16, 2009: Shove

Amanda

He's standing at the door.

"I need Chelsea to come downstairs and clean," he says to us.

I know what he is going to do with her down there. Does he think I'm stupid? I'm so tired of him lying to me and sneaking around like a snake. Gina has told me what happens when he asks her to "clean," and she has asked me if I could try to stop him. She says he listens to me.

As he takes her by the arm to lead her downstairs, I stand up with Joce in my arms and block the door to the hallway.

"I know what you really want with her," I say. "If you want to clean, I'll come downstairs and help, too."

"Shut up," he says. "She's coming with me."

"No! If she's going, I'm going, too."

I'm standing right in front of him, looking up into his eyes. I'm mad, and he's getting furious.

"Get out of my face!" he shouts.

"No!" I shout back. "I'm coming downstairs!"

He shoves me hard, and I fly backward onto the bed with Joce still in my arms. She is startled and starts crying. I'm stunned—he's never done anything like that before in front of Jocelyn.

"Shut up and stay here!" he yells, slamming the door.

June 2009: Bracelet

Amanda

It's Sunday night, close to midnight. Jocelyn is still up watching TV. He just left our room and didn't chain me. I guess he's coming back, or could he have just forgotten? When he's home on Saturday and Sunday he's started leaving us off the chains, a welcome bit of freedom. It's less hassle for him because he wants us to go downstairs to clean and wash clothes, and he doesn't have to keep locking and unlocking us.

But when he leaves the house or goes to bed, he never forgets to chain us.

Maybe since Jocelyn was still up he didn't want her to see him put the chains around my ankle. It's harder and harder to hide them from her. She's two and a half now and starting to ask questions, like the other day when the pink blanket I had covering my chains slipped off.

"What's that?" she asked.

"It's my bracelet," I said, as casually as I could.

We haven't talked about it, but I can tell he doesn't like Jocelyn seeing that he locks us up. And he knows the chains make it harder for me to take care of her. He was in our room the other day, and Jocelyn was in

the far corner and wanted me to come play with her, but she was a couple of feet beyond my reach.

Our door opens, and he walks straight through our room and into
Gina and Michelle's bedroom. I can hear him chaining them up. Then
he comes to us.

"Good night, Pretty. Give Daddy a hug," he says, giving Joce a big squeeze.

Then he leaves and locks my door from the outside.

I catch my breath. *He didn't chain me.*

I turn off the light and snuggle up with my baby. It's been six and a
half years since I have been able to fall asleep without being shackled.

Gina

This is how messed up things are here: today he didn't chain me and
Michelle, and instead of being happy, I'm scared. I noticed a couple of
weeks ago that Amanda was unchained. But just because he took hers
off, it doesn't mean he'll take mine off. He has different rules for each of
us. I wonder if I should remind him to lock me up, because if he gets
mad when he realizes he forgot, he'll take it out on us. He'll smack me
and yell about how he can't trust me, or maybe put me in the basement.
He'll make it my fault. But it sure does feel good to walk around without
dragging that rusting chain.

"Maybe it's not a mistake," I say to Michelle. "Maybe he'll let us off
the chains because of Jocelyn. He still locks the door, so he knows we
can't go anywhere."

Another day comes, and he says nothing about the chains. Then another
and another, and no mention. Every time he comes in I stay on my bed with
my leg under the blanket so it's not obvious that I'm not chained.

The room is tiny, so it's not like I have tons of room to move around,
but now I can exercise. I start doing a few push-ups, sit-ups, and squats,
and it feels great. I hide our chains under a piece of plastic so we don't
have to look at them.

It actually feels strange, like I'm suddenly missing part of me. But it's
a wonderful strange. It's so much easier to sleep without the chain. I

keep lifting my right leg and shaking my ankle—no sound! I love that the chain is gone, but somehow I don't feel free of it. I have bruises and scars on my right ankle that I'll probably have forever.

"I don't have you on the chain anymore because I trust you," he finally says one day, out of the blue. "But if you do anything, it's going back on, and I will hang you upside down by your ankles."

June 25, 2009: Michael Jackson

Gina

Michael Jackson is dead; that's so sad. He walks in while we're watching the news about it.

"Good," he says. "That's one less nigger on earth."

God, he is so hateful.

October 2009: Oprah

The Oprah Winfrey Show came to Cleveland to film a short video segment about Amanda, Gina, and Ashley Summers, another missing Cleveland teenager. FBI agent Phil Torsney described each of the cases on camera, pointing out the places where the girls had been seen last.

"What's been hardest for me is just that Amanda has been gone for too long, and I want her home," said a tearful Beth, wearing a white T-shirt with Amanda's picture.

Nancy was thrilled to talk about her daughter on such a popular show, happy that Gina's photo would be seen by millions of people. But as the crew set up lights and cameras in her living room, she was overcome by emotion as she showed them Gina's clothes and stuffed animals.

"Not knowing is what's tearing us apart," Nancy said. "But I fight. I'm never going to give up."

Christmas 2009: "We're a Family"

Amanda

"Here, Pretty, do you want to play with some snow?" he says, handing her a bucket filled with snow that he brought into the house.

She's so excited! She's never played in the snow. She wanted to go outside, but he said no and instead brought her the bucket, which she loves.

He has been doing more fun things with her. In August he took her outside for the very first time, and she sat on his four-wheeler ATV. A few times the two of them went into the yard at night to look up at the stars, and once all three of us sat in his Jeep and listened to music. She had never been in a car before and loved playing with all the buttons on the dashboard.

Last month she helped him rake leaves in the backyard. She loved the smell of them and the feel of the cold fall air. And she loved being with her daddy.

"We're a family," he says to me.

I never know how to respond to that. He's Jocelyn's father. But my family is my family, and he never will be. I want Joce to feel as much love as possible, and when I see him being so kind and loving with her, it makes me think he's not all bad. I can let him feel like he's family if that's what it takes to make Joce's life better.

He bought her a nice card for her third birthday and wrote in it: "Princess, May God bless you, and give you good health, and keep you safe always," addressing it, "To my beautiful little girl Jocelyn." Beneath that he drew three little stick figures of two parents holding hands with a small child and labeled them "Daddy," "Mommy," and "Pretty." He gave himself a hat and me long hair, and we all have big smiles. We read it out loud to her, and she hugs us both.

2010: Cutting

Gina

Look at the blood. I was opening a can of beef stew in the kitchen, and I cut my right pinkie. I run some cold water over it, and it stings. I can see all the way down to the bone. I've never cut myself so deep before.

It doesn't hurt, though, and I just stare at the blood flowing from it. It's like I'm getting hypnotized by the sight.

He comes over, looks at it, and says, "It's not that bad."

I barely hear him. I can't take my eyes off the cut. It's made me forget where I am. When I'm looking at it, it's the only thing I think about. I don't think about him or the disgusting things he does to me all the time. I can just block all that out, and I like the feeling.

All it's taken is this one little cut. Nothing that's going to kill me.

It's better than banging myself in the head. I've been doing that since I got here, but a lot more lately. I punch myself as hard as I can in the side of my head, then pull my hair until it really hurts.

I'm so frustrated by this place, and by him. And Amanda.

Sometimes we get along fine, but usually she doesn't talk to us. And it's so much easier for her in here. It's like they are a little family, and we are garbage.

I have almost no control over anything, but nobody can stop me from cutting myself.

I start with a butter knife.

I drag it across the inside of my forearm, where it's soft. I don't go deep, because I don't want to really hurt myself. At first I just scratch a little, then I put more pressure on it, and then pull the knife across my arm quickly and just hard enough to get it bleeding.

Look at the blood. Little drips of red on my soft, white skin.

It's working again. My mind flies away, and all I think about is the warm blood dribbling down my arm.

I lick it; it tastes salty.

"What are you doing?" Michelle asks. "Stop it."

"Don't worry about it," I tell her. "It's none of your business."

I've discovered that little white plastic knives from McDonald's are perfect. Their edges are just sharp enough to break the skin.

Just a couple of quick cuts, and I draw blood. I've been doing this every once in a while for months now. Michelle hates it and always tells me to stop. But she can't make me.

My mom used to tell me that if I saw anyone at school cutting herself, I was supposed to say something right away. She said it was a cry for help.

I don't think I'm crying out for help, I'm just trying to have a few minutes of peace in here. But I don't know. I just saw a show on TV about cutters. They said it's dangerous and that the only way to stop is to deal with your problems directly. Instead of cutting, they said it's better to talk to whoever is making you so sad or mad.

I can't talk to him about this. But maybe I should talk to Amanda. She's making me feel bad, too. He says she can't stand me. Why?

So I push open the door between our rooms. She's sitting on the bed, alone. I guess Jocelyn must be out with him. I stand in the doorway and look at her.

"I have something to tell you," I say. "I cut myself, and it's because of you."

Amanda

Gina's at the door, and I wonder what she wants. Usually she wants to play with Jocelyn. That's fine, as long as I don't have to spend too much time with her.

She and Michelle are such liars. They're always complaining to him that I'm not nice to them, so he yells at me. He's always putting me down. I'm so tired of being screamed at and called names all the time: stupid, fat, dork, retard, bitch, *pendeja*—a bad word in Spanish. Nothing I do is good enough: the fire on the stove is too high, or too low, or I used too much soap. He's always finding fault and always yelling. It's so demeaning and depressing and endless, and I hate that he does it in front of Jocelyn.

So that makes me mean sometimes. Most of the time I don't even talk to Gina and Michelle, or I snap at them about any little thing. They make being in here even harder. I wish it could just be me and Jocelyn trying to get through this together, like a tough little team.

But now Gina is staring at me, looking serious and sad.

"I cut myself," she says, "and it's because of you."

"What do you mean?" I ask.

She shows me the marks on her arm. Some of them look fresh. As I feel myself starting to well up with tears she tells me that I've been a real bitch to her, and that I tell him lies about her that get her in trouble. That isn't true, but I know I haven't been nice to her.

"I don't want you to do that because of me," I say.

"I'm so sorry. I don't want to hurt you. We get enough hurt from him."

It's like a slap in my face: I realize that there's no reason for us not to get along better. He did all of this to us. Having us not like one another is all part of his game.

"You have to stop doing that," I say, telling her that I read someplace that if you have a bad habit, you're supposed to find something else to do instead. I suggest that maybe she start wearing a rubber band around her wrist, and when she feels like cutting, she can snap herself hard with the rubber band instead. That way she can get a little bit of pain, but she's not really hurting herself.

She says that sounds like a good idea.

We talk a little more, and she tells me how hard it's been for her all these years. We're not different. It's not easier for her. She's not trying to make my life harder, no matter what he says. We're the same. She's going through exactly what I am.

I suddenly see her as another me. I'm sorry I didn't see it sooner.

I realize now that I can play an important role in this house. I'm a little older than Gina, so I think I can help get her through this, and maybe Michelle, too. Gina liked my rubber-band idea, and I bet I can think of other things to make this easier for her. It feels good to help. I'm becoming sort of the Mama Bear, and everybody needs help in here.

Gina

Amanda seems like she's sorry about me cutting myself.

And I like her rubber-band idea. I'm going to find one and wear it.

I go back into my room and lie down on the bed, feeling better.

I still think we are going to have problems. This place just makes you hate everyone and everything. But talking felt good.

February 10, 2010: Jane Doe

A man collecting recyclable cans in the desert outside Barstow, California, found a human head in a backpack. Forensic scientists determined that it belonged to a Hispanic female between fourteen and nineteen years old. Since it was discovered not far from several truck stops, they figured the girl could have come from just about anywhere.

The police contacted the National Center for Missing & Exploited Children in Virginia and then the Cleveland police to see if the Jane Doe might be Gina DeJesus, now missing for almost six years.

Detective Laura Parker took the call from the California police, and when she heard about what was found in the backpack, she buried her face in her hands and broke down crying. She prayed that the remains were not Gina's.

Police wanted to check dental records, but Gina had never been to a dentist, so there were none on file. They checked DNA samples that Nancy and Felix had supplied to police and discovered that the dead girl was not Gina. The head has never been identified.

March 25, 2010: No Simple Label

Amanda

At first I thought I could be nice to him just to get better treatment. When you stare at the same four walls day after day, any little thing is a big deal, like getting warm French fries instead of cold ones. But it turned out I needed more than that. I needed somebody to talk to. I remember the time I asked him for a hug and it actually felt good. I needed so bad to feel that.

I saw an Oprah show about a boy in Missouri named Shawn Hornbeck, who was kidnapped in 2002. They were saying he had Stockholm syndrome, a condition that made him start to identify with his abuser. Until someone has gone through this, they don't know how they would react. They can't understand that there is no simple label for what it feels like. You do what you have to do to survive, and it's multiplied by a million when you have a baby to worry about. I don't "identify" with my abuser. I have just done my best to cope, every day, for thousands of days in a row.

I don't think anybody is only one thing, and I don't think he is only evil. He can be a loving man and father. And if I can find warmth in him, I'm going to take it. Before he locks our door each night he gives Jocelyn a big hug and says he loves her. Then he kisses me good night, and it's okay.

I hope Beth will forgive me someday.

May 28, 2010: Ice Cream Truck

Amanda

We hear the ice cream truck again.

"I want to go get ice cream! Please! I want to go see the ice cream truck!" Joce keeps asking over and over.

"You have to ask Daddy," I tell her quietly.

Joce had been with him in the living room last summer when she asked him about the music she heard outside. He pulled back the curtain and pointed to the brightly colored truck and told her about the man who sells ice cream cones and Popsicles. But he didn't take her out to get one because he didn't want the neighbors asking questions.

So she stood inside watching a girl get ice cream until he closed the curtains. Then she gave a little wave and said, "Bye-bye, little girl! Bye-bye, ice cream truck!"

She never forgot that music and now, whenever she hears it, she starts jumping around and begging to go out. But he always has an excuse.

She's starting to get restless in this house. He began taking her outside last year when the next-door neighbors moved away. He told me I could watch from inside the back door when he took her onto the driveway. I cried as I saw the sun touch my baby's face for the first time. She was two and a half years old.

Now she's always asking to go outside. Sometimes he lets her ride her tricycle or run around near him when he works on his cars in the backyard. She copies everything he does, even pretending to shave. I'm worried about her copying too much from him and tell him not to say bad words around her. And I want to make sure that she says "please" and "thank you" and "excuse me," things he never does.

She's learned that if she wants to go out she has to get his permission, not mine. Even if she wants to leave our bedroom and go downstairs, she knows we have to wait for Daddy to unlock our door.

Now she's trying to be patient, waiting for him to come upstairs so she can ask him about the ice cream truck. It's probably on the other side of Cleveland by the time he finally climbs the stairs and unlocks our door. As soon as she hears his footsteps, she starts jumping around the room.

"Daddy, Daddy, I want to go out and get some ice cream!" She's begging him.

"No, Pretty," he says. "We can't go out right now. Maybe later."

June 18, 2010: Emily's Baby

Amanda

He's taking a bath when he says he wants to tell me something.

"Is it bad?" I ask.

"Yeah," he says, "and you have to promise not to hold it against me."

This can't be good. He's never said anything like that before. And what could he possibly tell me that I would hold against him more than kidnapping me for seven years?

"Okay, I promise. What is it?"

"It's my daughter Emily," he says. "She sliced her baby's neck and tried to kill herself."

"Is the baby alive?" I ask. How could Emily have done that?

"Yeah," he answers. "She's okay. It happened a while ago, but now Emily is going to prison for twenty-five years."*

He's told me before that Emily's had lots of problems with depression and mental illness. But I can't believe she would do something like this.

"I'm sorry," I say. I can't think of anything else.

"Maybe this is God's way of punishing me for doing this to you guys," he says.

He thinks everything is about him.

---

*Emily Castro and her boyfriend had a daughter in 2006. They were then living together in Fort Wayne, Indiana, but he moved out and left the baby with Emily, who was nineteen. The day after he left, Emily took the baby into her garage and slashed her neck four times with a knife. Her mother, Grimilda Figueroa, who was in the house at the time, discovered what was happening, ran out into the street with the bleeding infant, and flagged down a driver, who called 911. The infant survived. When police found Emily covered in blood and mud, she told them she had tried to kill herself by cutting her own neck and wrists with the same knife she had used on the baby, then tried to drown herself in a nearby creek. In June 2010 she was convicted of attempted murder and sentenced to thirty years in prison, with five suspended. She appealed later that year, arguing that the court mistakenly ruled her competent to stand trial. Her appeal was denied.

August 4, 2010: Police Next Door

Amanda

It's ninety degrees. He's outside working on his motorcycles, and Jocelyn is next to him playing with the dogs. Gina and Michelle and I are sitting in the little room off the kitchen, near the back door, which is open. This is as close as he'll let us get to fresh air on this hot day. Even though we're inside, he still makes us wear disguises—hats and wigs and sunglasses— just in case someone can see us in the doorway.

Suddenly he's hurrying back in with Jocelyn, warning us, "Be quiet!"

Over his shoulder, in the yard next door, I can see a bunch of cops with their guns drawn. It looks like they're raiding the neighbor's house.

Standing in the doorway, blocking us with his body, he calls out, "What's going on, Officer?" He wants to seem like he has nothing to hide. He's too smart to rush inside and shut the door, in case that looks suspicious.

We're so close to the police. They're just over the fence. I think about screaming, but he's right next to me. I've never seen him so nervous, and it terrifies me. I'm paralyzed.

Gina

I'm in a long black wig and sunglasses when he comes in and tells us all to be quiet. From where I'm sitting, I can't make out what's going on out in the yard, but I can see that he looks scared.

"Shut up and go upstairs—NOW!" he orders. "And don't make any noise!"

As we run upstairs to our rooms I ask Amanda, "What's going on?"

"There are police in the yard," she says.

I wish I had known. Maybe I would have screamed. But then again, maybe not. If I had tried to yell and it didn't work, I don't know what he might have done. I don't need any more punishment from him.

November 19, 2010: Slap

Gina

He brings home a couple of packages of sliced ham from his mother's house. The expiration date has passed, and she told him it was too old to eat, but of course he thinks it's fine for us. I heat up the meat in one of the bags, and it's actually okay.

When he comes back into the kitchen I ask him, "Do you want me to cook the second bag?"

"Where's the first bag, dumbass?"

I'm sick of being called "dumbass" and "retard." I'm sick of him calling me *prima*, which means "cousin" in Spanish, because I'm not related to him. And he's always pushing and poking me, shoving me and touching me. He loves to smack me with whatever's in his hand, like a newspaper or the cardboard tube from a roll of wrapping paper. He's like a fly that keeps landing on me that I'm not allowed to swat. He thinks it's funny, but he's pushing me over the edge. Being called "dumbass" again finally makes me snap.

"I cooked it, dumbass!" I shout at him, surprising even myself.

He slaps me in the face. And then I shock myself at what I do next: I smack him hard in the face with the bag of ham, and the slices fly all over the floor. He grabs my wrist and slaps me harder in the face. This time it really hurts.

"You have to learn not to talk back to your elders," he says.

"I don't care how old you are," I answer.

"The next time you do that," he warns me, "I'm going to punch you in the face. Now pick up that ham and cook it."

I take the ham from the floor and wipe away the dirt before I throw it in the pan. I'm smiling to myself. My face stings, but it felt so good to hit him. I've been dreaming about doing that for six years.

Christmas 2010: Nothing Normal

Amanda

"Look at the camera, Pretty. Over here!"

He's standing in the corner of the living room shooting video. On special occasions when Jocelyn is all dressed up, like today, he gets out his old video camera and films her.

Joce is a little confused about where she is supposed to look, then covers the lens with her fingers, and we both laugh.

The living room is usually dark, but he put up a six-foot white artificial Christmas tree with blinking white lights, and a disco ball that casts multicolor reflections all over the room. He brought Joce a birthday cake with coconut frosting, and we decorated it with little candy canes and four candles on top. He went crazy buying candy and snacks. We put Reese's Peanut Butter Cups, Tic Tacs, Oreos, and cheese puffs out beside the cake.

I've tried to focus on making this the best birthday party ever for Jocelyn and I have to admit, he has been a big help. He bought her a lot of toys and even got me wrapping paper.

We sing "Happy Birthday" to her, and she blows out the candles.

"Are you ready to open your presents?" I ask her as he keeps filming.

"Yes!" she says, and runs over to start ripping the wrapping paper off the old cardboard box that we filled with presents. She pulls out a big coloring book.

"Look, Daddy!" she says, walking it over to him and holding it up for the camera.

Then she takes out a box of graham cracker treats.

"Look, Daddy!"

She likes this game of showing all her presents to the camera and finds some Barbie clothes, a paint set, and some treats.

"What do you have there, my love?" he asks her. "What is that, strawberry granola bars?"

She walks back and forth from the present box to the camera, showing him her Elmo book, and her VTech V reader, a small toy computer that helps kids learn to read.

"Put on your Santa hat," he says, and she does.

Gina and Michelle are watching from behind him. He doesn't allow them to be on camera, and he usually doesn't allow my face to be on, either, but he's in such a good mood today I guess he doesn't care.

"Pretty! I love you, my love!" he says. "Birthday girl!"

He walks around with the camera and focuses in on family photos on the walls. There's one of his four kids, and another one of his grandkids.

I get a knife to cut the cake, but I should have known better.

"Go put that knife away," he snaps.

He is obsessive about knives—but does he really think I'm going to stab him in front of Jocelyn? There have been so many times when I've wanted to kill him, but right now is not one of those moments.

He hands me the camera and he sits on the chair with Jocelyn in his lap eating an ice cream sandwich. He's wearing a black fedora hat and the red long johns that he gave me to wear right after Jocelyn was born. He's smiling and snapping his fingers to "Feliz Navidad" on the radio.

Then they both sing along with José Feliciano: *"I wanna wish you a Merry Christmas, I wanna wish you a Merry Christmas, I wanna wish you a Merry Christmas from the bottom of my heart."*

There is nothing normal about this. But at least Jocelyn is happy.

February 9, 2011: A Talk

Amanda

He wakes me up before seven. He's usually gone by now, but I guess there's no school today or something—why is he still here?

"C'mon downstairs for a while so we can talk," he says.

Jocelyn is still sleeping, so I pull the blanket up over her, put on my slippers, and follow him. It's still dark out. He gets orange juice out of the fridge, puts some old doughnuts on the table, and tells me to sit. He has the strangest look on his face.

"I want to tell you why you're in this situation," he finally says. "I just want to explain it to you, so someday you won't have to wonder why." He pauses for a moment and then continues: "I have a sexual addiction. I've had it since I was a kid."

He tells me when he was young he got hooked on porn, obsessed by it. He also says that he was molested by a neighbor when he was a little boy.

"That must have been hard," I say, trying to act sympathetic.

"I've never told this to anybody else," he adds.

"Why are you telling me?" I ask. Of course, he's told me all this before—I guess he forgot.

"I just wanted you to understand," he says.

I've never seen him this emotional. He's not crying but he's choked up. He's saying everything very softly, like it's painful for him to get the words out. I don't know what to think.

"I'm going to resign from my job. It's too stressful. And I want to spend more time with Pretty before I take you both back home," he says. "I don't know how or when this is all going to end. Maybe in a few years."

He talks for more than an hour, until it starts to get light outside. He's never spoken to me for this long, and he doesn't seem like he's ready to stop. He does seem depressed and says that he's getting more and more headaches from the stress of leading this double life. He loves his grown daughters and doesn't get to see them that often. I know he and his son have never gotten along. He talks about his ex, Nilda, and how he beat her.

"She didn't know when to shut up," he says.

"That's no excuse for hitting her," I tell him. "You could have walked away."

"No, you don't understand," he says. "She would piss me off so bad."

That poor woman.

He has been acting different lately, talking more and buying more food and clothes for us. It's been a long time since he's hit me, but he's still rude and punishes me, like a few days ago when he wouldn't let me use the bathroom for two days because I was annoying him. It was back to using the trash can. He claimed I had started it because I wouldn't talk to him. I was mad because he keeps taking Gina downstairs to "clean" when Jocelyn wants to play with him. He should have been talking to her, reading to her, taking her out of the house, helping her have a bit more of a regular childhood. He should be acting like a parent, not a pig.

But right now I can't be too mad at him. He seems so sad and lost.

"You know," he says, "sometimes I don't even have feelings. I think I'm coldhearted. I don't care how people feel."

I have known that about him for years, but it's odd to hear him actually admit it.

"Well," I answer, "I don't know how you can do this to me and my family. I mean, you see my sister crying on TV. You see what this has done to my family and Gina's. Could you imagine going through that with your kids? What if your kids were missing?"

"You know what?" he says. "Sometimes I look at your family and I have no feelings about them at all. I know they're hurt. But it doesn't bother me. Like I said, I don't have feelings."

How can I respond to that?

I remember one day I heard people on TV talking about sociopaths. I had never heard that word before, but the description fit him so perfectly that I wrote the word down and later looked it up in the dictionary: *a person whose behavior lacks a sense of moral responsibility or social conscience.* And I thought: *That's him!* I started going through the whole dictionary to find other words to describe him and wrote some of them in my diary:

Censorious: Always finding fault, criticizing.
Despot: Person who treats those under his control in any way he cares to, cruel or unjust.
Fastidious: Not easy to please. Very particular.
Impenitent: Not feeling shame or regret. Not sorry for what he's done.
Imperious: Like a dictator, arrogant. Impolite.
Impudent: Not showing respect, shamelessly rude.
Sadist.

He is all those things.

"When are you going to let us go home?" I finally ask him after he goes on talking for another half hour.

"I don't know," he replies. "I don't have a date yet. But soon."

"You've been saying that for years."

I get up to leave and am actually looking forward to going back upstairs to Joce and having him lock us in. At least in my room nobody's crazy.

April 29, 2011: Royal Wedding

Amanda

Joce and I are watching the royal wedding. Prince William is so handsome, he looks like a king! And Kate is so beautiful. I'm not wild about her dress, though. I think it's too simple for such a fairy-tale wedding. I wish she were wearing something fancier, more amazing. But I love her tiara and how happy she looks.

I want a fairy tale. After this is over, I hope I can find a man who loves me and looks at me like I'm the only woman he ever wants to be with. I want a man who is kind and gentle. I want a husband who is my best friend and adores Jocelyn. I hope I will find my own prince someday.

May 2011: Haircuts

Amanda

He asks me to trim his hair. I don't know why, because Gina usually does it for him.

"I'm not a hairdresser," I tell him. "I don't know how to cut hair."

"Do it anyway," he says. "And don't mess it up."

He's obsessed with his appearance, always primping in the mirror. He asks me if this shirt goes with these pants, are these shoes okay, how does this outfit look? He has shoes and socks in red, white, and blue, like the Puerto Rican flag. He thinks they are stylish, but to me they're just silly.

Sometimes he wears eyeliner to make himself look like a cool rocker guy. He must have ten black leather jackets hanging up in the kitchen, and a whole collection of hats because they cover up his receding hairline. Like anybody cares.

He lies down on the bed on his stomach, with his head up. It's an awkward position for a haircut, and I'm having trouble. I don't know why he doesn't just sit in a chair. It's also hard because he makes us use the tiny kiddie scissors we have for our artwork—nothing sharp enough to hurt him.

As I'm trimming the back I accidentally cut a little bare spot, which I hope he won't notice. But as he checks the back of his head with a small mirror he starts screaming at me.

"What are you doing?" he asks, looking like he's going to explode. "Why did you do that? You did it on purpose!"

"I did not!" I say. "It's nothing. If I did it on purpose, I would have made it a lot bigger."

"Get upstairs!" he yells.

I run up the stairs to my room and sit with Joce. I'm worried about how he might react because he's always unpredictable when he gets this mad. I know he's going to come back and do something to me, because that's the way he is. He'll take his time and think of the perfect revenge.

All I can do is sit and wait, so Joce and I flip on the TV.

Three hours later I hear him stomping up the stairs. He barges in, wearing a hat to hide the bare spot. "It's haircut time," he says, with a crazy smile on his face. He's holding a big pair of metal scissors with black handles that I've never seen before. "You messed up my hair," he tells me, "so I'm going to get even."

"It was an accident!" I say. "Why do you have to do this?"

"Turn away—look over there!" he tells Jocelyn. He always does that when he doesn't want her to see what he's really like. She does what she's told.

He steps toward me, and I can see he wants to make this hurt. He grabs me and cuts a big bald spot on the top of my head, right in front. He jabs the scissors into my hair and keeps snipping.

"I know you did that to me on purpose," he says. "So now you can look at this every day."

"I didn't do it on purpose!" I can't believe he's doing this with Joce in the room. "And yours is in the back and small. This is really big and right in the front."

"It looks really nice," he says sarcastically, obviously pleased with himself.

I hate myself for ever getting close to him. I am so stupid. I can't believe I got fooled by him. He's standing there laughing at me. I grab my comb and try to push some hair over the bald spot. He takes his hand and messes it up again.

"How do you like it?" he asks and then opens the door to Gina and Michelle's room.

"Hey," he says, laughing. "You want to see her haircut?" They are trying not to look.

When he messes up my hair again, I go to kick him in his junk, but I miss.

"I'll punch you," he warns, holding up his fist. He looks at Jocelyn and leaves.

I'm so humiliated. Hair is scattered all over the bed. I try to comb my hair over the bald spot again, but it doesn't work. Joce is scared and hugging me.

Gina comes in and sits next to me.

"If it was me, I would go downstairs and look him straight in the face and say, 'It doesn't bother me,'" she tells me. "Don't let him beat you. Be proud, keep your head up. Remember what your mom would say."

She's right. Mom would tell me to quit crying and be stronger than he is.

June

Gina

He's cutting his hair again. He's so in love with himself. He spends more time looking at himself in the mirror than any girl does. He's always trimming his mustache and beard, cutting the little hairs out of his nose and ears, snipping his eyebrows.

He thinks he's so attractive. Dude, you're *old*. And fat and nasty and hairy. Looking in the mirror's not going to help! I wish I could say that to him, but I don't want to get smacked.

He usually makes me cut his hair. I bet I've done it fifty times, but today he's doing it himself. That's probably better, because we all remember what happened to Amanda a few weeks ago. She still has that bald spot, and it's going to take a long time for her hair to grow back.

Look at him. He's buzzing up and down and side to side with his electric trimmer. He must be in a hurry, because he's doing it way too fast. He can't see it, but he just messed up and shaved a bare spot in the back of his head. It's like the one Amanda gave him, except a lot bigger. When he realizes what he did, he turns to me.

"This is your fault!" he shouts.

"My fault?" I say. "I didn't do that. I was sitting right here and watched you do it."

"My machine never did that before," he says, furious. "You must have done something to it!"

"I didn't do anything!"

He's trying to fix the spot with the trimmer, but he's only making it worse. It kills him that his hair is going to look funny. But what's the big deal? He has a bunch of hats, so he can just cover it up.

"I'm going to jack you up like I did Amanda," he yells.

"I don't care," I tell him.

And really, I don't. I've already had my hair completely shaved in here. When Britney Spears shaved her head in 2007, right after my seventeenth birthday, I took his little electric trimmer and shaved my head too, hoping it would annoy him. And another time I gave myself a Mohawk, a little protest against him because he was always telling me that he liked my hair. The only problem with being bald was that he kept touching my head—not to hurt me, but just to feel the smoothness. It bugged me so much that I had to grow my hair back to get him to stop.

So what do I care if he messes up my hair now?

If I don't let it bother me, he can't hurt me.

* * *

Two days later he calls me into the kitchen and tells me he's ready to "jack me up good." "I'm going to chop you like I did Amanda," he says, waving the big scissors. "You want a Mohawk or a shaved head?"

He thinks he's scaring me. He made Amanda cry for days when he did this to her, and now he wants me to cry, too. No way, dude.

"Do what you want," I say, trying to sound bored. "I've had a Mohawk. Everybody has already seen my bald head, so I don't care."

He grabs my hair and chops a few pieces.

I don't move and look him right in the eye.

"Is that it?" I ask.

That pisses him off, so he starts cutting faster and makes a huge, ugly bald spot in the front of my head, just like Amanda's.

"That's a nice haircut," he says. "How do you like that?"

"Oh, you're done?" I say. "Good. Can I go play with Jocelyn now?"

I walk into the living room and say to Amanda and Jocelyn: "Look, I got a haircut! Isn't it beautiful?"

I'm laughing about it, which makes them laugh. Jocelyn thinks it's all just a funny game.

He comes into the living room and asks me: "What are you going to do? You going to shave your head?"

"No, I like it," I answer. "I'm going to keep it just like this."

He doesn't look happy and walks out, slamming the door and locking it.

That felt good. A little victory.

June 15, 2011: The Park

Amanda

He took Jocelyn to Roberto Clemente Park, just a few blocks away, for the very first time today, and though she was too scared to go on the swings, he took her down the slide on his lap. She is still getting used to the outside. I'm always telling her "I love you," and Jocelyn was so excited to see other kids that she was saying, "Hi, I love you" to everybody she met. She played with a little boy and girl at the park and kept hugging them. He said the other parents told him she was so beautiful and friendly.

He's been taking her out in his car, but today he actually got a car seat for her. He drove her to a bakery on Clark Avenue, where they gave her a free cookie with purple icing and sprinkles. Joce saw a little girl there with her grandpa, and she kept saying, "I love you" to her, too.

After that they went to the McDonald's drive-through and he told me that Joce asked the lady, "How are you doing?" And as they left, Joce said, "Thanks. Have a nice day!"

I love hearing how chatty she is. I've been worried that living in this house and being so isolated would make her afraid of people. It's good that he's taking her out more, because I want her to be normal and happy when we leave here someday.

July 14, 2011: Carnival

Amanda

They went to a carnival in the neighborhood today, and he came back with a video of her riding a little roller coaster. She was waving at the camera in his phone, saying, "Hi, Mommy!"

I started tearing up when I saw it, because it was one more little memory that I wish she had made with me.

"Mommy, why are you crying?" Joce asked.

I had to pretend it was nothing and went into the bathroom to dry my eyes.

"One day you'll get to do these things with her," he says to me. "You just have to wait."

If I hear that one more time, I will explode. I'm so tired of waiting.

It's summer, so he doesn't have to drive the bus and he's home a lot. Joce has been getting up early, waiting for him to come unlock the door and take her somewhere in the car. She's four and a half now, and it's harder to keep her in the house. They've been to Home Depot, where a lady told Joce that she loved her curls. He took her out to get us his version of dinner—KFC for chicken, Little Caesars for pizza, and Walgreen's for pop. They also went to Family Dollar, where he got her a new swimsuit and let her ride in the shopping cart, which she loved.

He makes her hide on the floor when they pull in and out of the driveway. I cried when he told me he taught her that. She must think it's perfectly normal for kids to do that, which makes me sad. But she loves going in the car, and she always returns all excited, describing what they did and who talked to her.

It's so weird to picture him waiting for her at the end of a slide or watching beside the monkey bars, acting like a normal parent. Other parents must think he's just some nice dad or grandpa. I wish they could somehow sense something wrong and report him to the police, but I guess I'm dreaming. I hate that he's the one who gets to do these things with her.

When they go out, I imagine what he's showing her: fire trucks, Lake Erie, the glass triangle of the Rock and Roll Hall of Fame. I keep extra busy until she comes back by finding tasks to do. I scrub the floors and tidy up. I write in my diary. I make tons of lists: names of my friends, birth dates of my relatives, favorite songs, sayings that make me feel good, like "Choose happiness" and "Know what you can and cannot change."

It's much better for me to keep busy. It's easier if I don't think too much.

July 30, 2011: Church

Amanda

Jocelyn prayed in church for the first time today.

He took her to a church festival where they had games and a crafts table for kids, and she made me a pink cross that she decorated with little hearts. He took pictures of her there with his phone. In one she's holding a little rod and is fishing in a kiddie pool filled with plastic fish. In another she's smiling and holding another little girl's hand. That's her favorite thing: meeting other kids.

She had never been inside a church before. I've taught her a lot about Jesus, but she's never seen an altar or rows of pews. She told me that she saw a statue of Jesus and hugged it—so sweet!

Then the two of them knelt down, bowed their heads, and prayed together.

I taught her to pray in this room. At night we kneel together at the side of the bed, fold our hands, and pray for "Mamaw," my mom. We pray for my dad and Beth and our whole family, too, then we climb into bed.

I bet she prays for my parents in church just like she does here.

I wonder what he says to God.

July 31, 2011: Praying

Amanda

It's a big weekend for Joce—today he took her to the lake for the first time!

Some guy had a kite and let her hold the string. It's been so hot—ninety-seven degrees. Last night I was fanning her with a cardboard box as she slept because it's so miserable in our room that we bake in here. I shut off the TV, the light, anything that might make it even one degree cooler. Joce's little cheeks get so flushed because there's no air. So I love the idea of her flying a kite in the cool breeze.

After the lake, she asked him to go to church and pray again. He came back with a picture of her with a statue of Mary, Joseph, and Baby Jesus. She says she really likes church. I hope she keeps taking him there.

August 24, 2011: First Day of School

Amanda

It's time to start kindergarten. Joce is almost five. Someday we're going to get out of here, and when she gets to go to a real school, I want her to feel she knows as much as the other kids.

Our room already looks like a tiny classroom. When she was very young, I began taping shapes, colors, and letters to the wall. I cut out pictures of animals from junk mail and magazines and taped them up, too. She would point to them and say "cow" and "horse" and "monkey." We played a little game where I would say the name of the animal in a picture, like "cat," and she would have to say it back to me.

He bought some jigsaw puzzles at a yard sale, with the Incredibles and Dora on them. She loves Dora. He also found some Barney flash cards, and we worked hard with those, so she knows her numbers pretty well.

I read to her all the time. We have only a few books, because he's so cheap. But after I begged and begged, he brought us more, and some of them even seemed brand-new. *Can You Tell Me How to Get to Sesame Street?* was her favorite. We must have read it ten thousand times: *"Elmo likes books. Fat books. Funny books. Bat books. Bunny books."* We also love Dr. Seuss's *Fox in Socks.* She likes the way it ties up her tongue when she reads it to me: *"Fox. Socks. Box. Knox. Knox in box. Fox in socks."*

But now it's time to make her learning more formal. I know the Cleveland Public Schools start today, because this is his first day back at work driving his bus. He left before six for the first time since last spring. Today it also means Jocelyn starts kindergarten.

I stayed up late last night getting everything ready. I have some work-sheets from schoolbooks that he found at yard sales or at Unique. He brings home books on math and reading, and one called *Hooked on Pho-nics.* I rip pages out of them to use as worksheets, and copy numbers and letters by hand and make my own. The books help me know exactly what kids are supposed to learn in different grades, and I have made worksheets for reading, math, and Spanish. It's simple stuff, because I want to make sure we start nice and easy, so she likes school.

He got Jocelyn a used pink-and-purple Dora fold-up table and an old kiddie lawn chair to use as her school desk. He bought a big white board, one of those dry-erase ones, with colored markers. I taped the whole alphabet, capital and small letters, to the bedroom wall. I am trying everything I can think of to create a real classroom.

I set my alarm for nine. Jocelyn rarely goes to sleep until after mid-night and I want to make sure we get up early. When the alarm buzzes,

I get up and get dressed, then I wake up Jocelyn. We use the little portable potty in our room, since the door to the hallway is locked and we
can't get downstairs to the bathroom. We have water in a gallon jug and
we brush our teeth with that. I cut the top off a plastic milk jug, which
we use as our sink. I put a packet of oatmeal in the microwave, add some
milk from our little mini-fridge, and we have breakfast.

"Are you ready?" I ask her after we finish eating.

"Yes!" she says.

She sits at her Dora desk and surrounds herself with her dolls, which
are almost as big as she is. She calls them her classmates. I write the date
on the whiteboard: Wednesday, August 24, 2011.

I sit on the bed facing her. We have a couple of little American flags,
and we hold them, which makes Joce feel grown up. "Please stand for
the Pledge of Allegiance," I say.

She stands at her desk, and as I take my place next to her, we both put
our hands over our hearts.

"I pledge allegiance to the flag," I begin, and Joce tries to keep up, *"of
the United States of America. And to the republic for which it stands, one
nation, under God, indivisible, with liberty and justice for all."*

She stumbles just a bit on "indivisible," but she's a quick learner.

"Okay," I say. "Please be seated."

We start by saying the date out loud, and then go over the days of the
week. We then practice naming shapes and colors. I cut out a triangle
from blue construction paper and write "blue" on it, and I tape it to the
wall. She works on coloring in shapes, and when she's done, I post her
work on the wall. She is so proud.

At lunchtime we have a sandwich that I made the night before. He
brought us some chips in a bowl, which I have to make last all week, so I
cover them with plastic to keep them fresh.

After lunch we play fun games and talk about things like pollu-
tion and safety. I warn her about never going anywhere with strangers.
I don't think she has any idea what I'm talking about, but someday
she will.

We say a few words in Spanish. I don't know much, but her dad speaks it to her all the time, so it's fun for her to learn some new words: "*Me llamo Jocelyn.*"

We finish for the day at around one o'clock because I think that's when real kindergarten ends for the day. After we fold up the Dora table and stand it up behind the whiteboard—I hate clutter—we play a game I call "time to go home." She puts on her little backpack and gets ready to leave, like they do at a real school. I explain to her about the safest ways to cross a street and then pretend to walk with her: out the door, down the street, cross at the corner, look both ways. She loves the imaginary trip. I pull make-believe keys out of my pocket, and she helps me unlock our pretend front door. Then we are home!

She drops her backpack, and it's time to do some exercises. I eat so much junk food that I need the workout, and I want to make sure that Jocelyn gets healthy exercise every day. So we stand and do twenty-five jumping jacks each. It's funny, and we laugh ourselves silly.

October 2011: Depression

Gina

I don't want to get out of bed. I don't want to eat.

"Chelsea! Chelsea! Let's play!" Jocelyn is at my door again, begging.

I keep my eyes closed and pretend I'm sleeping. It's late afternoon, and the days are getting longer and harder.

Sitting on the floor and playing with Jocelyn used to be my favorite way to spend time. We played Go Fish, and I pretended to eat her fake little fried eggs and plastic sandwiches. I made her laugh when I turned my eyelids inside out.

She is the only happy person in this house, and I love her.

But I can't stand being here anymore, so isolated and cut off from the world. I am twenty-one. I was fourteen when he took me and I feel like I'm still stuck at fourteen. It's Halloween soon, and I want to be out enjoying it. I think of Chrissy and my other friends and I wonder if they have jobs and babies now.

I am sick of being in the same bed when he comes for Michelle, and then me.

I need this to be over.

"Please, please, stop," I ask him.

His response is to call me names. Retard. Sasquatch—he especially loves that one, because he says I have big feet.

He found a red metal stencil of the word "hope" at a yard sale and brought it home for us. I don't know why. It's pretty, and I have used it to trace "hope" onto all kinds of pictures and artwork. But now I've stopped feeling hope, so I've stopped writing it. I've even torn up some of the artwork that I was going to give to my parents, and I threw away the cut-off ponytail that I had been keeping in a plastic bag for my mom.

Michelle says no one will ever come and rescue us, and that we will all die here.

I've stopped imagining all the ways I can escape. I used to dream of killing him with the rat poison that he sprinkles in our room because of the mice in this house. I could never figure out how to do that, and I think it's a lot easier to talk about killing someone than to actually do it.

I'm having trouble breathing. I feel the walls closing in on me.

I'm done hoping that he will ever change. This is my life.

December 2011: Puppies

Gina

Three puppies were born in our room a few weeks ago. At first I was mad that he brought one of his backyard dogs, a Chihuahua named Dana, into the room with me and Michelle. Dana had just had one of her litter outside, and he carried her and the puppy indoors where it was warmer and put her on our floor. I didn't know what to do and just watched her pace back and forth, her paws dragging dirt all over the new little piece of carpet he had just given us. And then she had two more puppies with all of us watching. Jocelyn was so excited and named the puppies Lala, Ginger, and Kashla, after the dog we buried a few years ago.

He told me I was responsible for making sure they were okay and didn't bark, so that meant I was up night and day. The puppies had worms, and I had to tell him to get medicine. Amanda was worried that Jocelyn would get sick from this outside dog.

When they were old enough he gave Kashla and Ginger away to relatives, but he let me keep Lala for a while. After she was weaned, I started putting out food for her and playing with her. She was white and fluffy and comforted me. But then one day she nipped Jocelyn, so he gave her to one of his daughters. She was my pal. I miss her.

Castro's Story: A Prickly Musician

One day in early 2012 Tito DeJesus got a text message out of the blue.

Hey, I'm back in the scene. Do you need my strings?

DeJesus didn't recognize the number, but it was obviously a musician looking for work. Everyone knew DeJesus as "Titopiano," and he was well regarded and well connected in the Latin music scene.

Who is this? he texted back.

It's Ariel.

DeJesus laughed out loud. His old friend Ariel Castro had finally entered the twenty-first century—he was texting! Castro was one of the best bass players DeJesus knew, and they'd been playing together for almost twenty years. But he wasn't big on technology.

Whoa, Ariel, you're finally getting with it! he texted back.

Castro had fallen out of touch recently. DeJesus knew that too many bandleaders had gotten fed up with Castro's behavior, always showing up late to practices and gigs and arguing with them over their choice of songs. He was an excellent musician but prickly and arrogant, and a lot of people thought he wasn't worth the trouble.

DeJesus felt sorry for his old pal, so he called him back and invited him over to his apartment to jam. Castro showed up with a twelve-pack of Corona, and they went over a few musical charts and new arrangements, DeJesus on the piano and Castro on the bass.

Out of the blue, Castro asked, "Hey, man, did they find your cousin yet?"

"Who?"

"Gina. Did they find Gina yet?"

DeJesus then realized he meant Gina DeJesus. "Oh, Gina!" he said. "I don't know if she's actually my cousin. We might be related, but I don't know for sure. And no, man, the family hasn't found her yet. We're praying."

"Well, you know, I hope they do find her," Castro said. "I'm praying, too. It's a shame what happened to that girl."

Castro was more than a decade older than DeJesus, and had become a mentor to him. When they first met, Castro said he admired DeJesus's piano playing and told him, "Let's get you some gigs, let's get your name out there."

So they started playing gigs at local Puerto Rican hot spots, and in 2010 they played at the Fiesta de Luz, a big fund-raiser at Progressive Field, home to the Cleveland Indians. Someone took a picture of the band that day that shows the musicians dressed all in white, with Castro wearing glasses and a neatly trimmed mustache.

DeJesus always thought Castro was a little odd, "a weird cat." They often drove together to gigs at clubs in Youngstown, about seventy-five miles southeast of Cleveland. Even if he was offered a free hotel room because the shows ended so late, Castro always insisted on driving home to Cleveland, no matter the hour. Since Castro was often his ride, DeJesus accompanied him.

On the way home from Youngstown one night, Castro was driving his van down the highway when he said, "I gotta take a leak." DeJesus told him to stop at a rest area, but Castro said he couldn't wait because he was in a hurry to get home. When DeJesus suggested he just pull over and go on the side of the road, Castro suddenly said, "Take the wheel!" and opened the driver's side door.

"What the hell are you doing?" DeJesus shouted.

"Hold the wheel! Hold the wheel!" Castro yelled.

With DeJesus steering at sixty-five miles per hour, Castro unzipped his pants, pushed the door open a crack, and started relieving himself onto the highway. DeJesus never knew what was coming next with Castro.

DeJesus liked Castro but often found him to be an argumentative know-it-all who was easily upset when he didn't get his way, someone who argued for the sake of arguing. He always felt he deserved to be paid more than other musicians, and if he learned that others were getting a higher fee, he complained loudly.

He often raged that the world was against him, especially women.

The clubs they played together were often filled with beautiful women, and DeJesus watched with amusement as Castro hit on them endlessly, never missing a chance to ask one of them to dance. They were usually much younger and always shot him down, which infuriated him.

"Dude, man, you're a glutton for punishment. You look like an idiot with those girls," DeJesus told him.

"Fuck those bitches. Fuck them all," Castro said. "Don't they know who I am? I'm a musician!"

"Whoop-dee-do!" DeJesus said, teasing his friend. "You may be a musician, but you're a friggin' school bus driver. Who the hell wants to date a school bus driver? You're nobody special. Neither am I."

"Fuck you, Tito," Castro said.

April 8, 2012: Easter Dresses

Gina

We are all wearing the new sundresses I bought. Last week I saw a newspaper flyer with cute $10 dresses, and since Easter and both Michelle's and Amanda's birthdays were coming, I asked him if I could give him money to buy a dress for each of us. And he did!

Every so often he gives me money. Sometimes when he is in a good mood, and after I wash the floor or do other housework, he hands me cash, usually $5, saying, "You're going to need money when you get out."

I think it makes him feel less guilty. Some years I get more than others, but usually I end up with about $50, and spend it on special things like take-out Mexican from Chipotle or poster board. Sometimes he says no when I ask him to buy me something with that money, and sometimes he takes it and buys nothing.

The dresses were supposed to be a surprise, but I was too excited to keep them a secret, since I don't get the chance to share good news very often. I wanted to make sure I got ones they liked, too, so I asked Amanda what color she wanted. She said there was no way he'd actually get us something brand-new.

Of course, he got the wrong sizes, so the dresses were way too big for all of us. I hemmed them and made matching headbands with the extra material and elastic waistbands from his old underwear.

Today it feels good to wear something new as I say my Easter prayers. Every day my prayers are the same: I ask God to give my parents a sign that I am alive and to please, please, please give someone a sign that we are right here inside 2207 Seymour Avenue.

April 2012: Nine Years Gone

April 11

Amanda

"Daddy, I want you to take me and Mommy to Titi Beth's house."

I'm floored. Out of nowhere, Joce tells him she wants to visit Beth. Puerto Ricans say *titi* for "aunt," which she's learned from him.

"I don't know where they live," he says, dodging her question.

"Mommy, do you know where they live?" she asks.

"I'm sorry, baby," I tell her gently. "They moved, and I don't know where they live now."

"But I really want to go to Titi Beth's!" she says. "I want to play with Mariyah and Marissa and Devon!"

"You're just going to have to wait," he tells her.

He goes in the other room, and Joce starts grilling me.

"Mommy, where did you live before I was born?" she asks.

"I lived in a nice house with Beth and Mamaw."

"Do you remember what it looked like?"

"I do. I haven't been there in a long time, but I had a pretty room, just like we have here."

She's been asking more and more questions like this lately, and I'm sure it's because she's tired of being in this house. She goes out with him a lot, but she knows that other kids do more things. She sees it on TV and at the park. Other mothers come outside and play, but hers can never go with her. She's beginning to figure out that this is not normal.

April 21

He says he wants this all to end in a shootout with the police. He knows someday he'll have to pay for our kidnappings, but he's so afraid of going to prison that he would rather be shot dead by cops. He says he has his gun ready. I hope someday that the cops do find us, and he gets his wish.

I'm watching the morning news because it's the ninth anniversary of my kidnapping, and there's a story about me and Gina. Lately she, Michelle, and I have been talking more, and we've drawn a lot of pictures together. Last year, when he cut off my hair, Gina really helped me through it, and we've been getting along better since then.

I let Joce stay in the room when news about me is on. Beth comes on, talking to a reporter, and she looks skinny.

"Is that Titi Beth?" Joce asks.

"Yes, that's her. Wave to her!" I say, and we both wave at the TV.

Joce steps right up to the screen and talks to Beth.

"God bless you, Titi Beth, and one day we'll get to see you and be with our family," she tells her. Then she turns to me and says, "Don't worry, Mommy, we'll see them soon."

My sweet child. I've never explained the whole situation to her, but she knows enough to want to comfort me.

It's Saturday, so he's not working. He comes up to our room at about noon.

"They showed my nieces and nephew on TV today," I tell him. "I love seeing them. They are growing so much."

"Yeah, Daddy, they're looking for Mommy," Joce says.

He looks at me, furious. He points a finger right in my face and says, "You're in trouble! Stay in this room! Don't come downstairs!"

He slams the door and leaves. I'm not supposed to tell Jocelyn what's going on here, but as she's gotten older, it's become harder to hide things from her. I probably shouldn't have let her watch the news reports about me and Gina, since she's not even supposed to know our real names, but I was too excited to see everybody on TV. I wait all year for the news on April 21, and I always record it on my VCR so I can watch the tapes of my family when things get really miserable.

We're hungry, but I don't dare go downstairs to make us lunch. He's too unpredictable when he's this mad, and now I hear him coming back.

"Go downstairs!" he says to Joce, and she does what she's told.

"Why are you letting her watch those videos?" he yells.

"It was nothing. I couldn't help it," I answer. "She heard it on the news. If I wanted to tell her something, I would have done it a long time ago."

"Shut up," he says, pushing me across the room. "Show me your tape!"

He sits there as I push the Play button and watches the recording I just made of the news, with Beth and her kids, and all the people looking for me and Gina.

"Give me the tape," he says.

"No! I want to watch it later, and I want to record the news tonight."

"You're done recording," he says, pulling the tape out of the VCR and throwing it into the closet so hard that it smashes against the wall and cracks at the corner.

"You bastard!" I scream at him.

"If I take her out and she says anything to anybody, you're in for it," he warns me and then storms out again.

I grab the tape and check to make sure it still plays. It does, thank God. He always does things like this. I was feeling good watching Beth on the news, then he ruins my day again. And he scared Joce half to death.

She comes back up after he leaves, and I hug her for a long time.

I'm so afraid that one of these days he's going to kill me. Then what will happen to Joce?

April 22

My family had a vigil for me last night, and I record the coverage of it on the news this morning. I am sure he'll check to make sure I didn't disobey him and record anything new, so I have a plan: If he asks, I'll show him the smashed cassette and hide this one.

When the news comes on, I make Joce close her eyes and turn around, and I put the TV on mute. I have to make sure she doesn't see or hear any more of this.

"Okay," I tell her. "It's over now, so you can open your eyes."

"Was our family on TV?" she asks.

"No, not this time. Maybe they'll be on another time."

I hate lying to her, but I'm afraid of what he might do.

She reaches into her little bag and pulls out her last piece of gum. She almost never gets gum, so it's a special treat.

She holds it out to me and says, "You don't have anything to celebrate your birthday, so this is for you."

"Time stands still for me—it seems like yesterday, but then it seems like forever."

That's what Beth said at my vigil, the night before my twenty-sixth birthday. I keep hearing her words in my head and I write a poem for her:

It seems like time stands still.
I feel like the world is turning and leaving me behind.
Sometimes it feels like Day One because I remember it all.
Sometimes it seems like an eternity, because my heart misses them so much.
For me, time stands still. I didn't even get to see my nieces grow into young girls.
I hear people outside laughing, kids playing and cars driving by.
Everyone else is living their lives while I'm just stuck here waiting to be by your side.
Every day I wonder, what's it going to be like for us.
All I know is I'm ready for a new life.

Castro's Story: Burying Nilda

On the evening of Sunday, April 29, 2012, family and friends gathered for a wake for Nilda Figueroa at the Walter Martens & Sons Funeral Home on Denison Avenue.

Nilda had died four days earlier of complications from her brain tumor while she was visiting her daughter Arlene in Fort Wayne. The official cause of death was an overdose of oxycodone for the chronic pain. She was forty-eight.

When Castro entered the funeral home, he was met with whispers and angry stares. Nilda's family blamed him for her death. Her male relatives wanted to take him outside and show him what a beating felt like, but Nilda's sister Elida and some of the other women persuaded them to stay calm. Nilda's and Castro's children were there, and nobody wanted violence at the funeral of a woman who had endured so much of it.

Castro's daughter Angie greeted him. She believed he was sorry for the way he had treated her mother. But Nilda's side of the family didn't say a word to him and stared angrily as he approached the open casket.

As he stood over Nilda's body, he said, loud enough for Elida and others to hear: "Man, she was a good cook."

Elida found his comment inappropriate, one final slight from the man who had brutalized Nilda for so long. But she swallowed her anger to keep the peace.

Castro didn't kneel or say a prayer, or show any sign of emotion, but did manage to take a cell phone photo of Nilda's body without anyone noticing.

Nilda was buried the next day under sunny skies at Riverside Cemetery, less than a mile from her old house on Seymour Avenue. Wearing his black leather motorcycle jacket, Castro stood alone behind the mourners.

May 3, 2012: His Ex

Amanda

Tonight we're sitting in the garage. It's been 90 degrees and hotter in the house, but it's a little cooler in the garage, even with the hats and wigs he's making us wear. Jocelyn is watching kid movies on a TV that he plugged in out here, and he and I are talking about Nilda.

He says he still can't believe that she's gone. He woke me up early the morning it happened to tell me. He was upset, but I'm not sure why, because he always told me he hated her. He was so frazzled the morning she died that he burned the bacon and filled the house with smoke.

He abused Nilda in this very same house. I guess after she left, he missed having a woman to treat like his property, so he started kidnapping other women.

I feel bad for his kids, because their mother is gone. I know what that's like. He complained that her family bought her a cheap casket. That's pretty ironic, coming from the cheapest person I know. But he seemed genuinely sad as he showed me her memorial card and a weird cell phone picture he took of her body in the coffin.

May 5, 2012: Flyer

Gina

He's wearing his tight BE MY VALENTINE underwear again. Gross.

Whenever it's hot, he hangs around the house in a tank top and his underwear. And his favorite pair are the Valentine's Day ones, red bikinis. Whatever, dude.

"Gimme a massage," he says, lying on the couch in the living room.

He makes me do this for hours, rubbing his shoulders and his back and his stinky feet, like I'm his slave. But at least it puts him in a good mood, so it's not worth fighting about.

"Oh," he says casually, "I saw your mother a little while ago."

"Really?" I say, startled. "Where?"

"She was out on Lorain and 105th passing out flyers," he says. "I asked her for one."

He says that he was driving by on his motorcycle when he saw her, so he stopped and asked if there was anything new on my case.

I'm so mad that he was out there talking to my mom. That's like laughing in her face. I want to strangle him, but I just keep rubbing his shoulders.

"Where is it?" I ask. "Can I have it?"

"Sure, I don't care," he says. "It's in my jeans pocket in the kitchen."

I find his pants folded over the back of a chair. I reach into the pocket and find a piece of folded-up paper. I open it and I see in big letters, MISSING PERSON: GEORGINA "GINA" DEJESUS, and six little pictures of me at different ages.

I start crying. An hour ago, this paper was in my mom's hands.

I finish massaging him and then go upstairs. I'm going to decorate my flyer, and I hope someday I can show it to my mom.

I cut out little paper hearts, cover them with red glitter, and glue them to the flyer. I carefully cut out one of the little photos of me. I'm going to put it in a pretty picture frame I made.

I'm so, so hungry all the time. I must weigh under a hundred pounds now, probably thirty less than when I got here. I take some grocery-store ads from the newspaper and cut out pictures of food I dream about: a strawberry ice cream sundae, a thick ham-and-cheese sandwich, a pile of onion rings, and a Hershey's chocolate bar. I glue the pictures of food to the bottom of the flyer and tuck it away in the little blue backpack where I keep my most precious things. I'd love to hang the artwork up on my wall, but Jocelyn can read now, so she would ask too many questions about why it says I'm missing, and he would go crazy.

Jocelyn doesn't even know my real name. To her, I'm Chelsea.

But I know who I am.

I am Georgina DeJesus. And my family loves me.

June 2, 2012: Graduation

Amanda

Yesterday was Jocelyn's last day of kindergarten classes, so today we're having a graduation ceremony.

I made her a black graduation hat out of construction paper and a "certificate of graduation" that was very formal and fancy. Where it said "teacher," I signed my name.

We all get together in our room: me and him, Jocelyn, Gina, and Michelle. I ask Jocelyn to stand up, and I read the certificate out loud: "This is to certify that Jocelyn Jade Berry has graduated from kindergarten."

She stands up wearing her hat and steps forward to get her certificate. We all applaud, and she says, "Thank you."

I'm so proud of her. She has worked hard all year. We had school five days a week, following the Cleveland Public Schools calendar exactly. We took vacations when real school was out for Thanksgiving and Christmas and spring break.

She has learned so many words and numbers and studied all kinds of practical things, like healthy eating. I tried to make it fun. I'd say, "*A* is for alligator," and bounce a little plastic ball to Joce. She would say, "*B* is for balloon," and bounce it back. We would try to get through the whole alphabet without missing a word or dropping the ball.

It wasn't always easy. There were plenty of days when she was sick of me, sick of school, sick of the same old everything every day, and it was hard to hold her attention.

One day in November he brought her home a lunch from school, a little brown paper bag with a sandwich. I guess they were giving away extras, and she was so excited that it came from a real school.

"I want to go to real school now. Can I, please?" she asked him.

"No," he said, but she kept begging him and asking him why not.

"It's not time yet," he told her.

"When is it time?" she asked.

"I don't know. You just have to be patient."

We have lots of nice food for the graduation ceremony. He had a year-end party at work yesterday, and he brought us a big dish of leftover pasta and some pop.

He also found hundreds of pages of first-grade worksheets that were being thrown away, which will be a big help when we start school again in August. Oh, God, I can't believe I'm just assuming that we'll still be here in August. Will this never end?

But for the moment I try to make sure Joce enjoys her big day, and I tape her graduation certificate to the wall.

He opens the pop, and we eat the pasta. We're all so proud of Jocelyn and happy for her. I can't remember another time when we were all in one room eating, talking, and laughing.

July 6, 2012: Pool Time

Amanda

I've been getting more and more upset about not being able to go outside with Jocelyn. He sees me quietly crying when they come back all excited about their latest adventure. So maybe because of that, and maybe because Jocelyn is asking why Mommy never goes outside, he says we are all going swimming today!

He gets the plastic pool—the same one I sat in when I gave birth to Jocelyn five and a half years ago—from the attic, drags it out the back door, and puts it in the bed of his pickup truck. With poles and a blue tarp he builds a screen around it and then fills the pool with water from the garden hose. He comes back inside and tells me to put on a wig and sunglasses. I stand at the door while he checks again that no neighbors are outside, and motions for me to dart out.

"Mommy's coming outside. Yay! Mommy's coming outside!"

He tells her to quiet down. Jocelyn loves playing dress-up with the wigs, and my long black hair only adds to her glee that I am outside playing with her.

I sink into the pool, wearing a T-shirt and a secondhand bikini bottom he bought at a thrift shop. He probably paid fifty cents for it, since there was no matching top. I begin splashing around with Jocelyn in her cute little two-piece suit and don't know what feels better, sitting in cool water on a blistering July day or looking up at the blue sky instead of the moldy ceiling of my room.

Jocelyn is happy and she sees that I am, too.

For hours, she pretends to fish with her plastic rod and sprays me with her squirt toys. "Look at me, Mommy!" she says, pretending she's swimming.

He fires up his little grill, the kind you can set on a table, and cooks hamburgers and hot dogs. He is in an unusually good mood and puts some chairs in the garage so we can stay outside and eat. He even hands me a beer after he's had a few himself. After a while he goes inside and lets Gina and Michelle out of their locked room, gives them wigs and hats, and they join us. We all fit in the pool if we fold our legs just right.

I don't mind the itchy, hot wig. I don't mind that he keeps telling Jocelyn to keep her voice down. I don't mind that he doesn't let us stand up in the pool because we are taller than the tarp and someone might see us. I've learned to try to make any comfort last. For five hours I have been out in the fresh air. For years I have been inside dreaming about coming outside, hopping the fence and screaming for help, and now that I'm here I don't do a thing but breathe the air and play with my daughter. I am not going to do anything to make him change his mind and take away this tiny bit of happiness.

It's been a good few days. On the Fourth of July he blew off some firecrackers in the backyard, and Joce loved that. He got sparklers, and he and Joce ran around with them in the dark while Gina, Michelle, and I watched from inside the house.

The more Joce goes out, the harder it is to keep her inside. She rides her white Little Tikes scooter with purple wheels around the backyard while he works on his cars. When he brings her to yard sales to buy toys and clothes, people sometimes ask who she is. He usually says that she's his girlfriend's daughter, but he's careful not to go to the same park, McDonald's, or library with her too many times. She loves to rent *Hannah Montana*, Looney Tunes, and *Beverly Hills Chihuahua* at the library and wants to watch them over and over again, but he told me he's worried that a nosy librarian might ask her where she goes to school.

She will be six years old soon and she's realizing more and more that there's something wrong with the way we live. Whenever she goes out with him, the last thing she sees is him locking me, Gina, and Michelle in our rooms. He tries to hide his temper from her, but she's seen how he can turn angry in a second and hit one of us. She knows that only she can go in Daddy's car. The rest of us have to stay inside.

A few days ago she didn't understand why she had to stay quiet upstairs in our room while Angie's two little boys were playing downstairs. Angie's husband had fallen off a roof and was in the hospital, so he was watching his grandkids. Joce could hear them and was desperate to play with other children. He's shown her pictures of Angie's kids, and even tried to explain that they're actually her nephews, even though they're all about the same age. But when they came over, he told Joce she had to stay upstairs.

"Maybe another time," I told her when she kept asking why. "Daddy said not this time."

It didn't make sense, and she knew it.

July 19, 2012: Digging for Amanda

Amanda
I wake up and turn on the TV. Channel 3 has breaking news:
SEARCH FOR AMANDA BERRY.
Some guy in prison told the police that he killed me and buried me in an empty lot at West 30th Street and Wade Avenue. That's two blocks from here! They're showing footage from the news helicopters flying

right over my head. I hear them! *Come get me! I'm alive! You are so close!* I wish I could smash a hole in the roof and signal to the helicopters. If only they could see me. There are swarms of police and men in FBI jackets watching the big backhoe digging for me. If I could bust out of here I could run over there in two minutes.

It's making me insane that they are so close. But I'm going even crazier worrying about Beth. She thinks they are going to find my bones.

He sits on my bed to watch the news and after a while says, "This is crazy."

He usually laughs when the police are chasing the wrong lead, but this time he is nervous and fidgety because they are so close by. I think it also scares him that my disappearance is still such big news nine years later. He keeps hoping people will forget about me.

He gets in his car and leaves, making sure to lock us in our rooms.

There's live coverage on every channel and I watch all day. They have the whole search area covered with a big tent and cadaver dogs sniffing for my body. The streets are filled with people who have come to watch, and I scan the crowd looking for my family. Channel 19 shows a photo of the guy who gave the tip, Robert Wolford. I stare at his face, trying to remember if I've ever seen him. I'm sure I've never met him. I wonder why he's making this all up.

The helicopters are still hovering, so loud, right over my head.

He comes back from the scene and says he stood watching them dig for my body with the rest of the crowd, trying to blend in, to see what was happening and to hear what the neighbors were saying.

"It's right down the street. It's right there!" he says, pointing in that direction.

At seven p.m. channels 3 and 8 are still airing it. Aunt Susie, my mom's sister, is there, only a couple of blocks from me. They play old interviews with Mom, and it's good to hear her voice. I miss her so much. I'm happy to see Gina's mom, Nancy Ruiz, out there talking on the news, too. She's a fighter like Mom, and it's nice she's supporting my family. That means a lot.

A few reporters have gone back to our old house, which looks vacant, and the grass is kind of tall. It's sad to see it empty, but I know Beth must have a nice new place somewhere.

They're interviewing some guy who says we all grew up together, but I don't remember him. They say Beth is too upset about the dig to go on camera, and that makes me cry.

Now they have my mom's friend Terry talking about the family. She brought a pretty paper butterfly to leave there in case they find my body.

July 20

It's day 2 of the dig and I'm still on the news all the time. A police officer just told reporters that they're 95 percent done but haven't found anything. They brought Wolford to the site to point out where he buried me, but now they suspect he's been lying. I'm glad they're figuring that out.

They interview my mom's sister Theresa at the Burger King where I used to work. She's crying and upset, which makes me cry more, and she says the whole family is watching on TV but that they just can't bear to go down there. The newscaster reports that Beth is so stressed that she's in the hospital. Oh, no!

Gina's mom is still there watching them dig and saying, "I am hoping it is false."

He's watching the TV with me and suddenly says, "Hey, there's Pedro!"

His brother Pedro is on the Channel 8 news. He's wearing a flowered shirt and sunglasses, shorts, and a straw hat, pointing at the dig site and saying, "That's a waste of money."

His brothers have been to this house a few times, but they have no idea we are here. I think Pedro is just one of those guys who likes to complain, so he's mad that the city is spending money digging for a lost girl. But what a weird coincidence that he's picked out of the crowd to interview about the case.

Finally, they call off the search. There's a press conference and a police officer says that everybody wants closure, wants to know what happened to Amanda Berry, and the good news now is that there's still a chance she will come home: "There is still hope that maybe somewhere, there is a girl still alive."

I waited all day to see Beth, and now she's on, saying, "I'll wait forever for Amanda to come home." On the news I see Marissa and Devon playing on the couch at Beth's house. And I see Beth has a new tattoo on her right arm—it looks like an RIP for Mom. Someday when I'm out of here, I'm going to get a tattoo for my mom, too.

So many tears are running down my cheeks—happy and sad ones at the same time. But now there's more bad news: my grandma Diane, my mom's mom, died. And my dad's in the hospital in critical condition, but they don't say why. I had no idea.

"Well, it's about time he croaked, right?" he says when he hears the report about my dad.

He knows just what to say to hurt me the most.

"That's just wrong," I answer. "You shouldn't say things like that."

"I'm just telling you the facts," he says.

"Oh, are you going to say that about your brothers when they die young? Because they're drunks!"

He thinks about that for a minute.

"You're right," he says. "I guess maybe I'm coldhearted."

He has been talking more and more lately about being "coldhearted," like it's some medical condition that excuses whatever horrible things he says or does.

Gina has been especially kind through these two strange days of watching police dig for my body. She drew a yellow cross and wrote on it: "Always believe in hope. Even through the hardest times."

And tonight we all held hands—me and Joce, Gina, and Michelle—and prayed for my dad. Then before I put Joce to bed, she and I prayed again for him and the whole family.

I'm scared that this bizarre dig is the closest the police will ever come to finding me. I force myself to stop thinking that way and decide that this whole thing is a message from God. Some guy in prison makes up a story, and it leads the police to within two blocks of me. I have to believe it's a sign that the end is near.*

July 30, 2012: Searching for Jaycee

Amanda

Joce and I are sitting here in our room playing Grand Theft Auto on the TV. She likes to drive around in the cars, but I don't allow her to do the violent stuff, like shooting people.

He comes in and asks me to go on the Internet with him. We got Internet access in the house a few months ago, but the only way I can

---

*Robert Wolford, who was serving twenty-six years for murder at a southern Ohio prison, sent a handwritten note to Cuyahoga County prosecutor William Mason in Cleveland on July 19, 2012, claiming that he had killed Amanda and buried her body:

> I am writing this letter because I have a confession to make that has been eating me up for the past nine years. I killed this girl her name is Amanda Berry. Me and her were seeing each other at the time. She had a boyfriend. She told me that she was going to tell her boyfriend that she has been cheating on him with me. So I waited for her to get off work then I killed her. . . . It's eating me up. I want her family to have the chance to rest. So I will tell you where I put her. I dug a hole on Clark and put her there.

Wolford was fifteen at the time Amanda went missing, so they were roughly the same age. Wolford was in prison for murdering a man in a drug deal at the same place where he said he buried Amanda. Of most interest to the FBI was the fact that the spot he identified fell within the area in which Amanda's cell phone had last been used.

Tim Kolonick and two other FBI agents drove to the prison in Lucasville to pick up Wolford, who was tearful and repeatedly said on the four-hour ride back to Cleveland that he was sorry he had killed Amanda. He told them he and Amanda had been dating for about six months, and that he killed her because she threatened to tell her boyfriend, DJ Diaz, about their relationship, and he didn't want trouble. So, he claimed, he had poured gasoline into Amanda's mouth until she died, then stuffed her body into garbage bags and buried her.

When after two days the digging turned up nothing but chicken bones, Wolford admitted he had fabricated the story. The police and FBI never figured out why, but ultimately they concluded that Wolford might simply have wanted a chance to get out of prison for a few days.

In January 2013, a judge added four and a half years to his sentence.

use it is with him, since he never lets the keyboard out of his sight, even taking it with him when he leaves the house.

I've been hearing a lot on TV about Jaycee Dugard, the girl who was kidnapped for a long time in California. She's written a book and she's doing interviews. I want to know how she's coping now that she's free. How are her kids doing?

"Let's search Jaycee Dugard," I say.

He says okay, but tells Jocelyn she has to go in the dining room and play because he doesn't want her to see it. She answers in pretend Spanish—she hears him speaking Spanish all the time, especially when he's on the phone, and she tries to imitate him—and skips off into the dining room.

As he and I read about how Jaycee was taken by a guy who was doing meth and who heard voices of demons, he says, "That guy was crazy."

Jaycee was held captive in a shed in the guy's backyard and she had two kids with him. It was hard for her to talk to the police after they found her, because he made her so afraid for so many years. I know that feeling. There have been times when I thought about screaming for help, like when the police were raiding the house next door a couple of summers ago. But I felt so beaten down and frightened that I couldn't open my mouth.

Jaycee says she was scared of the outside world. I know that I'm frightened that something will happen to Jocelyn when we get out of here. Will I ever be able to let her have a sleepover at a friend's house or go shopping?

Even he has warned her about strangers. "Never get in a car with somebody you don't know," he tells her. He says that when they go out, she's friendly with everybody. I guess that's good, but it makes me worry, like Jaycee worries about her kids.

We read more about Jaycee and I say, "This is just like what happened to me."

"It is similar, because she had the kids," he agrees. Then he looks at me and asks, "Are you going to write a book about this?"

"I'm not sure," I answer. "Do I want to write a book and relive all this?"

Someday, when I get out of here, I know some people won't be able to understand why I didn't figure out how to kill him or escape. It's going to be hard to explain how fear paralyzes you. And I have Joce to worry about. If I fought back and he killed me, she would have only him to raise her, and I can't let that happen. People are also going to say there was something wrong with me because I allowed myself to get close to him. I can't help what people say, but I'm the one who went through this, and only I know what I've had to do to survive and to create the best possible life for Jocelyn.

"If you write a book, are you going to tell the truth? Are you going to say that you had feelings for me?" he asks. "'Cause if you don't, you shouldn't even write it. It won't be true."

"I am going to tell the truth," I say. "I'm going to tell people what you did to me. I will tell them about all the rapes."

"I never raped you," he says.

I hate it when he says that. Does he really think that because I'm not screaming and hitting him every time, it's "consensual"? He loves that word.

"Yes, you did," I tell him. "You rape me all the time."

He knows what he's doing is wrong; that's why he locks us up and keeps us hidden. But I don't want to get him mad, so I drop it. Sometimes he is kind to me, and I do feel close to him.

"If I write a book, I'm not going to lie," I say. "If you want people to know I care for you, fine. I'll say that. But it was only like that after I had a kid with you. It wasn't like I got here and said, 'Oh, I'm so in love with you and I want to be here.'"

He turns off the computer and tells me, "You got in my car willingly. You got into bed with me because you wanted to. I never raped you. It was always consensual. I never did anything wrong."

"I'm going to tell the truth," I say again.

August 30, 2012: Bedbugs

Gina

I wake up itching. My arms and legs are covered with little red bites, which is weird because I don't know how mosquitoes could possibly get in the house. The bites are incredibly annoying and are driving me crazy. Michelle and Amanda haven't been bitten at all.

"I think you have chicken pox," Amanda says.

"No, I had chicken pox when I was nine," I tell her. "I definitely remember that. I missed a lot of school."

"Maybe the measles?" she wonders.

She says I should stay away from Jocelyn in case I'm contagious.

Over the years we have all had colds, fevers, and stomachaches. He is around schoolkids all the time and gets sick, and then his germs race around the house. But I often wonder what he would do if one of us got seriously ill, or broke a bone or had an appendix attack? Even if he found an emergency room far from Cleveland and the doctors didn't recognize us, he knows we would tell people and he would go to jail. Getting sick is just not an option. He would let us die.

In the heat this summer I had a lot of breathing problems and was making a scary wheezing sound. I have allergies and told him I thought it was from the mold and dust in my room. I was suffocating and needed some fresh air, and though he wouldn't open the boarded-up window in my room, he cut a round hole in the ceiling to the attic and opened the windows up there. He rigged up a fan that was supposed to suck the hot air out of our room, and it did help a bit.

When I show him the spots all over my legs and arms, he goes to the drugstore and buys some skin cream. It calms the itching enough for me to sleep, but when I wake up, I freak. Now my face, neck, back—every inch of me—has red dots. And then I spot the problem: a plump little bug crawling on the bed. Bedbugs! So gross! I just saw on TV that there are tons of them these days.

I show the bug to Michelle, and she jumps off the bed. I trap it on a piece of tape so I can show it to Amanda and him.

"I can't sleep on this bed anymore!" I tell him, showing him the dead bug.

"Why are they only biting you?" he asks.

"I don't know! Maybe they like my blood. But I can't sleep here!"

Now I wish I hadn't asked for a new bed. A few days ago I helped him carry a box spring and mattress upstairs. I had been begging him to get us a new bed because the one I had to share with Michelle was so miserable—an old mattress on the ground. It had been on a frame, but the wooden slats kept falling out, so finally we just put it on the floor. But the mattress was lumpy and even he didn't like it.

After I told him I wanted a regular bed like Amanda's, he found a queen-size one on a curb that somebody had thrown out. The mattress was so comfortable that when we brought it upstairs he hollered to Amanda to ask if she wanted it. She pretty much gets first choice of everything. She took it, but I didn't care, because then we got her mattress on top of the new box spring from outside, so we were way better off than we had been.

But now, as I itch from head to toe, I realize the box spring must have been full of bedbugs. I sit on the little plastic portable toilet in our room, since the bed takes up most of the room, and there's nowhere else to sit. I don't want to be on that mattress. Last night I dreamed that a bug with a huge face was laughing at me.

I hate this place. Why is this happening?

He returns with rubbing alcohol and bleach-soaked rags and tells me to help him wash down the mattress and box spring.

When Amanda got her new mattress, before we even knew about the bedbugs, she asked for a sheet of plastic and duct tape to wrap it. She's always so worried about germs, and Jocelyn sleeps in that bed, too. Now he realizes what a good idea that was, so he does the same thing to our mattress and box spring. Amanda keeps telling him to hurry, because bedbugs move fast.

"The bugs will never get out," he says, putting more and more duct tape around the mattress. "They are locked inside."

October 25, 2012: Encounter

Amanda

"I saw Beth and her daughters at McKinley School," he tells me. "I looked at her, and she looked right back at me."

This is just like last year when he saw Beth in line at Marc's. It makes me think about what a small world Cleveland is. McKinley is just a few blocks from my old house, and I'm only a couple of miles away. We all live in one big neighborhood, so why can't anyone find me?

I wonder if Beth feels anything when she's close to him. Something strange, or maybe familiar?

November 6, 2012: Fired

Amanda

My mom would have been fifty today. I kissed her photo this morning fifty-one times: one for each birthday, plus one for luck.

Mom's birthday is good luck for President Obama—he was reelected today! I've now missed the first three elections when I would've been old enough to vote. I can't wait to vote someday.

It's early evening and time to exercise. We jog every night now. He thinks he's getting fat and the doctor told him he has high blood pressure, so he's suddenly a lot more health-conscious.

We turn on the music and jog in circles from the living room to the dining room and into the kitchen, over and over for an hour, all of us in a line. He goes first, then me, Joce, and Gina. Michelle usually stays in her room, because whenever she's with him they get into a fight. Gina and I have learned it's easier if you don't talk back to him.

We look ridiculous jogging, especially him. He likes to wear his sweatpants with the waist pulled way up high. He says that makes him sweat more, which makes no sense, but it sure makes him look funny.

Today he's not wearing his old straw cowboy hat, just a bandanna around his head. The jogging feels good. Sometimes it's so goofy that it's fun. Gina and I pretend to kick each other as we run, and he mixes in salsa steps. We laugh at how idiotic he looks.

But then later it feels awful again, and the moments when we were smiling and pretending everything was okay are all gone. Gina has felt less and less like jogging lately.

She's become more depressed these past few months, and sometimes she doesn't even want to get out of bed. I really have to beg her to get up. Joce gets bored with the jogging, too, so she doesn't want to do it for too long. But I think it's helping me feel better. I'm trying to eat less junk, too, but it's hard.

Ever since Joce was born, but especially in the last year or so, he's been buying healthier food. His doctor told him to eat more fruits and vegetables, and while he still cooks a lot of rice and beans, he makes me steam broccoli or green beans or kale, something green every day. He read on the Internet that kale is good for you, so he has that a lot. He suddenly has cucumbers and carrots in the fridge, and fish. He's started growing peppers and tomatoes in the backyard.

But it's annoying, because the good food is only for him and Jocelyn. The rest of us still have to eat a lot of McDonald's and other junk because it's cheaper. He buys apples and oranges and bananas, but we're only allowed to eat them if they start going bad.

He still has a sweet tooth, though, and loves chocolate so much that he keeps huge Hershey's bars with almonds in the fridge. Mainly those are just for him, but sometimes he gives us a little.

I go into the kitchen to get a drink of water after jogging when he walks in looking happy.

"I finally got fired today," he says with a smile, holding up a letter from the Cleveland Public Schools saying he's been terminated. This has been his plan for a long time. He's been more and more worried that driving a school bus was too risky, that he would make a mistake at work and the police would come here again.

One time in 2004, he left a kid alone on the bus while he went to have lunch. He got suspended and he said two cops knocked on the front door to talk to him, but he wasn't home. I must have been upstairs, chained in my room, because I never heard anyone knocking.

He says if he quit, he wouldn't have gotten as much money, but now he can collect unemployment, and it's better for his pension, too. He says he's been egging on his boss for a couple of years, getting smart-mouthed with him and trying to get fired. Last Valentine's Day he went shopping at Marc's. He left his school bus in the parking lot and went in wearing his driver's uniform. His boss was in the store and told him he wasn't supposed to be doing personal errands with the bus.

"He said he was going to fire me, so I said, 'I don't care. Fire me!'" he tells me. Another time he got into trouble for making an illegal U-turn with a bus full of kids.

"This way I can spend more time with Joce before all this ends," he adds.

He's been saying stuff like that more and more lately, talking about "the end," but he never says exactly when that will be. I think he's trying to figure out how we could all go home. I've said to him I could just say that he wore a mask all the time, so I didn't know who he was. I keep telling him: I don't have to tell anybody about you. But he knows better.

"I can't take you home yet. I don't want to go to jail," he says. He is obsessed by prison and watches *Lockup* on MSNBC all the time. I know it scares him.

"Look at us," I say. "We're in jail. We've been in jail for years."

He hates it when I say that.

"This is not jail!" he snaps. "You are not in jail!"

He lives in his own little fantasy world.

On Sunday he took Joce to the Westfield Mall for the first time, where she got to ride a little kiddie train, and he bought her these cute Skechers called Twinkle Toes that light up. He paid $40 for them! That was surprising.

She wanted to get her ears pierced at the mall, but he said no. He would have to sign a permission form, and he didn't want to put his name to anything. But he took her to a photo booth, and the pictures of them together are actually nice. So finally I can put a photo of her up on my wall now—the first one I have of her. I've been dying to get one, and it's taken until she's almost six years old.

Joce is starting to feel these walls closing in. She feels stuck in here. She asks all the time to go out with him to the festival at St. Rocco's Church, or shopping, or anywhere. She wants me to come, too. I always say I have to clean or just, "I can't go right now." He jumps in, too, and says, "Mommy has things to do here. She'll come next time."

The other day Joce told me that she wants to move to a bigger house with more space for her to run around. She's growing up, and that is complicating things for him.

"We can't keep living like this," he says.

"No, we can't," I agree. "You should take us home."

It's only a matter of time until Joce tells somebody about how she and her mom and some other girls live in this house. She wants her friend Tiffany from the park to come over to play and doesn't understand why we always say no.

She's been crying more lately when it's time to go upstairs, and gets so bored in the bedroom that sometimes she just walks around in circles. She doesn't want to play with her toys, because she's sick of all of them. It's often so hot in this room that he sawed a four-inch hole near the bottom of the door to let in more air from the hallway. So now Jocelyn will sit and look out the hole for hours, waiting for her daddy to come home. She knows that until he returns we have to be locked in, and it's starting to upset her more.

She asks all the time why we can't go downstairs to wait for him, and I have to answer: "You know we can't open the door, we have to wait for daddy to do that."

"I know," she says sadly. She has never known anything else.

She's also learned my real name. One day she saw the gold necklace that I wear sometimes that has a charm with my name on it.

She sounded it out: "A . . . man . . . da," and asked, "Is that your name?"

"Yes, but you can't say anything to Daddy," I told her. "That will be our secret, okay?"

"Okay, Mommy," she said, hugging me.

"I wonder what they'll call me," he says.

"What do you mean?"

"When this is over, I wonder what they'll call me in the newspapers. Maybe the 'Cleveland Kidnapper'? Or maybe 'The Monster.'"

One minute he's saying what a happy little family we are, and the next he's talking about what a huge crime he's committed. I think he's getting worn down by leading this double life. He has so carefully built and guarded his secret world inside this house, and he knows that Jocelyn, the person he loves most, is the one who could bring it all crashing down.

He's clearly trying to imagine how this will all end. It's like a monster just up ahead in the fog. He can't quite see it yet, but he knows it's there waiting for him.

Thanksgiving 2012: Perfect Little Family

Amanda

I've told him how much I want turkey for Thanksgiving, so he got up really early today and went to Save-A-Lot, since they're open twenty-four hours, and bought a bunch of frozen turkey legs.

We can't cook a whole turkey because we don't have an oven, so frying the legs will have to do. I don't even like turkey that much, but Thanksgiving isn't the same without it, and I want to make sure Jocelyn learns all these traditions—at least as much as possible in this place. It's sweet of him to help me.

Joce woke up before six to watch cartoons. She's been excited because I've been building up Thanksgiving for weeks, and I've put turkey decorations all over the place. She's becoming more aware of the significance of things, including being grateful on Thanksgiving for food and health.

He put the TV in the kitchen so we could watch my favorite, the Macy's Parade, while we cook. I love watching the big floats in New York. I've never been on a plane and hope I can see the parade in person someday.

While Gina and I start picking the meat off the thawing turkey legs and putting it in the frying pan, he and Joce go out in the backyard to rake leaves. Since he got fired he wants to be with her all the time. "She's everything to me now," he keeps saying. "She's the reason I keep going."

When they finish their raking, we all dance to music in the living room. I want to be with my family more than anything on Thanksgiving, but this is the best I can do today.

He and Joce love rice and gandules, so we heat them up in the rice cooker, make some instant mashed potatoes and a box of stuffing, and warm up a can of corn in a pan.

We all sit down to dinner in the kitchen and finish with a special treat: pumpkin pie with Cool Whip! I feel like a whale because I ate so much, just like I used to at home. God, I miss that feeling of being home on a lazy, happy holiday. Watching him sitting here with us, smiling and content, it's suddenly so clear to me: he wants that feeling, too.

He had a lousy family life growing up, and a terrible relationship with his ex. Maybe that's partly what this has all been about, why he stole our lives, why he let me have a baby. He wants that perfect little family he never had. He's created his own world and he doesn't realize it's fake.

I feel sorry for him. I'm grateful that he went out of his way today to make us happy. I have never felt closer to him than I do at this moment.

But I also know that if I had the chance to kill him right now to get free, I would do it without a second thought.

January 2013: Pile of Chains

Amanda

It's been three years and seven months since he stopped shackling me like a dog, but he won't take the chains out of my room. I hide them from Jocelyn under some blankets and in the toy box, but this space is so small and they're so big and bulky. The other day, when I took the blanket that was covering them off to wash it, Jocelyn noticed them and asked why they were in our room.

"They're just there, that's all," I said. That was good enough for now, but how much longer can I keep saying things like that to her? I just want them out.

"No," he says. "Leave them right where they are."

"Can I at least put them under the dresser?"

"I told you, leave them where they are."

I know what he's doing. He wants them here as a reminder of my six years living in chains, a silent warning about how easily he could put me through that again.

When he leaves the room, I slide them under a plastic bin. He didn't say anything about not putting them under there.

February 2013: Invisible

Gina

The headphones help. At night, I put them on and lie on my bed, listen to music, and try to forget where I am. I used to have to shut off the music so Jocelyn could go to sleep, but now, with these headphones he gave me, I can listen to music all night. Staying up late makes it easier to sleep away these horrible days.

For years if he wanted sex he just woke me up. But something is happening to him. He doesn't wake me up anymore. He hasn't touched me in months.

He still fights with Michelle. I've given up trying to explain to her that there are times to stay quiet, little things to do and not do, so you don't rile the monster. I've run out of ways to help her.

In the past I would say, "Please stop hitting her!" when he went after Michelle, and he would say, "Oh, we're just playing," and stop pushing her around. But now it's like I'm not even here. He doesn't listen to me. He doesn't stop.

I feel invisible.

People are outside, walking and driving by. I wonder if my mom is at my aunt's house just down the street? How can nobody know I'm here?

I'm so worried that this is how the whole rest of my life will be.

My friends have had their *quinceañera* and Sweet Sixteen parties, graduated, found jobs, and maybe even gotten married. It's hard to think about the nine birthdays, the nine Christmases, and all the fun in between that I've missed with my family and friends. I was in seventh grade when I walked into this house. Now I'm twenty-three.

The days are going by more slowly. It's getting harder in this tiny, smelly room. I hate being locked up in this closet waiting for him to open the door and give me the privilege of using the toilet downstairs.

Michelle says we are never leaving.

I used to like to sing and dance with her to the music on our radio. When Rihanna or Adele came on, I knew all the words and got up and danced around the room. Even with the chain on my ankle, it felt good. Now I feel like a block of ice in a freezer. I used to daydream about loud, happy reunions with my family. Now all I can see in my head are images of being old and gray and still here.

When I stand in front of the mirror, I look the same, just a lot thinner. My family and friends would know me in a second, but I'm a different person now. I was never sad before.

"Come on, Chelsea. Think positive!"

Amanda is at my door, trying to get me out of bed. She says I'm spending too much time lying down and I have to move around, and that I have to think of something, anything, that will make me smile.

"Come over here with Jocelyn and me," she says. "Look at all the things I'm going to buy when I get out of here."

On her bed are pictures of shiny white kitchen appliances and pretty dresses that she's cutting out of newspaper ads. She says there are tons of pictures here, and I should pick what I'm going to buy someday, cut it out, and keep it as a reminder of good things ahead.

"Look at these shoes! Look at all this nice food!"

I miss my mom's cooking and all my relatives sitting around our table. I miss being able to get up and go to the refrigerator when I'm hungry. I see Amanda's picture of a big ham sandwich. I sure would like one of those, and the roast beef sandwich, and all the fruits.

Amanda spends hours every week copying down recipes from Martha Stewart and other cooking shows. I asked her why she spends so much time pausing and rewinding the same show over and over just to get the exact amount of flour and cinnamon or whatever. And she says someday she is going to walk into a grocery store and buy whatever she wants and make all these recipes.

Plus, she says, she needs to occupy herself, or she'll get depressed. She keeps telling me I need to keep busy and in motion. I know she's right, because misery is taking over my mind. It's gotten harder and harder to get out of bed in the evening when he wants me to jog around the house. I don't want to get up, and I sure don't want to be near him.

"Please get up, Chelsea. Will you color with me?"

Jocelyn wants to play, but even that is hard.

I used to make her laugh. Now she is trying to do the same for me.

When I ask him when I can go home, he always says, "One day." But that day never comes. I am so tired of his lies. I used to like to go downstairs to do the laundry or the dishes just to get out of this room. Now when he makes me go down to clean, I only want to go back to bed. I don't want to be around people. When he sends me back upstairs and locks me inside this closet, I feel relieved.

Finally, I think, I can lie down.

Castro's Story: A New Sister?

On April 10, 2013, Ariel Castro and his eldest daughter, Angie, sat in the McDonald's at Westown Square, within sight of the Burger King where Amanda once worked and the corner from where Gina disappeared.

They had been drinking coffee and chatting for a long time, and Angie thought something seemed strange. Her father would stop talking and hold her gaze, start to speak, then stop and look away. It seemed as if he wanted to tell her something, but couldn't quite get it out.

Then, finally, he pulled out his cell phone and showed her a photo of a little girl, about five or six years old.

"She's cute—who is that?" Angie said, curious and suspicious, because the girl looked almost exactly like her sister Emily at that age.

"It's my girlfriend's daughter," he said.

Angie knew her father had dated women now and then since her mother had left him seventeen years earlier, but she didn't recall hearing about anyone recently. She wondered if her father was struggling to tell her that she had a new sister.

"Is that your kid?" she finally asked. "She looks a lot like Emily."

"No, no," he said quickly. "She's my girlfriend's kid, but I'm not the father."

"Are you sure?" Angie asked him.

"It's not my kid," he said, clearly trying to end the conversation.

Angie knew her father met a lot of women at the clubs where he played, and she felt uncomfortable asking questions about who he might be sleeping with. But she was anxious to know more about this little girl.

"You can't just have a kid out there and not be sure if you're the father," she told him. "You need to get a DNA test."

"I told you," he said, annoyed now. "It's not my kid."

Angie took a long look at her father. For her entire life he had been very good to her. When she was a kid, he bought her what she needed, talked sense into her, made her laugh. After she got married, he was always there when she needed help with her kids or projects around her house. She suspected that he'd never really gotten over her mother, despite their tortured relationship, and she had come to regard him as a quirky, older bachelor set in his ways. He often canceled family plans at the last minute, claiming his allergies were flaring up. He didn't want her or her husband to go upstairs in his house, because he said he had too much stuff up there. She knew he was a hoarder, constantly buying unnecessary junk at yard sales, bargaining old shirts down from a quarter to a dime. But she sensed there was something he wasn't telling her about this child.

"If there's another one of us out there," she told him, "I need to know about it."

He put his phone away and changed the subject.

April 12, 2013: Recurring Dream

Nancy and Felix stood courtside at an NBA game between the Cleveland Cavaliers and the New York Knicks, looking up at Gina's picture on the big screens hanging above the 20,000 fans gathered at the Quicken Loans Arena in downtown Cleveland. At a special half-time presentation the announcer asked the crowd to look at the photos of several missing Ohio children, including Amanda and Gina, to see if any of them looked familiar.

Nancy knew her neighbors and friends thought she was delusional to keep believing that Gina was alive after so long. She could see that they didn't believe her, even pitied her, when she insisted that one day her daughter would walk through her front door. Though Nancy had never lost faith, the pain of the past nine years had taken its toll. She had lost nearly ninety pounds and Felix had suffered a heart attack. Doctors told them stress was making them sick, but they stayed in the public eye every chance they had.

When people came up after the Cavaliers game to offer condolences, Nancy told them there was no need because her daughter was not dead.

She had been having a recurring dream that she was sure was a sign that she was right. In the dream, Nancy would walk by Gina's school and see her daughter eating lunch, sitting on the grass and leaning against the building, smiling and waving at her.

It woke Nancy up night after night, frightened, but more convinced than ever that Gina was still alive.

April 12, 2013: Demons and Facebook

Amanda

"This is going to be over soon," he says.

For so many years I clung to that lie, long after I actually believed it. I've always tried to wire my mind that way in here: focus on the hopeful thoughts, push out the negative ones.

But today I answer: "I don't believe you."

I'm finished with telling him what he wants to hear, tiptoeing around and trying to keep him from getting mad.

He still won't let us go up and down the stairs by ourselves. And when he leaves the house, he locks this place down like a prison. He rigged a homemade alarm on the front door, with wires and an old clock-radio, and he says it will go off if anybody tries to open the front or back door. And he never forgets to bolt my door. So no, I don't believe this is ending anytime soon.

I'm surprised he doesn't blow up at me but seems to want to talk. Jocelyn is downstairs playing, so it's just the two of us.

"No," he tells me. "It's true. This is going to be over soon. But I'm worried about what's going to happen to me."

He should have thought about that before he kidnapped us, but he's right to worry, because I don't see how this can possibly end without him either dead or in prison. He knows he can't just let us go free, because we would turn him in. He keeps saying he hopes it will all end with a gunfight—suicide by cop.

In a way, I think he's confused about who he is. Is he a sadistic rapist or a doting father who loves his little girl? He knows he is both, and that must be terrifying. He keeps talking about how his headaches are getting worse.

"I realize that you're scared, but you need to be punished for what you've done to us and our families," I tell him. "You say you have a sexual problem, but that's no excuse. You should be punished. If you had to go to court and my mom was still alive, what would you say to her? Would you apologize?"

He thinks for a minute and says, "I would tell your mom I'm sorry. But I wouldn't take any of this back. I would do it all over again because of Pretty."

His love for Jocelyn has blinded him to reality: Taking his daughter shopping once in a while doesn't make up for the fact that he's holding her hostage. But as Joce has gotten older and become more aware, he's started to see things through her eyes. It's challenged his perceptions. It's harder to convince himself that what he is doing to us isn't wrong.

"I love Pretty, and it makes me sad to think that someday you're going to get married, and she'll have a stepdad," he says.

"I *am* going to get married," I tell him. "I want to meet a man who'll treat me well, and to fall in love, and to live happily ever after. I want more kids."

"I know you're going to find someone who loves you and takes care of you," he says.

A couple of days ago he told me that he showed Joce's picture to Angie and said it was his girlfriend's kid. He told me Angie said Jocelyn's photo looks like Emily, and Joce says his brothers, Onil and Pedro, have seen her driving around with him. Doesn't anybody in that family think there's something funny about him spending so much time with this little girl, or that they never see the girl's mom?

April 22

Today I turn twenty-seven, and I feel nothing but anger and resentment.

I never finished high school, or learned to drive. I haven't talked on a telephone since I was sixteen. I have spoken to only four people in ten years, and one of them is my kidnapper. I wonder what it's like to send a text or an e-mail or use an iPad or Twitter—all the stuff I see on TV. I hate him for sealing me off from the world, especially today, on another lost birthday.

I have changed so much in these ten years. I'm stronger and more aware of the importance of kindness—to the person giving and receiving it. Life is too short to be mean to people. I've learned how to be patient. I appreciate all the little things that add up to a life. If I get out of here, I'll never look up at the sky, walk down a street, or wade in the lake without thinking how lucky I am. I know now how everything can disappear in a second.

But still, it's hard. Yesterday marked a full decade that I've been inside this house, and I was so anxious to see my family on TV that I set my alarm to catch the 5:30 a.m. news. But there was nothing. I thought the tenth anniversary would be a big story. But there was nothing on the noon and 6:00 p.m. newscasts either. Has everyone forgotten me?

I spent most of the day trying to comfort Joce, who had a bad toothache. Her gums were swollen, and she barely slept. I didn't know if it was an infection, so I kept rinsing her mouth with saltwater.

"I might have to take her to a dentist," he told me after seeing how uncomfortable she was.

He's never said anything like that before. I still doubt that he'd actually have taken her, because it would have been too risky. It doesn't matter now anyway, because during the day her pain went away and I think she's okay.

Finally, on the 10:00 news, there was a story about me. I'm so glad they remembered. Even after all these years I still cry when I see Beth on TV. She was at a vigil for me outside Burger King, but there was hardly anybody there, just a few people standing in a little circle and holding candles. Gina's mom and dad were right in front.

The news report was short, and they cut away quickly to the big news of the day: a garbage strike. I guess people can't keep hoping for a miracle forever.

May 1

"Hey, Nandy, come look at this," he says.

I walk over to the living room computer, where he's looking at Facebook.

There I am! Somebody created a Facebook page about me, with my picture and a lot of information, including my height and weight, when and where I went missing. It says nobody should give up on me. I'm so happy I feel like screaming, because I thought people had forgotten me.

They list all the people who liked the page, and one of them is Angie! She helped him set up his own Facebook account a couple of months ago. His profile picture shows him wearing a hat—like always—and a necklace, which has a little marijuana leaf charm at the end. He doesn't smoke that much weed, but he thinks the charm makes him look cool.

We were looking at Facebook a while back and we saw there was a page for Gina. But there wasn't one for me then, so somebody must have just created it. I wonder who cared enough to do that. It's hard to keep thinking that everything is a sign that something good will happen, because I'm tired of being disappointed. But this has given me such a boost that I have to believe that God is telling me not to give up hope that someday I will be free.

I write an entry in my diary, addressed to my mom and Beth, telling them about all this, and saying, "Keep faith!"

I flip over to the last page of my diary notebook, where I start a wish list.

Beneath it I write the two things I want more than anything:

1. *To have my mommy back.*
2. *To be home with my family.*

May 6, 2013: Escape

Amanda

"Daddy's gone! Daddy's gone!"

Jocelyn is shouting as she comes running up the stairs. She can't find him anywhere and she's confused.

Our bedroom door is unlocked. Whenever he leaves the house, he's always careful to lock us in, so he must be somewhere downstairs. But I can't help her look for him, because going down on my own would be breaking one of his most serious rules. I don't want the chains back.

"Go check the backyard," I tell Joce. "He's probably out there."

It's a warm day, so he must be outside messing around with his cars or motorcycles.

Joce heads back down the stairs, wearing a long black wig because she loves playing dress-up. She peeks out the back-door window, which is locked from the outside. I hear her little footsteps as she races around the ground floor, looking in every room.

She climbs back up the stairs, huffing and puffing, agitated that he seems to have left without her. She likes to go for drives in his little blue Mazda Miata with the top down. He loves that car. He sold it last year, but then he bought it back from the same guy a couple of months later because he missed it.

"Daddy's blue car is gone!" she says.

I freeze.

No him? No car?

Could this really be it? My chance to escape after all these years?

Gina

Michelle and I are in our room, watching a Hilary Duff movie, *According to Greta*.

The door to Amanda's room is closed, but I hear Jocelyn say he's not home. I hear her running around the living room and kitchen looking for him. But if he's really gone, why is their door unlocked? How did Jocelyn even get downstairs? He always locks the door.

Michelle and I look at each other: *Oh, my God. Maybe this is the day. Maybe we can actually get free.*

"Let's run!" I say.

"You want to do it?" she asks.

"Yeah! Let's do it!"

But then I stop, wondering if he's testing us to see if we'll run. He's always threatening that if I try to escape he'll hang me upside down.

"It could be a trap," I say. "Let's just stay put."

We don't say anything to Amanda.

Amanda

I tiptoe barefoot out into the hall, listening for any sign of him. But I'm too scared, so I hurry back into my room.

I want to get out of here, but I don't want to risk getting killed. I don't want him raising Joce. But then I think about Beth and all she has endured, and how I have to get back to her.

He's taken away all my electricity for not speaking to him, so I can't imagine what his punishment would be for trying to escape. But I missed a chance to get away seven years ago when I was in the van—I hesitated instead of pushing that gas pedal. I have regretted that ever since and I can't let it happen again.

I leave Joce in the room and make my way as quietly as I can halfway down the stairs, trying to peek into the living room to see if he might have fallen asleep on the couch and Joce didn't spot him. I can't see him anywhere. The radio isn't on. That's weird. He almost always leaves it blaring when he leaves. Is he hiding down there?

I'm wasting too much time thinking. If he's really gone, I have to move now!

I run back up to my room and pull on my high-tops.

I don't say anything to Gina or Michelle. If this doesn't work they might tell him I tried to escape. But I also don't want to risk getting any-one else hurt, so I'm not going to involve them.

If he catches anybody, it will be just me, alone.

Gina

There's a little knock on our door that sounds like Jocelyn.

"No," I hear Amanda whisper, "leave them alone." So we don't open the door.

We don't hear anything else, and I wonder if Amanda may be trying something. But I'm not sure. That would be crazy.

I turn back to Hilary Duff on TV.

Amanda

I gently pull Joce away from Gina and Michelle's door, then crouch down in front of her and whisper.

"Mommy's going downstairs for a minute to do something, and I'll be right back," I tell her quietly. "You stay right here in the room. But if Mommy yells for you, then come downstairs as fast as you can."

"Okay," she says, a little anxiously, "but what are you doing?"

"Just stay here until I call for you," I tell her. She knows something is going on. She has never seen me downstairs by myself.

"Can I tell Chelsea and Juju?"

"No, we're not going to tell them right now. Just wait here."

I step back out in the hall and over to the head of the stairs. I know I have to go right now, but I am so terrified that I can't make myself move.

Mom, please give me a sign. Give me strength if the time is right.

And just like that, I swear I feel something, like my mom is pushing me.

I go.

I start down, as slowly as I can, one step at a time on my tiptoes. I'm shaking. I can barely feel my legs, and my heart is beating out of my chest. I make it to the landing. I'm terrified he is going to pop out of nowhere.

But I see no one. I hear nothing.

My lungs feel like they're on fire.

I run across the living room to the front door, which is blocked by a big outdoor swing he brought inside that we sit in sometimes. I shove it aside just enough to squeeze by and get to the front door.

I see all the wires connected to a clock-radio and I realize I've forgotten the alarm. Will it go off?

It's too late to worry about that. I have to try, so I turn the door lock.

No alarm!

I don't see any other locks, so I pull on the wooden door.

And it opens.

In ten years I have never seen this door open more than a crack, when he reaches out to get the mail.

I scream: "Jocelyn! Jocelyn! Come down here!"

She scrambles down the stairs and I pull the door all the way open. We're free!

Wait, what's this? There's a storm door, and it's chained shut with a padlock! I had no idea this was here!

I start pushing and shoving and banging it, but it won't move.

Jocelyn sees how desperate I am. She has never seen me like this. She senses my terror.

"Mommy! Mommy! What are you doing?" She starts to cry and screams, "I want Daddy! Where's Daddy? What are you doing?"

"Shh," I tell her. "Shh. Just be quiet."

I'm getting more frantic. Every second feels like an hour.

Finally I manage to push the storm door open just enough to get my hand out, and then my whole arm, which I begin to wave like crazy. I can't see anyone on the street, so I scream out the door: "Help me! Help me! I need to get out of here!"

There has to be somebody out there. And they have to hurry.

All I can think about is him coming back.

"Help me! Help me!"

Gina

We hear noises from downstairs. The front door is right below our room, and there's loud banging and Jocelyn is screaming.

It's definitely a beat-down. He must have caught Amanda trying to escape and he's beating her. We strain to hear more.

"Nandy?" I call. But she's not there.

"Oh, no, she got caught," I say to Michelle. "He's coming for us next."

Amanda

Oh, thank God! Here comes a guy. He sees me and steps right up onto the porch.

"Can you help me, please!" I scream.

He looks confused, maybe even scared.

"Please," I beg him, "help me!"

But he just stands there, looking at me and the door. He can see there's a chain and that I can't get out. Why doesn't he do something?

Finally he gives the door a little pull. It doesn't move.

"Help me! I'm Amanda Berry! I've been kidnapped for ten years! Help me!"

An older lady comes by on the sidewalk, sees what's happening, and waves her finger at us, saying, "No, no, no."

What? What is she doing?

She's motioning for the guy on the porch to step away from me.

This can't be happening. These people aren't going to help me?

"Help me! Help me! I'm Amanda Berry!" I shout again.

I have never screamed so loud. I keep waving my arm.

The guy steps down off the porch. He's walking away from me!

"No! No! No! Please help me!"

Joce is standing behind me, screaming and saying, "I want my daddy!" But if her father came back right now, he would kill me. Why is this guy leaving? Why won't he help?

Now another guy has walked in front of the house, a tall black guy. He's asking the old lady what's going on. She tells him that I can't be Amanda Berry, because Amanda Berry died years ago.

No! I'm right here. Who cares who I am? Can't they help me?

The tall guy comes up on the porch and pulls on the door a couple of times.

"Oh, man, this thing is locked," he says.

"Please," I beg him. "Please help me!"

He looks closely at the door from top to bottom and then, noticing something, starts to kick at the bottom panel.

"Go ahead," he tells me. "Finish kicking it out, Mama."

I hadn't thought of that. I've been trying to push the whole door open. But he's right. Maybe I can just kick out this bottom panel. It's just flimsy cheap aluminum.

"Go on, Mama!" he says.

Why doesn't he kick it in for me? He's just standing there watching me. Why won't anybody help me? I start pounding at the panel with my sneakers, kicking and kicking until finally I smash out enough of it for me to squeeze through.

I crawl outside and then reach in and pull Joce out after me.

"I want my daddy!" she's screaming. "Where's Daddy?"

We're out but we're not safe.

"I need a phone!" I scream as loud as I can.

"Okay, okay," the tall guy says. "I've got a phone in my house."

He lives right next door and starts to run there. I'm right behind him, carrying Joce, who's clinging to me and wailing.

He opens his front door, picks up his cell phone, and dials 911. I wait in the doorway and look around. It's dark inside, spooky, with not much furniture. I've just escaped from one scary house, and am not taking Joce back inside another one, so I bolt back out onto the sidewalk.

A few people have gathered on a porch across the street to see what all the commotion is, so I run over there, still carrying Joce, who won't stop screaming.

"Please," I tell them. "I need a phone!"

I haven't seen this woman before, but I don't think she speaks much English. She doesn't say anything, but she looks concerned. She hands me a phone and I dial 911, watching up and down the street for the blue Miata.

Finally a police operator picks up.

"Cleveland 911. Do you need police, fire—"

"Hello, police? Help me! I'm Amanda Berry!"

"Do you need police, fire, or ambulance?"

"I need police!"

"Okay, and what's going on there?"

"I've been kidnapped and I've been missing for ten years, and I'm, I'm here, I'm free now!"

"Okay, and what's your address?"

"2207 Seymour Avenue."

"2207 Seymour. Looks like you're calling me from 2210."

"Huh?"

"Looks like you're calling me from 2210."

"I can't hear you!"

"It looks like you are calling me from 2210 Seymour."

"I'm across the street; I'm using the phone."

"Okay, stay there with those neighbors. Talk to the police when they get there."

"Okay."

"Okay, talk to the police when they get there."

"Okay. Hello?"

"Yeah, talk to the police when they get there."

"Okay, are they on their way right now? I need them now!"

"We're going to send them as soon as we get a car open."

"No, I need them now before he gets back!"

"All right, we're sending them, okay?"

"Okay, I mean, like . . ."

"Who's the guy you're trying—who's the guy who went out?"

"Um, his name is Ariel Castro."

"All right. How old is he?"

"He's like fifty-two."

"All right, and uh—"

"I'm Amanda Berry! I've been on the news for the last ten years!"

"Okay, I got that, dear. And, you say, what was his name again?"

"Uh, Ariel Castro."

"And is he white, black, or Hispanic?"

"He's Hispanic."

"What's he wearing?"

"I don't know! 'Cause he's not here right now! That's why I ran away!"

"When he left, what was he wearing?"

"Who knows!"

"The police are on their way; talk to them when they get there."

"Huh? I need—okay."

"I told you they're on their way; talk to them when they get there, okay?"

"All right, okay."

"Thank you."

"Bye."

Maybe three minutes pass before the first police car pulls up. Before it even stops I run over to it, yelling at the cop who's driving, "I'm Amanda Berry!"

Two officers step out of the car, and one of them says into the radio that they found Amanda Berry.

"Is there anybody else inside?" he asks me, with a startled look on his face.

"Yes!" I shout. "There are two more girls in there!"

They look shocked and they start running toward the house.

"Wait! Can you please put us in the car or something, in case he comes back?" I'm terrified, and Joce is still out-of-control crying, so they tell us to sit in the back of the cruiser.

By now the whole street has begun filling up with police cars, and cops are running everywhere. Some of them are breaking the storm door open and going inside.

A cop comes to take me and Joce out of the police car and walks us over to an ambulance, and we sit inside.

There are so many cops here now. He can't get to us anymore.

Gina

We hear sirens outside, but I don't pay any attention. We've been hearing them for years, and they never come for us.

A couple of minutes pass, and then we hear somebody climbing the stairs.

"Shut this door!" I tell Michelle. "I think he's coming for us."

We're terrified. We close the door and throw our weight against it. There's no way we're strong enough to keep him out, but we have to try. What is he going to do to us?

Somebody in the hall is shouting: "Cleveland police! Cleveland police!"

Michelle pushes the door open and runs through Amanda's room and into the hallway. I hear her yelling, "You saved us! You saved us!"

I'm still hanging back, just out of sight inside Amanda's room. Maybe they are fake cops. Maybe it's just some of his friends in costumes.

I peek around the corner and see two cops in uniform, a man and a woman.

Michelle has jumped up into the man's arms, and she's holding on tight. Then he gently puts her down, and she jumps up onto the female officer, shouting hysterically, "Please don't let me go! Please don't let me go!"

"I'm not letting you go," I hear the officer say.

I look out from the corner a little more, real slow, and I meet eyes with the guy cop.

"What's your name?" he asks me.

"Gina DeJesus," I tell him.

He looks like he doesn't believe me, so I say my full name.

"My name is Georgina DeJesus."

He looks as if he's just seen a ghost and says into his radio, "We found them! We found them!" Then he stares at me for a while and says, "We've been looking for you for a really long time."

They keep telling us that we're safe now, but I'm still not sure.

"Do you know who kidnapped you? What does he look like? Is that him?"

They're pointing to a picture on Amanda's wall, but it's Amanda's dad, not him.

"If you want pictures of him, you have to go downstairs to the kitchen and look on the refrigerator," I tell them.

I take them downstairs to show them. There are cops all over the house. When we get to the kitchen, Michelle is already there, pointing out the photos.

We ask if we can go upstairs to get a couple of things, so they take us. I grab my blue book bag, which is filled with a lot of my drawings and letters. I want to show them to my mom and dad. I want to take some of the clothes that I sewed myself, but I don't have time to grab them, because they are hurrying us outside.

We walk through the front door, which is all smashed up. There are so many people outside, cop cars and flashing lights everywhere.

It's so bright that it hurts my eyes.

Amanda

The cops bring Gina and Michelle into the ambulance. Michelle's very emotional and is lying on a gurney, having trouble breathing. Paramedics in light blue gloves are telling her to calm down and breathe slowly.

I'm just sitting here with Joce, watching them, with Gina next to us.

"I'm so glad you're okay," Gina says to me. "I was worried you got hurt."

The ambulance crew puts a black band on my arm to take my blood pressure, and it nearly squeezes my arm off. We haven't been to a doctor in ten years. Joce has never even met one.

A guy comes into the ambulance and tells us that he's an FBI agent, and that his name is Andy Burke. "You guys look the same," he says, smiling. "The only thing is that you look a lot thinner. We've been looking for you for a long time."

A nice police officer named Barb Johnson then joins him.

"So," she asks me, "you're really Amanda Berry?"

"Yes, I am," I tell her.

It feels strange after so many years to talk to a total stranger.

"Who's this little girl?"

"This is my daughter, Jocelyn."

Joce has calmed down now and she's looking around in amazement at everything and everybody in the ambulance.

"So this is his daughter?" she says.

"Yes."

"And you're really Gina DeJesus?" she asks Gina.

"Yeah," Gina says.

She's smiling. I haven't seen Gina smile in months.

Gina

"You did this? You got us out?" I ask Amanda, sitting next to me in the ambulance.

"Yeah, I did," she says. "I was so scared. Then I thought of my mom and my sister and I couldn't let any more time go by. So I did it."

"Why didn't you ask me for help?" I ask her.

"Because if I got caught, I wanted it to be me alone," she says. "I didn't want him to catch you, too."

Wait until he finds out it was Amanda who got us out.

"It's the one you trust most that screws you over in the end," I tell her.

We both laugh at that. It feels real good to laugh.

The cops are looking for him, and they tell us we never have to see him again.

Jocelyn has calmed down now and is happily babbling and excited about being inside an ambulance. She's trying to show me something, but when I don't pay attention, I hear her say: "Gina! Gina!"

It's the first time she has ever said my real name. She must have heard the police say it.

I'm not Chelsea anymore. I am free.

It seems like it takes forever, but the ambulance starts moving.

We drive to the corner and turn left.

We are off Seymour Avenue, finally and forever.*

---

*Cleveland police officials reprimanded the dispatcher who handled Amanda's 911 call. He was cited for not staying on the line until police arrived. His supervisor also noted that he "could have demonstrated more empathy and could have been more compassionate in [his] dealing with Ms. Berry."

Neighbors have offered differing views of the escape and who deserves credit for helping Amanda. The first man who stepped up onto the porch, Angel Cordero, who was visiting Altagracia Tejeda, said he kicked the door open for Amanda. The second man on the porch, Charles Ramsey, Castro's next door neighbor, said he was the one who kicked in the door. Ramsey's account is more widely known because he became an instant global celebrity for several colorful television interviews he gave. (Cordero does not speak English.) Amanda said Ramsey helped her by giving her the idea to kick out the door's bottom panel and calling 911 for her. But her memory is that she kicked the door out and freed herself. The FBI, which had offered a reward of up to $25,000 in the case, decided not to give out the full amount, but did give some money to both Ramsey and Cordero.

Part Four

May 6, 2013: Arrest

Dan Brill and Mike Hageman were taking a domestic violence report on West 47th Street when their radios started buzzing.

The two veteran police officers looked at each other: The radio traffic was urgent; something unusual was happening. Hageman stepped outside the house to listen as Brill finished taking the woman's statement.

"It sounds like they found Amanda Berry," Hageman said when Brill returned to the car.

"You gotta be kidding me," Brill said.

Nearly every cop on the west side of Cleveland knew Amanda Berry's name and face. For ten years, her photo had been up on the wall of the Second District headquarters, on telephone poles, and on highway billboards. Everyone wanted to believe she was still alive, but cops know these long-term missing-person cases typically end when someone discovers bones.

But now the excited chatter on the police radio was saying that Amanda Berry was alive and safe on Seymour Avenue, just a few minutes away.

"Be advised, suspect Ariel Castro, fifty-two-year-old Hispanic male, is driving a blue Mazda Miata convertible," the dispatcher announced.

Brill and Hageman knew that half the police cars in Cleveland were already on Seymour Avenue, so they decided to look for the Miata. They started driving east on Clark Avenue, a busy main road not far from Castro's house. And there it was: just up ahead, a blue Miata was pulling up to a stop sign with two Hispanic males in their fifties in the two-seater convertible.

As the police moved closer, the driver of the Miata saw the cruiser and made eye contact with the officers. Brill and Hageman were waiting for "the look," the expression they see on the faces of car thieves, drunk drivers, or any other driver who doesn't want to attract police attention: a guilty look, then a careful effort to direct their attention anywhere but at the officers.

The Miata driver did none of that. He seemed totally calm.

He headed down Clark Avenue and then turned right into a McDonald's parking lot.

Brill radioed in the license plate: FHY4669.

The confirmation came quickly: It was Castro's 1993 Miata. "That's the male we're looking for," the dispatcher said.

The officers pulled up directly behind the car and turned on their overhead flashing lights. The two men in the car turned around, clearly bewildered. Hageman and Brill approached them, asked for IDs, and told them to keep their hands in plain sight. Ariel Castro was the driver, and his brother, Onil, was in the passenger seat with a dog on his lap. The cops ordered them out of the car.

Ariel said nothing, but Onil seemed confused. "What's going on?" he asked. "What did Pedro do?"

Onil told the officers that if their brother Pedro, who had a severe drinking problem, had gotten into some kind of trouble, they could find him at his house, where he lived with their mother. He demanded to be released.

"We will explain this all to you," Brill said. "But right now we need you to cooperate with us."

Onil was still holding the dog, and the officers saw that there was another dog in a plastic milk crate in the space behind the seats. Onil was still complaining loudly about being stopped when the officers told him to put both dogs in the crate.

As they handcuffed both men, Ariel Castro was silent.

Officer Tom Connole pulled up in a second patrol car and quietly updated Brill and Hageman: "He held three girls kidnapped for ten years. One of the other ones is Gina DeJesus."

Brill was shocked. Not only was Amanda alive, but so was Gina, whose disappearance was just as well-known in Cleveland. So they had been together all these years.

The officers put Onil in their patrol car and Ariel in Connole's vehicle. They were each read their Miranda rights, and when Ariel Castro was told he was being held on suspicion of kidnapping, he seemed stunned. He started to speak, but then stopped and slouched down in the patrol car.

The brothers were taken to the Second District police headquarters, a five-minute drive from Castro's home, and locked up separately. Ariel Castro was placed in Cell 22, a tiny room with a concrete floor and yellow brick walls. Previous occupants of the cell had scratched their colorful street names into the bars over the years: Baldy D, Bobby 104, Lil Bryan. Castro sat there silently. In another cell across the room, Onil was mouthing off to the officers, demanding to be freed and insisting he had done nothing wrong.

Police had found their brother Pedro passed out drunk in his backyard and arrested him as well. He now lay on the floor of a third cell, still sleeping it off.

All three men were given dark blue "paper suits," which are generally used for prisoners who are a suicide risk. The police had taken that precaution because the case was so extraordinary and was already drawing overwhelming media attention. Onil was furious about being forced to change clothes, but Ariel quietly slipped into the outfit while officers changed the unconscious Pedro.

The Cleveland police and FBI did not want to make any procedural missteps in such a high-profile case, so they decided to wait until the next morning to question the suspects. For the next few hours, until well after midnight when Castro was transferred downtown to the Justice Center lockup, police, FBI agents, and other officials came to his cell door to catch a glimpse of the man accused of such breathtaking crimes. Throughout it all Castro sat silently on a wooden chair beneath the cell's neon light.

He never asked a single question about why he was being held.

May 6, 2013: Reunion

At the moment Amanda was kicking out the door of 2207 Seymour Avenue, Nancy Ruiz was preparing dinner for her sister Janice three blocks down the street. Janice lived there with two other sisters, a nephew, and his family. She had suffered a stroke a week earlier and had been released from the hospital that afternoon. The house had been in the family for about fifty years, and its fresh white paint and tidy yard made it stand out on an otherwise run-down block.

Nancy was cooking a chicken stew while Janice rested in her bedroom. Her doctors had said that Janice needed quiet, so Nancy had drawn the curtains and shut off her phone and the TV to make sure nothing disturbed her.

Outside, though, Nancy heard a commotion—sirens and people shouting. She didn't think much of it, but then the door swung open and her older sister Sandra burst in and shouted, "They found three girls in a basement down the street!"

Nancy froze.

"Oh, my God," she said. "Is it Gina?"

"I don't know," Sandra said. "But we have to go!"

They took off down the street and parked near the corner of West 25th Street, right behind Cesi Castro's Caribe Grocery. Cesi and his wife, Norma, were standing outside the market watching the chaotic scene— police cars with flashing lights, TV satellite trucks, a gathering crowd.

As she passed, Nancy quickly hugged Norma, whom she had known since she was a teenager, and began running toward the police cars. She ducked under the yellow crime-scene tape and saw Andy Burke, an FBI agent who had been working on Gina's case from the beginning.

"Please," she said to him, "just tell me! Is it Gina?"

"Yes, it is," Burke said.

"Oh, my God!" Nancy shouted. "Oh, my God! They said there's a baby. Is it hers?"

"No," he told her, "it's not hers."

She fell into his arms and they both started crying. "They're in that ambulance right there," Burke said, pointing toward the emergency vehicle pulling away down the street.

"You have to go to Metro Hospital," Burke told her. "That's where she's going."

Cleveland Deputy Police Chief Edward J. Tomba, who had just arrived, put Nancy and Sandra into his cruiser and tore off, sirens blaring, toward the hospital.

Gina

We've only been in the ambulance for a few minutes when we pull up to Metro Hospital. They wheel Michelle in on the gurney, but Amanda and I walk, and she's carrying Jocelyn.

I was sick so many times inside that house and wanted to go to a doctor, but now here I am at this huge hospital, and all I want to do is stay outside and breathe the fresh air for hours.

Doctors lead us into a big room with three beds that says TRAUMA 16 and TRAUMA 17 over its doors. The whole wall is glass, so we can sit on the beds and see the nurses' station and all the doctors and cops rushing around.

They put Amanda and Jocelyn on the bed at one end, Michelle in the middle, and me on the third and pull curtains around each of us. A doctor examines me and tells me I weigh a hundred pounds—thirty pounds less than when I was kidnapped. Then I hear a voice I haven't heard in nine years.

"Gina!"

It's my mom.

A cop is helping her make her way to me because she almost fainted when she saw me.

"Hi, Mommy," I say, very quietly.

Neither of us knows what else to say, so we just hold each other. My mom keeps looking at me and touching me, checking me out to make sure I'm really okay. She's smiling and crying at the same time.

A few minutes later my dad runs in and hugs me, and then my sister Mayra.

There must be a hundred police and FBI guys in the hallway, some of them looking through the glass and others who come in to say hello. Some of them are crying and a couple of them even fall to their knees, sobbing.

My mom and I can't stop hugging.

"Mommy," I ask when we finally pull apart, "do you still make mashed potatoes, fried chicken, and corn?"

"We can make it tonight!" she says.

"I want to go to the mall," I tell her.

"We'll go tomorrow!" she says.

Then I remember that I have something for her.

"Wait, Mommy, wait," I tell her. "I gotta show you something."

I get the book bag I took when we left Seymour Avenue and pull out a "missing" flyer of me, the one that he got from her and that I decorated with glittery hearts and pictures of food.

"Look what I have," I say, handing it to her.

"Oh, my God," she says.

She recognizes this flyer, and she's starting to put it all together.

I think if Ariel Castro were standing here right now, she would kill him.

Amanda

Where is Beth?

I wish she would get here. I'm dying to see her. Gina's family has been here for a while, and a nice woman named Yvonne Pointer is talking to Michelle.

The nurse says Pointer's daughter was murdered in 1984, and now she's an activist who helps victims of violence. She's sitting on the bed with Michelle, holding her hand, and they are singing: *"Lift every voice and sing, till earth and heaven ring."*

The doctors keep poking and pulling at me, checking my heartbeat and blood pressure. I weigh ninety-two pounds, and I was one-twenty when he took me. They take swabs from my mouth and Jocelyn's to check our DNA.

The nurses bring us a sandwich, chips, and juice. They ask Jocelyn what her favorite food is, and she says, "KFC!" So somebody runs out and gets her some. She's excited but takes one bite and realizes it's the spicy kind. Too hot for her, so she gulps down water.

And then I see Beth.

She's walking through the nurses' station but hasn't noticed me yet.

She looks so skinny, even thinner than I am. But it's really Beth! And my aunt Theresa and my cousin Melissa!

Beth looks through the glass window and finally catches sight of me.

She starts pushing her way through the chaos until she finally reaches me, and we hug. We're both crying hard, and Theresa and Melissa put their arms around me, too. Jocelyn is sitting on the bed staring at all this. I don't think she has any idea what's going on.

"Who is this?" Theresa asks.

"That's my daughter, Jocelyn," I say.

"Well," she says, "tell her to come over here!"

So Jocelyn joins in the hug, and I introduce everyone. She knows exactly who they are because I have been talking about them for her entire life.

"Is Daddy okay?" I ask Beth. "I heard on the news he was really sick."

"Yeah," Beth replies. "He's okay."

"And what about you? You're so skinny. Are you okay?"

"Don't worry," she says. "I'm fine."

An FBI agent named Tim Kolonick comes in and introduces himself.

"We've been looking for you for ten years," he says.

"I know. I saw you guys on TV. Thanks for not forgetting us."

He looks at Jocelyn and asks her name. "She's gorgeous," he says, smiling at her.

In a few minutes the police ask me to come to a separate room and answer questions. I tell Jocelyn to wait with Betsy Martinez, a nurse who has been taking good care of us. I can tell Joce is getting more comfortable, because she's running all over the place, with her face all red from a cherry Popsicle somebody gave her.

"I've got a joke, Miss Betsy," she says to the nurse.

"What's your joke?"

"Why did the chicken cross the road?"

"I don't know. Why?"

"To get to the other side!! I got you!!!"

And she laughs and laughs and laughs.

Amanda

They ask me if I want a shower.

God, I would love a shower, a long one, without worrying about someone pawing me. Just a hot, peaceful shower. I can't remember the last one I had. It used to be my favorite thing.

Today—Monday—was my bath day anyway. He had a schedule in the house. It depended on the season and the weather, but usually Jocelyn and I got to take a shower every four or five days. Tonight it was going to be our turn to go downstairs to use the shower.

They lead us to a big bathroom. It's so clean! I close the door and lock it, and Joce and I stand under the hot water, soaking and shampooing and scrubbing. It's been ten years since I have been able to use all the soap and shampoo I want. I close my eyes and breathe in the sweet smells. I'm so happy it almost makes me cry.

As we're scrubbing, the diamond stud in my ear falls out and slips down the drain. He used to wear it and then gave it to me. This seems like a fitting moment to have that little trace of him disappear forever.

We dry off with fluffy towels and put on some clothes that a nurse gave us. She says it was stuff that her family had outgrown. When I escaped from the house, I was wearing a tank top and a pair of baby-blue pants that Gina had sewn for me out of fabric from an old dress. Now Jocelyn is wearing a Disney princess dress and I'm in a track suit. I can't wait to buy brand-new clothes that nobody else has ever worn.

We walk back to the big room in the emergency ward, and I see Teddy, Mariyah, Marissa, and Devon standing there along the wall. The last time I saw Teddy was at Burger King the day I was kidnapped. I was so mad at him that day, but I'm so happy to see him now. And I can't believe how big the girls are.

My mouth drops, and I run over to hug them.

"This is Devon," they tell me, and I take a long look at this adorable little boy. I first saw him on the TV news as a newborn in Beth's arms, and now he's seven. I've been gone for his entire life.

"It's nice to meet you, Devon," I say, and we hug.

At around midnight they put my whole family into an FBI van and drive us to an Embassy Suites hotel in the suburbs. We have a two-room suite with FBI agents stationed outside to make sure nobody bothers us. They tell us there are reporters from all over the world at the hospital and on Seymour.

Jocelyn and Devon are bouncing off the beds and playing in the big closets like they've been friends forever, and Beth and I sit up talking. She tells me about Mom, and what it was like right up to the end. We make plans to go visit her grave. Beth says she didn't have enough money to get her a gravestone. I'm going to figure out how to fix that.

We never do get to sleep, and at about eight we wander down to the breakfast buffet. In the house, Gina and I would often daydream about a buffet where you could eat whatever you wanted and all you wanted. I eat pancakes and doughnuts and orange juice, and I ask the man at the omelet station to make me one with ham and cheese and onions. I can't believe how much I'm eating. I haven't seen this much food in ten years. So many choices!

Then, back in the room, in a bed with big pillows and soft sheets that smell like soap, I fall into a slumber so deep and happy that I could sleep forever. And for the first time since I was sixteen, I'm actually looking forward to waking up.

May 7, 2013: *Nos Vemos*

On the morning of Tuesday, May 7, Cleveland police officer Larry "Chiqui" Guerra brought a suspect into the Justice Center in downtown Cleveland. As he was turning the man over for fingerprinting and booking, he heard a familiar voice call out in Spanish from behind him.

"Hey, Chiqui! *¿Qué haces? ¿Cómo estás?*"

Guerra turned and saw Ariel Castro in a holding cell, lying on a mat on the floor, his hands clasped behind his head, smiling.

Guerra took a step back in surprise. He had known Castro all his life. Their families were both from Yauco, and they had grown up together in a Puerto Rican neighborhood a few streets away from Seymour. Castro was seven years older, but he and Guerra hung out in the same places, including the Caribe Grocery.

Castro's uncle Cesi and Guerra's father were friends and they'd often take young Chiqui to Indians baseball games. When Guerra graduated from the police academy, Cesi Castro bought him a military-style flashlight worth more than a hundred dollars.

Guerra played the *güiro*, a percussion instrument made from a hollowed-out gourd, and he would always join in the *parrandas*, the Christmas music parties in the back of Cesi's shop. He had seen Castro there at one of those celebrations just five months before, drinking a beer.

Guerra had always thought that Castro was a little odd and obsessively private. Guerra had never met his wife or his children. Castro would never engage in conversation much beyond small talk. He was friendly enough, but you always knew not to ask him too much because he wouldn't answer.

Guerra had been at home when he heard the news, and he thought of all the times he'd talked to Castro while he had the girls locked in his house. He thought of the hundreds of times he'd driven by 2207 Seymour and towed illegally parked cars off that street. It was his neighborhood, and the man accused of this unbelievable crime was his friend.

Now here was Castro, smiling at him from the mat on the floor, looking as relaxed as a man in a backyard hammock.

"*¿Ariel, qué pasó?*" said Guerra.

"I really fucked up," Castro said, sounding tired.

"Hey," Guerra warned him, "I'm not just Chiqui in here. I'm a policeman. Whatever you say, you might want to think about it."

"I don't care," Castro said. "I'm a victim here, too."

"How can you say that?"

"I didn't take those girls," Castro told him. "They came with me. I didn't make them do anything." He stood and started pacing around in the cell as he talked. "I was abused, too, as a kid."

"Well, I don't know about that," Guerra replied, his anger rising. "But it doesn't give you any excuse for what you did. Dude, it's been ten years. You even know Gina's father. Everybody knows Felix. How could you do this?" Guerra felt the crime personally, as his brother had married a relative of Gina's, and their daughter and Gina had been close friends.

"I didn't make them do anything," Castro insisted. "I didn't rape them. They did this willingly. They wanted to be with me. And another thing, when can I see my daughter? I should be able to see her."

Guerra was growing increasingly disgusted, and asked, "How did you keep this a secret for ten years? Did your brothers know anything about this?"

"My brothers didn't know anything about this. Nothing," Castro answered. "It was hard, but this was my little secret, and I'm glad it's finally over. I know I'm going to die in prison, but I didn't do all that stuff you guys say I did."

Guerra looked at Castro staring back at him through the bars and saw that he was cool, unemotional, and resigned. And Guerra thought to himself, he's been living this lie for so long that he actually believes it.

"All right, man," Guerra said. "I'm done talking to you."

"Okay, I'll see you later," Castro replied.

"*Nos vemos,*" Guerra said—see you later—though what he was really thinking was, "*Para el carajo.*"

Go to hell.

May 7, 2013: Confession

On the morning after his arrest, police searched Castro's house and found ninety feet of chains. They seized padlocks, deadbolts, and a clock-radio and wires rigged up as alarms connected to the front and back doors. In a drawer in the kitchen they discovered a note handwritten by Castro with the heading "Confession's [*sic*] and Details." The four-page document, printed on lined notebook paper, was filled with misspellings and scratched-out words.

The first page was dated with odd precision: "4-4-04, 8:06 a.m.," forty-one hours after Gina's abduction. The letter apparently took him four days to finish, because the final page was dated "4-8-04, 2:05 p.m."

The rambling note was in turns confession, suicide note, personal history, and rambling fatherly advice to his children.

He wrote that he had been "abandoned" by his parents, that an older boy had sexually abused him when he was a boy in Puerto Rico, and that his mother had been so physically abusive there were times he "wished she would die."

He said that he was married at age twenty and that the "marriage was a failure from the beginning." He claimed that Nilda was "abusive" and would hit him and "push me to the limit."

"I hit her back," he wrote. "She put me in jail, only to get me out and apologize to me. This happened a couple of times, but the name calling and arguments were always there." After she left him he said, "I lived alone for the most part . . . I had good sex drive. I was in a relationship with a woman for about two years."

He then described kidnapping Michelle and Amanda, claiming, "I treat them well and make sure they eat good."

"I don't understand why I keep looking for women out in the street. I already had two in my possession," he wrote. He said that Michelle and Amanda were being held "against their will because they made a mistake by getting in a car with a total stranger."

Though he expressed no remorse about taking the first two women, he did seem more troubled about Gina: "I had no idea Gina was so young, she looks a lot older," he wrote, adding that he didn't know that Gina was "the daughter of Felix, a school classmate of mine."

The bottom line is, I am a sexual predator who needs help, but I don't bother to get it. I live a private life. I function around others like a normal person. I've been having problems with my head for a long time. I feel depressed, dizzy and short term memory loss. I really don't know what's wrong with me. To the parents of these three woman [sic], I would like to say, <u>I'm very sorry</u>. I am sick.

When I wake up in the morning, I don't feel like I'm really hear [sic]. For some reason I feel I can't concentrate. This is a big problem in my everyday life. I just want to put an end to my life, and let the Devil deal with me.

Castro wrote that he planned to let the women go "when I feel I have arranged everything so my family knows what to do after I take my life." He noted that he had about $10,000 in a bank account and another $11,000 in cash hidden inside his washing machine.

I would like this money to go to the victims, for they deserve every red cent of it. Again, I apologize (sorry) to everyone this whole ordeal has affected.

To my children, please be strong and make the right decisions. Just because you may think you know someone do not get into their vehical [sic]. This was the case of Amanda + Gina.

Grimilda; please do your best to insure my babies are safe. If possible, move away (far away).

As I write this letter on 4-8-04 at 2:05 pm, my simptoms [sic] are clearly bothering me (dizziness and not really feeling like I'm hear [sic]). Also, Depression. <u>I know I am sick</u> (Mentally).

May 7, 2013: Fallout

While investigators searched Castro's house, other officers scoured the neighborhood to make certain they weren't missing any accomplices or clues. Across the street and three doors down from Castro's house, police arrested Elias Acevedo Sr., a convicted sex offender who had moved in with his mother but failed to register his new address with police. He was jailed for that offense, and while he was incarcerated police linked his DNA to an unsolved 1993 rape. The further they looked into that case, the more they also began to suspect Acevedo in the unsolved disappearance of Christina Adkins, who was eighteen and pregnant when she went missing in January 1995.

Encouraged by the fact that Amanda, Gina, and Michelle had been found alive after so many years, FBI agent Andy Burke began reviewing cold cases. Burke noticed inconsistencies in police reports about Adkins's disappearance—one witness seemed to have given police a false name and date of birth. After pulling the original files and reinterviewing people involved in the case, Burke discovered that that witness was Acevedo.

Acevedo ultimately confessed to killing Adkins, as well as Pamela Pemberton, a thirty-year-old whose body was found in 1994. He then led police to an area off I-90 near downtown Cleveland and pointed to a manhole cover. When officers lifted it, Burke shined his flashlight twenty feet down into an old concrete storm sewer and saw Christina Adkins's skull.

May 7, 2013: Interview

Twenty-four hours after his arrest, still in his paper jumpsuit and slippers, his hands cuffed in front of him, Ariel Castro shuffled into a small interrogation room on the ninth floor of the Justice Center, the headquarters of the Cleveland police and Cuyahoga County courts.

At 5:28 p.m., two interrogators—Dave Jacobs, a veteran officer in the Cuyahoga County Sheriff's Office assigned to the FBI's Violent Crimes Task Force, and Andy Harasimchuk, a Cleveland police sex crimes detective—entered the room, showed Castro their badges, and began questioning him. Castro sat with his chin resting in his shackled hands, his elbows on the table, sobbing softly and dabbing his eyes.

"Whatever you need to know," he said quietly, "just ask me questions."

He spelled out his name. He said he had an ornate tribal tattoo around his left bicep and tried to lift his shirt to show the detectives but couldn't manage it with his hands cuffed. He said he was five-foot-seven.

Jacobs handed Castro a paper with his Miranda rights and asked Castro to read them out loud.

"'You have the right to remain silent,'" Castro started, but then his voice broke and he started crying loudly. "I'm worried about my little girl. How's she doing?" he asked.

Jacobs assured him that Jocelyn was fine.

"I miss her so much already," Castro said, wiping his eyes. "She knows I was always there for her. I'm sorry. I'm glad she finally got her freedom."

Castro finished reading the Miranda form and signed it, along with another document granting his consent to speak to police without a lawyer being present.

The interrogation began with Castro giving some family history about his late common-law wife, Nilda Figueroa, and their four children. He said his job as a bus driver was hard and, "I would just come home stressed out."

His account was delivered as matter-of-factly as if he were answering questions from a bank teller. But he broke down again when he mentioned Jocelyn: "My daughter was born there. It just worked out so well. She's a miracle baby."

Jacobs asked him to describe the day he abducted Michelle. He said he offered her a ride home from the Family Dollar store at Clark Avenue and West 30th Street. He couldn't remember what year it was.

"I'm just so screwed up in my mind," he said. "Anybody in their right mind wouldn't do something like this."

He described chaining Michelle in his basement. Jacobs asked if he had had sex with her, and Castro replied, "That was the whole intention."

"I'm selfish and cold-blooded," he said. "Having four kids, and now five, I can't understand how I did these things. I'm a father. I'm a grandfather."

When the officers asked about Amanda, Castro started sobbing again.

"I'm going away for a long time; I know it," he said. "I just want to tell you whatever you need and tell the truth. . . . Maybe my information can help other kids or other women."

He said he did not know Amanda before he abducted her. He told them that he was dropping off his daughter Arlene on West 110th Street when he saw Amanda walk by in her Burger King uniform: "I noticed Amanda smiling towards us and I was attracted to her. So I says 'bye' to my daughter and I pulled out of the driveway and I went the way Amanda was walking." He pulled up next to her, rolled down his window, and asked her if she wanted a ride. "She said yes, surprisingly," Castro recalled. "She thought my daughter was still in the van." Castro then said he "tricked her" into coming to his house and described how he began having sex with her on that day.

"A week or two later I called her mom. I think I said something like, 'I have your daughter and that she's okay, and that she's my wife now,'" he said, crying again.

There was rarely any interaction between Amanda and Michelle, Castro said, because he told them not to talk to each other.

He described Jocelyn's birth in the plastic wading pool, and how he cut the umbilical cord, froze the placenta, and eventually buried it in the backyard.

While Amanda named her Jocelyn Berry, he considered her last name to be Castro.

The interrogation then turned to Gina, and Castro recalled that he went to Wilbur Wright Middle School looking for Arlene on April 2, 2004, when he noticed Gina on his way in.

"I was attracted to Gina. She was showing her cleavage," he said.

He spoke briefly with a security guard and then went inside the school, but when he couldn't find Arlene, he left. Fifteen or twenty minutes later, he recalled, he was driving down Lorain Avenue when he saw the two seventh-graders walking together near the corner of 106th Street.

Castro said he knew Gina was the daughter of Felix DeJesus, and he would see them together at school assemblies and shows. But he said on the day he abducted Gina, he didn't realize it was her: "If I'd a known then, I would have just dropped her off."

Castro turned his car around and drove past Arlene, who did not see him, and pulled up beside Gina near the corner of 104th Street. "I did something very cold-blooded to my daughter; I passed her to get to Gina," he said, breaking into tears again.

He told the interrogators he was surprised that police didn't see him on surveillance footage when he went into Wilbur Wright Middle School that day: "They could have cracked the case right there."

Castro said he had not planned to abduct anyone that day. It was an impulsive decision, and he was surprised when Gina got into the car with him, though he couldn't remember how he convinced her to come into his house.

"We stayed downstairs for a while, then we went to the basement," he said.

Jacobs asked how he persuaded her to follow him there.

"I just asked her," he said.

Jacobs asked what happened there.

"We were just talking," Castro replied. "She was complying with everything. All three of them, they were just so compliant. To this day, I don't understand how they would get into my vehicle and got into my house with no questions and without a struggle."

He repeatedly used the word "consensual" to describe his sexual relationship with his captives. He claimed he had never been violent and that none of the victims had ever cried while he was having sex with them.

Castro said he would sometimes take the women outside into the backyard, but always made them wear wigs, baseball caps, and sunglasses.

Jacobs asked if he was concerned they would try to escape.

"I gained their trust," he said. "They were surprisingly willing to do what I asked."

Castro described how he would occasionally have guests over to his house. "I would tell them be quiet, because, 'I don't want you to get in trouble,'" he said. He did not have to say things like, "I'm going to beat your ass," "because by then I had felt them out. I kind of knew what I could get these girls to do."

On the day the women escaped, Castro told the officers, he had gone to his mother's house to wash his car. He said he told Jocelyn, "I'm going to Grandma's, and she's going to cook for us, and I'll bring some back."

Amanda's room was unlocked because Jocelyn had been complaining about being locked inside all the time, he said.

"Yesterday, I know I let my guard down."

He never took Amanda, Gina, or Michelle out in his car, he said, but he often went out with Jocelyn. His brother Pedro had seen them in his car a few times, and Castro told him she was his girlfriend's daughter. A few days before Castro was arrested, he said Pedro had walked into a Burger King while he and Jocelyn were eating breakfast, but his brother thought nothing of seeing Castro with the child.

"I never took her to my mother's house," he said. "I wanted to so bad. I wanted her to meet her, but she never met her."

Jacobs asked Castro about a cross in the backyard of Seymour Avenue and some freshly turned dirt. Castro said he had buried two or three pet dogs in the yard, and the newly dug earth was for a greenhouse he had started building.

Jacobs asked if anything else might be buried in the yard.

"If you're trying to get at, 'Am I a serial killer?' I'm not," Castro said.

"I don't think you are," Jacobs said.

"I'm a sexual predator," he said. "They say if you do it once and you continue doing it, you're a predator."

"What if you only do it once? In your mind, what does that make you?" Jacobs asked.

"Probably just an offender," he said. "I kept doing it over and over."

Jacobs asked how Castro managed to keep the whole thing secret for so long.

"I don't know how I pulled it off," he said.

* * *

After two hours of talking, Castro asked when he could eat.

Jacobs and Harasimchuk said they would take a break and get Castro some food. As they were leaving the room, Castro stopped them.

He said he had about $40,000 in his 401(k) account from the Cleveland Public Schools, plus cash hidden in a black bag inside a broken Kelvinator washing machine in his basement. He was worried that "corrupt cops" searching his house would steal it.

Another officer brought Castro a slice of pizza and a bottle of Coke. Sitting alone in the room, with the surveillance camera still recording him, Castro had trouble picking up the pizza with his cuffed hands, and put his face down into the plate and ate it. When he finished, an officer brought him a second slice.

A half hour later, the two interrogators returned.

Castro asked if they found the money in his basement and told them, "I would like as much money to go to the victims as possible, and my daughter."

Jacobs showed Castro a series of photographs of the women, taken the previous night at Metro Hospital. He asked him to identify the first one, and Castro started sobbing heavily.

"My baby's mama, Amanda," he said. Through his tears Castro told Jacobs, with obvious pride, that he had helped her quit smoking.

He then identified Gina and Michelle, and crying again, said, "I was just so tired of this double life and I wanted freedom for them."

Jacobs asked Castro about his sexual history. Before he abducted the three women, he recalled, he used to pick up prostitutes on Lorain Avenue and bring them back to his house.

He said he had "lost sexual interest" in his three captives by the end, because "I just didn't find them attractive." He had not had sex with Amanda or Gina in "eight months or a year," and only rarely had sex with Michelle, although he admitted to having two videos on his phone of him having sex with her the previous week.

Jacobs showed Castro the letter dated April 4, 2004, two days after he abducted Gina, that police had found in his kitchen.

"In case something ever happened to me, I wanted you guys to see that I'm a victim," Castro said, explaining the letter, referring again to his claim that he was sexually abused as a child.

He said he never intended to have a child with any of his captives, but he never used any form of birth control. He claimed all three women "wanted sex all the time . . . they would ask me for it." When Amanda became pregnant, he said, "We just dealt with it." He called her "an excellent mom."

During the course of the four-hour interview Castro never apologized for what he had done and cried every time Jocelyn's name was mentioned.

"I miss my daughter dearly, but on the same token, she has her freedom now," he said. "And they have their freedom."

May 9, 2013: Starting Over

Amanda

The FBI says we need lawyers, and they're sending over ones they say we can trust. I'm staying at Beth and Teddy's house on West 129th Street, and there are satellite trucks and TV cameras outside. The police are keeping the media away from the front door and we have our shades drawn. Beth went out yesterday and pleaded for privacy, but this doesn't feel like privacy.

The lawyers, Jim Wooley, a former federal prosecutor and partner at Jones Day; Henry Hilow, a former assistant county prosecutor and partner at McGinty, Hilow & Spellacy; and Heather Kimmel, associate general counsel of the United Church of Christ arrive, and we meet in the living room with Jocelyn, my aunt Theresa, Beth, Teddy, and their kids. The room is filled with stuffed animals, flowers, and cards that people have sent from all over the world. Jim and Henry start making jokes about each other and they actually make me laugh. I cover my mouth with my hand because my teeth are so yellow and gross after ten years without seeing a dentist. I can't wait to get them fixed.

"Is there anything we can get for you or bring to you? Anything at all?" Henry asks.

I'm not sure what a lawyer can do for me, but there are two things I need.

"My mother doesn't have a headstone, and I would like to get her one. And I want a birth certificate for my daughter."

"We can do that," Henry says.

May 13, 2013: Graveyard

Amanda

A week after my escape I'm finally going to see where my mom is buried.

I wanted to go yesterday, because it was Mother's Day, but the FBI said that all the news people would be expecting me to do that, and I'm not ready to face the cameras.

So now Joce, Aunt Theresa, and I are on our way to the cemetery a few miles outside Cleveland. So many wonderful memories of my mom flood back as we drive past the pretty trees and fields along the road.

Jen Meyers, a victim specialist with the FBI, is driving us in her van. Jen recently worked with families in the school shooting at Newtown, Connecticut, and she's been great to talk to about how to cope with what happened to us. She has been with us practically every day since the moment we got out, and I'm glad she's the one taking us out here.

We don't know exactly where Mom is buried, but Aunt Theresa has a section and plot number, and she knows that it's close to my grandma's grave. We walk across the grass trying to find the spot, and when we finally do, what I see makes me break down.

Somebody has laid fresh flowers on my mom's grave, with a note: "Dear Amanda, We hope that your mom knows you are home." It's signed by someone I don't know.

For ten years, I lived in a world controlled by one selfish man. Now I live in a world of kindness, where total strangers help me and ask for nothing in return.

I explain to Joce that this is where her grandmother is buried.

"She's in heaven, but this is where her body is," I tell her. "So we're going to come here and visit her all the time."

"Okay, Mommy," she says quietly.

It's cool, barely fifty degrees, and rays of sunshine shoot through the big trees around the gravesite. I look around at the perfectly mowed grass and think my mom would approve.

I crouch down and whisper, "Mommy, I'm home."

August 1, 2013: Sentencing

On August 1, Ariel Castro took a seat in a downtown Cleveland court-room, wearing an orange prison jumpsuit and shackles. He looked like an unremarkable middle-aged man with wire-rimmed glasses, a reced-ing hairline, salt-and-pepper beard, and a bit of a paunch.

Castro had already pleaded guilty to 937 felony counts, with many details of the indictment drawn from Amanda's diaries, and today was his sentencing hearing. Cuyahoga County Prosecutor Timothy J. McGinty, an outspoken former judge, said 937 was a "conservative" number of the possible counts against Castro. He described Castro as "evil incarnate."

In exchange for the guilty plea, McGinty had not sought the death penalty, and the case was wrapped up at remarkable speed—less than ninety days from arrest to sentencing. Castro had agreed to life in prison without the possibility of parole, plus a thousand years—a sentence intended to convey the community's revulsion at his crimes. McGinty also said it was a message to other criminals who might want to become famous by copying Castro.

All that was left now was for Judge Michael Russo to formally accept the deal at the sentencing.

Wooley, Hilow, and Kimmel wanted a low-key hearing. Given the extraordinary interest in the case, they had no desire to have Amanda, Gina, and Michelle endure a very public confrontation with Castro. The county prosecutor, an elected official who never shied away from the media spotlight, disagreed. McGinty said Castro's crimes should be aired as publicly and in as much detail as possible. He said he wanted to leave no doubt in Judge Russo's mind that he should approve the sentencing deal, and to leave a court record so damning that no judge, even decades in the future, would ever consider letting Castro out of prison. He wanted all the victims to testify.

Russo agreed to let the sentencing hearing go forward, and McGinty presented a series of witnesses, including psychiatrist Frank M. Och-berg of Michigan State University.

Describing Castro's treatment of Amanda, Gina, and Michelle, Ochberg said, "The damage done to them will not go away." But he called them, "marvelous, compelling examples of resilience."

Amanda and Gina did not want to see Castro and were not ready to speak publicly, so they declined to attend. They sent family members to read statements.

"The impact of these crimes on our family is something that we do not want to discuss with people we don't know," Beth told the judge. "Even if I wanted to talk about it, it is impossible to put into words. For me, I lost my sister for all those years and thought it was forever. And we lost my mother forever. And she died not knowing. . . . It is impossible to put into words how much it hurts.

"Amanda is not here today. She is strong, beautiful, inside and out, and is doing better every day. She's not just my only sister, but the best friend I have and the best person I know. She does not want to talk about these things. She has not talked about these things even with me.

"The main reason she does not want anyone to talk about these things, or be forced to talk about these things, is because she has a daughter. She would like to be the person who decides what to tell her daughter, when to tell her daughter, and how to tell her daughter certain things."

Sylvia Colon, Gina's cousin, spoke on behalf of the DeJesus family.

"To Ariel Castro's family, we are saddened that you are burdened with this horror and will unfortunately forever be tied to these atrocities. Please know that we do not hold you accountable and pray that you can one day be whole again. Continue to love and support one another—we promise you that with this recipe you will be triumphant.

"Our family recognizes it is not for us to judge or determine any punishment. Only a higher power can do that.

"Today is the last day we want to think or talk about this. These events will not own a place in our thoughts or our hearts. We will continue to live and love.

"We stand before you and promise you that our beloved family member thrives. She laughs, swims, dances, and more importantly she loves and is loved. We are comforted in knowing that she will continue to flourish. She will finish school, go to college, fall in love, and if she chooses, will get married and have children. She is where we will continue to put our energy. She lives not as a victim, but as a survivor. Her insurmountable will to prevail is the only story worth discussing."

Then she turned to the defense table and faced Castro directly.

"To Ariel Castro: *Que Dios se apiade de su alma.*"

May God have mercy on your soul.

Michelle stood before the judge and described the pain of being separated from her son. He had been placed in foster care before she went missing, and she had been working to regain custody when she was abducted. Then she addressed Castro: "I spent eleven years in hell. Now your hell is just beginning. I will overcome all that happened, but you're going to face hell for eternity."

Judge Russo asked if Castro had anything to say before sentencing.

For the next sixteen minutes Castro stood at the defense table, rambling in a soft voice, without notes, appearing to voice thoughts as they came to him, in no particular order. He had pleaded guilty to almost a thousand counts of horrendous crimes. But he sounded, for all the world, like a man whose feelings had been hurt by all the mean things being said about him.

He described being abused and said he was addicted to sex. He said that pornography had pushed him into "the art of masturbation," which he would engage in for "two or three hours a day nonstop." He claimed he had never been abusive until he met Nilda, whom he beat because "I couldn't get her to quiet down."

Castro insisted that Jocelyn had had a "normal life" and would probably describe him as "the best dad in the world."

"There was harmony in that home," he said.

"Most of the sex that went on in the house, probably all of it, was consensual," he told the court, insisting that his imprisonment of the three women did not involve violence: "I simply kept them there without them being able to leave."

"I just want to clear the record that I am not a monster. I did not prey on these women," he stated. "I just acted on the sexual instincts because of my sexual addiction. . . . I am a normal person. I am just sick. I have an addiction, just like an alcoholic has an addiction."

Finally he offered an apology: "I am truly sorry to the DeJesus family, Michelle, and Amanda. You guys know all the harmony that went on in that home. I ask God to forgive me. I ask my family—and I apologize to my family also for putting them through all this. I want to apologize to the state of Ohio, the city of Cleveland, for putting a dark cloud over the city. I just want to apologize to everyone who was touched by these events.

"I just hope that they find it in their hearts to forgive me and to maybe do some research on people who have addictions so they can see how their addiction takes over their lives."

He then criticized the FBI, saying: "I feel that the FBI let these girls down" because they questioned his daughter, Arlene, about Gina's disappearance, "but they failed to question me. If they would have questioned me . . . it's possible that it would have ended right there."

He apologized to the judge for taking up his time and then complained about Gina's cousin telling him in court, "May God have mercy on your soul," which he said was "uncalled for."

After alternating between describing the "harmony" in the house and saying how sorry he was, he concluded: "So again, thank you, everyone. Thank you, victims. Please find it in your hearts to forgive me. Thank you."

On the bench Russo could barely conceal his disgust. He accepted the sentencing agreement and asked Castro to rise as he issued the court's final word on his case:

"Sir, there is no place in this city, there is no place in this country, indeed there is no place in this world for those who enslave others, those who sexually assault others, and those who brutalize others.

"For more than ten years you have preyed upon three young women. You subjected them to harsh and violent conduct. You felt you were dominating them, but you were incorrect. You did not take away their dignity.

"Although they suffered terribly, Miss Knight, Miss DeJesus, and Miss Berry did not give up hope. They have persevered. In fact, they prevailed.

These remarkable women again have their freedom, which is the most precious aspect of being an American.

"Mr. Castro, you forfeited that right. You now become a number with the Department of Rehabilitation and Correction. You will be confined for the remainder of your days. You are hereby remanded for transport to Lorain Correctional Institution.

"Now for Miss Knight, Miss DeJesus, and Miss Berry, as well as your young daughter, we celebrate your futures. We acknowledge the faithfulness of your families, your friends, and all others in this community who so fervently believed that you were alive. On behalf of the judges and the staff of this court, we wish you continued success and a sense of peace."

Castro stood, and bailiffs led him out a side door of the courtroom.

It was the last time he would ever be seen in public.

August 1: Gravestone

Amanda

I'm watching the sentencing on TV at home with Jen Meyers from the FBI. I'm glad I didn't go down to the courtroom. I didn't want to give him the satisfaction of seeing me again.

Beth said what I wanted to say. And if I had been up there in front of the cameras and so many people, it would have been hard not to cry.

It makes me angry to listen to his ridiculous, delusional statements. I want to slap him.

"None of that is true," I say to Jen. "How can he say that?"

"That's just in his mind," she replies. "It doesn't matter what he says. You know what really happened."

While we're watching the sentencing hearing, Jen gets a text from Jim Wooley. He says the people from Kotecki Family Memorials, who donated my mom's grave marker, called to say it was laid at her grave today. It's a bronze stone with roses etched around the border, and a color photo of my mom, smiling.

My mom has amazing timing.

First I felt her pushing me toward the door the day I needed to find the strength to escape Seymour Avenue.

Now on the day he is finally being punished, her memorial stone, which means so much to me, arrives. She is the reason I'm still alive, and her spirit will get me through whatever lies ahead.

Gina

I wake up on my parents' bed and hear his voice on the TV.

I have a sex problem. I was a victim. Blah, blah, blah.

They were the same things he said in the house so many times. I'm glad I decided not to go to court. It's pointless to talk to him or to listen to him.

You know what? Even if he was a victim, he had the power to choose.

He didn't have to do what he did to us. If he was mistreated as a kid, it should have made him more aware of how important it is to treat other people well. Just because he abused me, I'm not going to go abuse somebody else.

He keeps talking—that voice! I heard it every day for nine years. I've had a few months without it, but now all his crazy talk is back. He says one thing and then the opposite. He did nothing wrong and treated us well, but he is sorry for what he did and wants to apologize.

He's telling so many lies, it's hard not to get angry. He keeps talking about the "harmony" on Seymour Avenue. Does he think people are stupid? He tied us up and forced all of us to say how much we wanted sex with him. He really is crazy if he actually believes we did.

I want to scream at him: "Nobody cares what you have to say! You're not going to convince anybody that you're not a monster. Maybe you weren't a monster every day, but you were most definitely a monster. You put me in prison. Now it's your turn."

August 5, 2013: Return to Seymour

Angie Castro Gregg walked back into her father's house at 2207 Seymour Avenue two days before it was scheduled to be demolished.

Cleveland officials wanted the house razed as quickly as possible, and to shred and throw in the dump all its contents, to prevent it from becoming a ghoulish attraction. The last thing they wanted was "House of Horrors" tourism.

Castro had agreed on July 29 to forfeit the home, but not before breaking down in tears and complaining to police that it was a "perfectly good house" and should not be destroyed.

Evidence had been removed, every inch of the house had been photographed, and the FBI prepared a wooden scale model that cost more to build than the value of the actual house. The electric company cut the power and a contractor had donated his services to tear the place down.

Before the demolition equipment arrived, Castro's family was given a chance to salvage any personal items. So now, with FBI agents watching, Angie climbed the stairs to the second floor, a part of her former home that she had not seen in fifteen years.

She had left this house when she was fourteen, after her parents split up. Although she had been back several times, her father had never let her upstairs. What she found there now made her shudder: Windows boarded over. Holes drilled in the walls. Missing doorknobs. Wires in strange places. Locks on the outside of the doors.

She felt sick. It was hard to imagine what sort of mind had devised it all, and it was worse to accept that it had been her own father's.

She walked into what had been her parents' bedroom and saw a child's drawings on the walls and clothes for a little girl, and realized Amanda and Jocelyn must have lived there. She was horrified at the thought of Amanda giving birth to a baby and raising her inside these four walls.

She walked into the little bedroom that had been hers. Pictures she had taped to the wall were still there, as were her elementary school plaques and awards. It was eerie to see her childhood memories in a place that had witnessed so much misery.

Angie collected as many old family photos and other personal mementoes as she could find, including her red dog puppet she found in the attic.

Just a few months earlier, she had spent several hours in the living room of this house helping her father set up his Facebook account, while Amanda, Gina, Michelle, and Jocelyn were locked away upstairs. She wished there had been a clue. A noise. A creak. A cry. Anything that would have made her suspect that something was wrong. If she had discovered the girls, or if her father had confided in her, she could have forced him to go to the police and let the girls go.

Over the years she had remained close to her father and talked to him often. But now she couldn't bring herself to face him. She hadn't gone to visit him in jail. She knew how persuasive he was, and that he would try to convince her that what had happened wasn't as bad as it sounded, so she cut him off completely.

Her mother had died the year before, and now she realized her father wasn't who she thought he was.

She felt like an orphan.

August 7, 2013: Demolition

Amanda

They are tearing down 2207 Seymour, and it's big news on TV.

There has been so much interest in that house that police built a security fence around it and have been guarding it around the clock. People have driven from all over to see it, causing constant traffic jams.

As a huge piece of heavy equipment with a giant mechanical claw rips off the front of the house, on TV I can suddenly see right into the room where he kept me for so long.

It's such a strange feeling. For so many years I dreamed of smashing those walls, ripping the wood off those windows—anything to get out of there. Now I'm watching this big machine do it for me, taking just a few minutes to destroy what had been my whole world.

Jen Meyers called and asked if I wanted to be there, or even just drive by in her car while it was happening. It was nice of her to ask, but Seymour Avenue is the last place in the world I want to be.

Gina stayed home, too, but I see Michelle is there letting some balloons go.

Tim McGinty, the county prosecutor, is being interviewed on TV and is explaining they want a "new and positive use" for the land, maybe a park. He says that they were going to use the $22,000 in cash they found in Castro's washing machine to pay for the demolition, but the company did it for free as a public service. He offered the cash to me, Gina, and Michelle, but we didn't want Castro's money, or anything of his.

I'm grateful that I will never see that house again.

Gina

I'm watching the news at our friend Janet Garcia's house. I didn't want to go to the demolition and face all the cameras and reporters. My mom said she could take me down there and hide me in a car, but then I'd feel like I was in captivity again. No, thank you.

My mom is there watching, and my aunt Peggy is actually climbing into the big crane. She takes the controls and smashes the claw straight into the second floor of the house, right into the bedroom where he held me. When the house starts crumbling, I can hear people cheering. I don't make a sound, but nobody is cheering louder than me.

August 2013: Downward Spiral

At 6:25 p.m. on August 2, the day after his sentencing, Ariel Castro arrived at the Lorain Correctional Institution, about twenty miles southwest of Cleveland—a standard first stop for prisoners from northern Ohio entering the state prison system.

At the county jail in Cleveland where he had been held since his arrest, he had told officials that he was suicidal. But during the medical and psychological screenings given to all new inmates at LCI, he said he had lied about wanting to kill himself because he had been scared of being placed in the general population and wanted to be in a cell alone. He said he had been depressed since his arrest, but that he had plenty of reasons to live, including his religious beliefs, his family, and his children.

"He appears quite narcissistic, but does not show evidence of mood, anxiety, or thought disorder," the medical officials who interviewed him concluded. Still, they recommended that Castro be placed on suicide watch and segregated to keep him safe, from himself and other inmates. Their report stated that his feelings about suicide could change "as the gravity of his situation begins to sink in."*

Three days later, on August 5, Castro was transferred to the Correctional Reception Center (CRC) in Orient, southwest of Columbus. That prison normally serves as the intake center for inmates from the southern half of the state, but officials made an exception to get Cleveland's most notorious criminal as far away from the city as possible.

Given Castro's infamy, Warden Rhonda Richard ordered a more extensive mental-health examination by prison doctors. Castro told them he was "upset" because other inmates had been shouting at him and harassing him. During the examination, Castro smiled occasionally and described himself as "always a happy person."

---

*This account of Castro's last days was drawn largely from reports by prison officials, the Ohio State Highway Patrol, the Franklin County coroner, and consultants Lindsay M. Hayes and Fred Cohen, corrections experts hired by the state to look into a spate of ten suicides in Ohio prisons in 2013, including Castro's.

The doctors found him "oblivious to the realities of his future situation, and . . . incredulous that the media and other inmates should treat him so poorly." Castro told them that he wanted to "do my time in peace." They concluded that he was a "low risk" for suicide, but they said that could change because prison life might "challenge his sense of entitlement and fragile grandiosity." Diagnosing him as having "Narcissistic Personality Disorder with Antisocial Features," they urged prison officials to monitor him closely for any changes in his mental health, "given his lengthy sentence, somewhat fragile self-esteem, and the notoriety of his crimes."

Accordingly, the warden ordered that Castro be kept in the prison's segregation area, in a cell by himself out of sight of other inmates. He would be allowed to leave his cell one hour each day for recreation, medical appointments, or meetings with prison staff. A supervisor would be present when his meals were delivered. Whenever he left his cell, Castro was to be handcuffed. Guards were required to go to his cell and check on him every thirty minutes. Those measures were intended to prevent Castro from harming himself or from being harmed by anyone else.

Castro's new home was the last cell on the second-floor hallway, or "range." It had two windows with a screen and two thick horizontal bars, a bunk bed, sink, toilet, and a little corner desk, a Bible, pen, and paper. From his sparse cell he could see no one, and no one could see him.

Castro started complaining almost immediately.

Guards said he was "demanding and pompous." He often sat naked in his cell, and he was constantly told to put on clothes when female guards were on duty. He refused to leave his cell for recreation.

He began writing journal-style notes, and in the first entry, dated August 10, he grumbled about a guard who "mistreats me, for no apparent reason." He hated his food, claiming that he found hair and plastic in his meals, and that they were always served "in a pool of water." He wrote that he flushed most of his meals down the toilet. He was dropping weight quickly, and inmates saw guards holding up his pants as they led him to appointments.

"I really think someone tampered with my food," he wrote on August 14, the day medical staff came to his cell twice in response to his complaints of chest pains, vomiting, and nausea. Guards who brought Castro his food showed him that his tray was randomly selected from a cart full of identical trays, but Castro continued to insist that it was being doctored.

His many concerns began to obsess him, and he documented them in his journal.

August 22: He asks for a mop to clean his "filthy" cell and toilet. He asks for clean bed linens and underwear, but "nothing gets done."

August 28: "I'm really getting frustrated."

August 31: "I will not take this kind of treatment much longer . . . I feel as though I'm being pushed over the edge, one day at a time."

Castro also wrote an essay called "A Day in the Life of a Prisoner."

I eat, brush, and go back to bed, get up, lay down, get up, lay down. This goes on all day. . . . I pace in my cell, meditate, stare at the walls as I daydream a lot.

I will never see light at the end of the tunnel, but that's all right, it's what I chose. . . . I've lots of time on my hands now to think and read, write, exercise. I want to make a bigger effort to try to commit to God.

I also get depressed and don't want to do anything but just lay here . . . Most of the guards here are okay, but the younger ones don't take the job seriously or they are rude to me for no apparent reason. . . . Sometimes I drift into a negative thought, I check myself and try harder not to go there.

He had two visits at this prison from relatives, including one from his mother. He was free to make phone calls but never did.

September 3: Last Day

On the morning of September 3, Brandi Ackley, a supervisor in Castro's unit, collected his underwear to be washed. She had often seen Castro naked in his cell, and that day she noticed that Castro's prison pants were loose and falling down. She left instructions for officers coming on duty later in the day to return Castro's underwear when it came back from the laundry.

At 1:30 that afternoon Castro was handcuffed and escorted by guards to a meeting with prison officials to discuss his request to be placed in "protective control," an even higher level of segregation and security. Castro was asking for that change due to "the high-profile nature of my charges" and seemed happy that this could involve a transfer to a prison closer to his family in Cleveland. He also asked about mail and family visits.

The prison officials recommended that the warden grant Castro's request.

He was returned to his cell at 1:52 p.m., and guards checked his cell periodically throughout the afternoon.

At 5:29 a guard and a supervisor left a dinner tray at Castro's cell. As they were walking away, Castro called them back and said there was a problem with his food. The supervisor again told him that his tray had been chosen randomly, but Castro refused to eat.

Guards checked his cell at 6:08, and at 6:30, a guard, supervisor, and nurse came to speak to him. He refused his evening hypertension medication, which prison doctors had prescribed after his arrest.

For the next two hours and twelve minutes, no one came to look in on Castro, even though regulations required checks be conducted every thirty minutes.

Alone in his cell, he placed a pocket-size Bible on his bunk and opened it to the Gospel of John, chapters two and three, which contain one of the Bible's most well-known verses: *"For God so loved the world that he gave his one and only Son, that whoever believes in him shall not perish but have eternal life."*

He laid out several pieces of paper on the small corner desk. On one he wrote out the names of his children, including Jocelyn, and his six grandchildren. He decorated it with hearts, flowers, musical notes, a cross, the words "Daddy" and "Mommy," and the exclamation, "God is Great!"

He carefully wrote the date, "Sept. 3, 2013," on another piece of paper and printed several Bible verses in large capital letters, ending with, *"For all are sinners, we all fall short of the glory of God."*

He stacked up ten pages of complaint forms, mostly concerning food and harassment by prison guards, which he had never submitted, adding a few pages of handwritten notes titled, "I Found God" and "A Day in the Life of a Prisoner Who Has Accepted God." In the neat pile he also placed a letter to his mother.

"Hi Mrs. Warden," he began another note asking for permission to call his mother. "She and I haven't spoken in nearly 3 weeks. I would like to speak to her, for I'm concerned of her well-being and she of mine."

He set a pair of glasses on the bed, straightened his shower shoes on the floor near the wall, and draped his towel neatly across the sink.

At 8:51 guard Ryan Murphy checked on Castro. He was standing near his cell door, staring directly at Murphy. They met eyes. Neither man spoke.

Castro wrote out one final complaint form: his underwear still hadn't come back from the laundry.

At 9:18 p.m., twenty-seven minutes after the previous check, guard Caleb Ackley looks into Castro's cell and sees him hanging.

Ackley yells to Murphy, who sounds an alarm and runs to join him.

Castro has tied a bedsheet around his neck and knotted the other end around the frame of the window screen. His orange prison-issue pants have fallen to his ankles.

The officers lift Castro to relieve the pressure from his neck and tear the sheet away from the window. They lie him on the floor while Murphy runs to get something to cut the sheet away from his neck. Several other guards arrive and start CPR, thinking he might still be alive.

At 9:22, prison medical officers arrive and take over the CPR. Castro is unresponsive, then . . .

9:25: Prison officials call for an ambulance.

9:49: The ambulance hasn't arrived, so they call again.

10:05: Forty minutes after the first call, ambulance medics arrive at the cell.

10:18: Castro is loaded into the ambulance and leaves the prison. Following prison protocol, he is handcuffed.

10:46: Castro arrives at the Ohio State University Wexner Medical Center.

10:52: Thirty-three days after he was sentenced to life in prison plus a thousand years, Ariel Castro is pronounced dead.*

---

*Three sentences in the first official review of Castro's death, conducted by prison officials, launched waves of speculation:

"His pants and underwear were pulled down to his ankles. The relevance of this finding is unclear. These facts, however, were relayed to the Ohio State Highway Patrol for consideration of the possibility of auto-erotic asphyxiation."

A far more exhaustive report, issued three months later by the Highway Patrol, rejected that possibility, concluding: "Other than the fact that Inmate Castro was discovered with his pants down there was no other evidence to support he was engaged in auto-erotic asphyxiation."

Officials said his beltless pants were too big, his underwear was in the laundry, and when he hung himself his pants fell to the floor.

A third report, by Hayes and Cohen, nationally recognized specialists in jail suicide, also found no evidence to support anything but a finding of suicide:

"The issue of clothing worn at the time of death only serves as a distraction to other facts in this high profile case. All the available evidence, including, but not limited to, the condition of the inmate's cell when he was found hanging (e.g., careful placement of family pictures and Bible), as well as the increasing tone of frustration and annoyance voiced in his journal entries, and the reality of spending the remainder of his natural life in prison subjected to harassment from others, points to suicide."

"In conclusion," Hayes and Cohen wrote, "based upon the fact that this inmate was going to remain in prison for the rest of his natural life under the probability of continued perceived harassment and threats to his safety, his death was not predictable on September 3, 2013, but his suicide was not surprising and perhaps inevitable."

Cohen interviewed four inmates who had cells near Castro's, who told him prison guards regularly harassed him. One said Castro asked a guard about his meal, saying, "What am I eating?" The guard allegedly responded, "You're eating shit," "You're a piece of shit," or "It's dog food." The inmates also claimed that when Castro asked about recreation, he was told by the officers, "You don't deserve it. Never gave them girls recreation." Cohen and Hayes were unable to confirm those accounts, and prison officials deny that Castro was ever mistreated.

* * *

At 3:45 the following morning, Franklin County Coroner Jan M. Gorniak began her autopsy at the county morgue. In the cool, clinical language of postmortem exams, Gorniak described an utterly unremarkable corpse:

> The body is that of a well developed, well nourished white male, compatible with the reported age of 53 years.

He was five-foot-seven and weighed 168 pounds, down from his weight of 178 when he arrived at the prison a month earlier. There were handcuff marks on his wrists; his right earlobe had a single pierced hole; and his nose, abdomen, lips, and internal organs were all normal. He had damage to his throat and bite marks on his tongue, which were consistent with Gorniak's official ruling about the cause of death: suicide by hanging.*

Her only unusual finding was an inch-high cross, in blue ballpoint pen ink, that Castro had drawn on the left side of his chest, directly over his heart, which looked like a small plea to God from a man who knew his Judgment Day had arrived.†

---

*The elected commissioners of Pickaway County, where the prison is located, complained that local taxpayers should not have to pay for Castro's autopsy. Gary Mohr, state prison director, noted that Ohio law calls for the cost of an autopsy to be paid by the county where the death occurred. But because of the notoriety of Castro's case, Mohr made an exception and reimbursed Pickaway County the $1,100 cost of the procedure.

†Prison officials placed guards Caleb Ackley, Ryan Murphy, and Matthew Gleason on probation. Murphy and Ackley were cited for failing to conduct all the required checks on Castro's cell on the day he died, and Gleason was cited for falsifying the log to make it appear as though they had looked in on him every thirty minutes. Prison officials concluded that their actions did not contribute to Castro's death.

Halloween 2013: Finding Peace

Amanda

It looks like a million kids are trick-or-treating on our new street, even though it's a drizzly evening. Joce is dressed up as Blueberry Muffin, one of the Strawberry Shortcake characters, with a blue wig and striped tights. She and her cousins step outside and fall into the happy parade.

I'm still getting used to this. I walk along the street behind her and I can't quite shake the feeling that I'm doing something wrong, that I'm breaking some rule, that I'll be punished for walking out the door.

For too many Halloweens, I wished I could take Jocelyn outside, but all we could do was trick-or-treat at Gina and Michelle's bedroom door. He kept the house lights off so no children would come knocking at 2207 Seymour Avenue.

I'm trying to forget all that and move on, but it's hard. Memories come from nowhere, unsettle me, and have a way of keeping me on edge, close to tears. But day by day it gets better. I love my new home and love that I'm living under the same roof as Beth, Teddy, and their three kids. They live upstairs, and Joce and I are on the first floor.

Beth found this house online. It was in terrible shape but in a nice neighborhood, and Freddie Mac, the federal mortgage agency, had taken it over during the recession when so many houses were going into foreclosure. Jim Wooley mentioned the house to Mary and Rustom Khouri, developers and philanthropists in Cleveland, and they persuaded Freddie Mac to quietly donate it to us. The Khouris helped pay for a complete renovation, and an army of volunteers—overseen by George Shiekh Jr., owner of Cleveland Tile & Cabinet, and one of his workers, Paul Irwin—worked for three months at no cost to us. Many other kind people with busy lives, including lawyers at Jones Day, helped to replace the roof, install new HVAC, and make the place sparkle, from the new hardwood floors to the bright-pink paint in Jocelyn's bedroom.

I placed three big words on the wall over the fireplace: LIVE, LAUGH, LOVE. They remind me of the promise I made to myself inside Seymour that when I got out, I would remember that every moment is a gift.

So many people in Cleveland, and well beyond, donated to the Cleveland Courage Fund, set up by City Council members Matt Zone, Brian Cummins, and Dona Brady. The fund raised nearly $1.4 million, from more than ten thousand individual contributions, some of them as small as one dollar. The donations came from all fifty states and seven countries, and it was split evenly among me, Gina, Michelle, and Jocelyn. I put Joce's money in a trust fund for her.

The Courage Fund money has bought me the time to concentrate on getting Jocelyn settled into our new life, and to learn all the ways the world has changed since I was sixteen. Whatever happened to pay phones? Now cell phones give you driving directions! There are so many things to get used to, like grocery stores. I load up my cart with food I used to dream about: strawberries, plums, kiwis, big boxes of Raisin Bran, and green beans. And, of course, ribs! I have to remind myself that I can just get a few things at a time and come back to the store whenever I want to, and he can't stop me anymore.

I make us the most amazing breakfasts of over-easy eggs, nice and yolky with bacon and sausage—just because I can. Sometimes when I'm cooking, I go out of my way to push the pan to one side of the burner. He always demanded that it be exactly in the middle of the flame and called me names if I did it wrong. It feels liberating to do things my way, not his.

I want to finish high school, but Jocelyn comes first. Classes at the neighborhood elementary school started only a couple of weeks after he was sentenced. I didn't think she was ready for what other kids might say, so I'm homeschooling her for one more year. We turned a small bedroom into a classroom that has lots of things we wished for on Seymour Avenue, like light pouring through the windows. We have a laptop and a printer, and a brand-new desk.

The walls are covered with harder vocabulary words:

Congruent: same shape and size.

Homographs: words that are spelled the same but have different meanings.

We study math, contractions, alliteration, proper nouns, the solar system.

I taped the alphabet to the wall, along with words that start with each letter. And at the start of every class we stand, as we did inside Seymour Avenue, put our hands over our hearts, and say the Pledge of Allegiance.

Gina and I have become closer friends than we ever were inside. It's like we've started over. Joce loves it when Gina comes to visit, and she uses my phone to text her silly messages. It's tougher between me and Michelle. We are very different people, and I think life is going to take us in different directions. We endured the unthinkable together and we'll always have that bond. I wish her happiness.

Joce has made new friends. Some of the little girls in the neighborhood come over to play, and I'm starting to let her go to their houses. But it's hard to let her out of my sight. When they play in the front yard, I sit on my new sofa and watch them out the window. I'm happy that she is stepping out into the world, but I'm also worried. Will she run into traffic? Will she be too trusting of others? Will kids be mean to her?

I don't sleep much. I lie with Joce until she falls asleep, then I get up and pace, walking from room to room, trying to settle my racing mind. Seymour Avenue is like a scary movie playing over and over in my head. Because he killed himself, Joce and I will never have a chance to confront him, so I'll never really be able to feel closure.

A few weeks ago Teddy, Beth, and I went to a yard sale and as we were loading the car, Teddy teased me and called me a "dumbass." He was just joking, but I felt like I'd been hit by a train. I choked up and started crying.

"What's wrong?" he asked. "Are you okay?"

I snapped at him: "Don't ever call me that again! He used to call me that, and I hate it!"

Poor Teddy was just joking, but hearing that word triggered something completely overwhelming inside me.

I don't go out all that often. When I do, people recognize me. Everybody means so well, but it's awkward when strangers walk up and hug me. I'm not sure what to say or how to act. I'm seeing a counselor, and she says it will take time to heal. One minute I feel whole and strong, and the next minute I feel like I am breaking.

I think about what it all means, who I am after ten years in that house. I know I'm more aware of other people's pain. I am a believer in the power of hope—in myself and in God. But I still don't know why this happened to me, or what lies ahead for me and Joce.

After all those years locked up in a house dreaming of getting out and being with other people, sometimes all I want to do is be by myself at home.

So at night I pace, trying to figure it all out, looking for peace.

December 11, 2013: Moving On

Gina

My tutor and I meet at a Cleveland Public Library with big windows, where I can see the snow falling outside. Diane Cook, a retired teacher, tutors me several hours a day and helps me with other skills, too, like budgeting money and studying for my written driving test.

Today we're working on reading. I never finished seventh grade, so I have a long way to go to get my high school diploma. I'm twenty-three and sometimes I think it would be easier to just quit and get a job. But every time I say that, my mom nearly jumps out of her skin. She wants me to finish school, period.

I know she's right, so here I am, making my way through *The First Part Last* by Angela Johnson, a novel about teen pregnancy. I turn to page seventy-five and start reading out loud and keep going until I reach the last line of the chapter: "Nothing has changed, but everything has."

"What does that mean?" my teacher asks. "What's changed?"

"He's growing up, maybe," I say.

This is how I am rebuilding my life, one page at a time, one day at a time.

I don't cry much. Amanda is still a fountain of tears, but everyone is different. I try to push my locked-up years out of my head, erasing him from my mind and filling it with new and happier memories. At least that is what I want to do, and it seems to be working.

I'm starting a new life. The Gina I was, the Gina before Seymour, is gone. That innocent, introverted, and happy-go-lucky person doesn't exist anymore, and it's hard to let her go. But it's what happened. So instead of dwelling on that, I'm focusing on figuring out the rest of my life. Everyone changes, anyway. Sad and violent things happened to me, and because of that I think I can help other victims, like a young girl I met recently. I asked her what was wrong, and she told me about the bad situation she grew up in. She needed someone to listen to her, and when she was finished I told her, "I'm glad that is over. Take it slow, day by day. Enjoy that it is not happening now. Enjoy the right now." She was grateful and said that if it worked for me, it just might work for her.

I appreciate everything now: new eyeglasses, a quiet bath, squeezing all the toothpaste I want onto a new toothbrush, my mom's pork chops. I have my own bedroom! Because of kind people who gave to the Courage Fund, my family was able to pay for an addition to our small house that my dad had been planning for years, and someone donated a privacy fence outside, too. I'll have my license soon and just bought a little Toyota so I can drive to the mall or over to Amanda and Jocelyn's. I couldn't believe all the funny license-plate frames they sell, and for fun I picked out one that says YIELD TO THE PRINCESS! It's hysterical when my dad drives my car.

While I was practicing driving, I drove my car into a really deep pothole the other day and messed up the front end. I am mad at myself for doing that, but I'm not letting it bother me. I've had worse problems.

I spend lots of time with my mom. We go to bingo and dance salsa in the house, but mostly we just hang out together. It's been hard for her to get used to the idea that I'm not fourteen anymore, not a kid to correct, to tell to sit up straight or not to stay out late. I understand why she still thinks of me that way, and that she wants to protect me, but I am so much older now.

I'm jumpy sometimes and wonder when that will stop. It happens over little things, sometimes just the sound of the front door opening. For years, whenever I heard a door open it was almost always bad news. My niece came close to me holding scissors the other day, and I asked her not to come near me with them again. She didn't know about how he would use them to chop off my hair.

Sleep can be hard, and sometimes I wake up in the middle of the night, kicking and crying and screaming "Get off of me!" My little dog, Lala, sleeps in my room. For the few months I had her on Seymour, before he gave her away to his relatives, she slept beside me, between my legs, or even right on my pillow. Lala was in the car with him and his brother when he was arrested, and she ended up in an animal shelter. One day on the TV news, I saw her there. I told my lawyer, Heather Kimmel, that I would love to have her, and she went and rescued her for me.

I have very few things from the Seymour years. I threw away all my clothes. I have Lala and some notes and poems I wrote to my family: "I hope to see you soon so we can sit outside and watch the moon."

I love walking outside and looking up at the sky. It may be my favorite thing. It always cheers me up to gaze up and see the sun or the moon. I wish everyone would realize how much they would miss it if they couldn't go outside for years.

My nieces talk about Twitter, what they are googling, and how to use the GPS on their cell phone. When I first got out of Seymour Avenue, I had no idea what they were talking about, but I'm catching up with all that changed in the world between 2004 and 2013. A lot of my school friends have jobs and babies.

I feel closer to God. There were times inside when I lost my faith, or nearly did, because I couldn't understand why God would let this happen to me. After I got out, I went to Our Lady of Mt. Carmel Catholic Church and I knelt there and prayed and asked God to forgive me for doubting Him.

I also said a prayer to Nilda Figueroa. When he first kidnapped me he told me this was all her fault, that if she hadn't left him he wouldn't have kidnapped me, Amanda, and Michelle. For a while I was actually angry at her. I guess I was mad at anything and anyone who I thought could have saved me all that pain. I had no idea then about all she endured, and so I asked her to forgive me for ever blaming her and told her I was sorry for what she went through. I also lit a candle for all missing children.

My parents took me to the Night Out Against Crime three months after I was freed. They had gone every year to hand out "missing" flyers with my picture. I wasn't ready yet to speak publicly, but my dad got up and said what I wanted to, that we were there "for every missing child that's out there."

I hope I'll be able to do more to help those kids soon. I am finding my voice.

May 5, 2014: Washington

Gina
Wow! The White House.

Our names are on the guest list, and two uniformed Secret Service officers greet us. One of them says it's amazing to meet us, but she's got that backwards: we're the ones who are amazed.

We were invited to Washington by the National Center for Missing & Exploited Children, an organization that helped our families when we were gone. They are giving us their Hope Award, which goes every year to someone who inspires hope for missing children. The big awards dinner is at the Ritz-Carlton hotel tomorrow night, on the one-year anniversary of our escape.

The center flew us all here. I came with my parents and our neighbor Charlene Milam, who has done so much for my family over the years. Amanda brought Beth and two cousins, Tina and Tasheena. Our lawyers, Jim Wooley and Heather Kimmel, flew with us, too, but they insisted on paying their own way since they have vowed never to take a cent for working with us. They are like family now.

I had never been on a plane before, and neither had Amanda. Everybody told us not to worry about it—it couldn't be easier, like sitting in your living room. Yeah, right! Our flight from Cleveland was so bumpy that people's drinks were flying out of their hands and hitting the ceiling. Even passengers who flew a lot said it was scary, their worst flight ever. Before I was kidnapped, I would have thought: What bad luck that my first flight was so horrible. Now, after learning to focus on the positive, I think: What good luck that we landed safely.

We walk into the White House and see the East Room and the State Dining Room and the Blue and Green and Red rooms. On Seymour Avenue we used to call our rooms by their colors. I never imagined when I was living in that miserable pink room that one day I would be standing in this famous Red Room.

I have never seen such wide hallways and grand staircases. When we come to a shiny banister I whisper to Amanda that I bet the Obama girls slide down it when nobody's around.

"I want a picture of me pretending to slide on it," I tell her.

So I climb up on it, and she gets her camera ready.

"Gina, be careful," Jim says. "You might fall."

And, of course, I do!

"I bet I'm the first Puerto Rican to fall in the White House!" I say, laughing.

Just then we run into Bo, President Obama's dog, in the hallway. He's adorable, and the guy walking him lets us pet him for a few minutes.

I'm thinking that this has to be the single coolest day of my life. Then, as we are getting ready to leave, someone tells us that Vice President Biden would like to meet us and wants to know if we can come back tomorrow.

May 6

Amanda

It's ten a.m. and we're back at the White House, though we come in at a different entrance than we did yesterday. Today we're going to the West Wing. The hallways are narrow, and there are people all over the place.

Everybody looks like they are in a hurry. We stop for a minute outside the Oval Office and peek in, but it's empty. I feel like I am on a movie set.

We're escorted to a little seating area to wait for the vice president and I ask to use the ladies' room. When I come out, I walk around a corner and whoa! I come face-to-face with President Obama, who's talking to Gina and Beth. It's really him! He is holding out his hand and he knows my name.

"Hello, Amanda," he says. "I heard you were coming to meet the vice president, and I wanted to make sure I had a chance to say hello. I want to tell you how proud I am of you, and that it's such an honor to meet you."

Then he asks, "Do you have time to take a picture?"

It's a funny question, since he's the busy one, but I know he is just being nice.

We pose for a few photos with the president and vice president. And then he is off, saying, "I've gotta go deal with this Ukraine thing." He's making a joke, but it reminds us of exactly where we are.

The vice president asks us to sit down and then sits forward in his chair, looking at Gina and then me, focusing in hard, like we're the only people in the world. "I can't begin to imagine what you went through," he says. "Nobody can begin to imagine what that was like." He tells us about a terrible accident in 1972 that killed his wife and daughter. His eyes are filling with tears, and we're all starting to cry, too.

"I didn't have the courage to deal with it," he says. "I just kind of quit. I didn't have the strength to confront it." He leans in close and looks me right in the eyes: "Like you do." Then he turns to Gina: "And you do."

I think to myself that it's amazing how he got over his pain and accomplished so much. If he can do it, so can I. He was twenty-nine when that accident happened, and I'm twenty-eight. I have a new life ahead. And he's right: After what I've been through, I can face anything. He's not afraid to cry, and I don't have to be either.

We talk for about forty-five minutes, and the vice president says he has to go, but he wants to treat us to lunch. So one of his aides escorts us to the White House Mess, which is not a mess at all. It's a fancy dining room in the basement. It's busy at lunchtime, and there are a couple of senators eating at the next table. I'm taking pictures of everything, including the presidential seal pressed into the butter—who thinks of something like that?

The room is so pretty, and we laugh and joke and sip bubbly water from crystal glasses, eating club sandwiches with white linen napkins.

Gina

The ballroom at the Ritz is absolutely huge.

More than five hundred people are sitting at round tables for the National Center for Missing & Exploited Children's dinner, all dressed in suits and fancy dresses. We're at a table near the front, listening to speakers, including two teenagers who helped rescue a little girl abducted by some creep in a van in Pennsylvania. I wish they had been around when we were taken.

We go onstage last, and John Walsh, the host of *America's Most Wanted*, whose son was kidnapped and murdered, introduces us. I'm so nervous. Amanda has a little speech written and she's been practicing it. I have a few ideas about what I want to say, but I haven't written anything down. I don't know if I'll be able to speak when I get up onstage. I have never spoken in public. I feel a little sick with nerves.

John Walsh finally says our names, and we step toward the microphone, with our families right behind us. I feel my heart banging in my chest.

Amanda goes first.

"It is really special to be here with Gina and our families. It means more than you'll ever know."

She starts tearing up and stops for a moment, then keeps going:

"I want to thank the center for everything they've done and continue to do—not just for us, but for all the missing kids and their families. If I could say only one thing, it would be this: Never give up hope, because miracles do happen!"

Now it's my turn. I am thinking I probably should just say "thank you," but at the microphone more words come out:

"Always believe in hope, even though sometimes it is hard to believe in hope. Just pray to God, and God will give you that hope."

I did it!

Everyone is standing, cheering and applauding for us. It's amazing. Amanda and I look at each other, and she smiles at me. I feel so alive.

Epilogue: Learning from Cleveland

The Cleveland case prompted the National Center for Missing & Exploited Children to convene its first-ever summit on long-term missing children.

In April 2014, nearly two hundred investigators, pediatricians, anthropologists, medical examiners, behavioral scientists, and others involved in missing-children cases gathered outside Washington to consider the question: "Are we doing enough?"

The officials noted that an increasing number of long-term missing children were being found alive, including in recent years Jaycee Dugard and Elizabeth Smart. But they also observed that none of those cases had been solved directly because of traditional police investigations into their disappearances. Amanda, Gina, and Michelle escaped on their own. Dugard was found when police became suspicious of her abductor for a completely unrelated matter. Smart was found when a viewer of *America's Most Wanted* recognized her abductor from a suspect composite made by Smart's sister.

About four hundred thousand children a year are reported missing in the United States. Most of them turn out to be runaways, and others are taken by family members in custody disputes. Those situations can result in violence to children. A stranger abduction, the stereotypical classical kidnapping, is more rare but there are still about one hundred cases a year. That means that every three or four days a child is kidnapped somewhere in America.

In cases where children have been abducted by strangers, the longer they are missing, the greater the likelihood that they are not alive. However, the center is stressing to law enforcement that, contrary to conventional wisdom, many long-term missing children may still be alive.

One young woman still missing is Ashley Summers, who was fourteen when she disappeared in July 2007, less than a mile from where Amanda and Gina were taken.

For years Amanda's and Gina's photos were shown alongside Ashley's, on "missing" posters, on the big screen at the Cleveland Cavaliers game, and on *The Oprah Winfrey Show*.

On the day Amanda and Gina escaped, Ashley's mother, Jennifer, heard that a third woman had escaped with them and she prayed it was her daughter. She frantically called Jen Meyers at the FBI, who broke the bad news.

One morning in September 2014, Amanda walked into the bagel shop where Jennifer Summers works. They didn't know each other, but Jennifer recognized Amanda immediately from having seen her on TV. She was struck by how Amanda, free after all those years, looked so radiant and happy.

And she wondered: *When will we find Ashley?*

2015

Amanda

Jocelyn now attends a regular school and has her own little desk, just like all the other kids. She loves school, and when she comes home she tells me the names of all her new friends and what they did at recess and circle time.

I still worry what others kids will say to her. Before she walked into a big classroom after all those years of being homeschooled, I asked my child psychologist to help me come up with the best way to explain to her more about her father. I didn't want a stranger to be the first one to tell her things she didn't know—or worse, to tell her their version of what happened before she could hear it from me.

I did tell Joce that her father had died, but not much else, and she never asked. I think that deep down she knew there were things she didn't really want to hear. She sees people stop me in the grocery store and ask, "Are you Amanda Berry?" and she saw my picture on the cover of *People* magazine, and all she says is, "Mom, you're famous!" but never asks why.

Before her first day of the second grade I told her that her daddy had a mental illness that caused him to do bad things. I told her that some people are sick in the stomach, and that Daddy was sick in his mind, and that was why he took me away from my family. For many years nobody knew if I was alive or not, and that is why people are now so happy to see me. And I also told her that he loved her very much. Her response was to hug me and tell me that everything would be okay.

Thanks to Joce, I also have new friends. I love her teacher, and we hang out sometimes. Joce loves her, too, and tells me, "You are my first favorite teacher, and she is my second favorite teacher." That makes me smile.

Joce has a best friend at school, and her mom and I have also become friends. We all went to a Cavaliers game and saw LeBron James. It's exciting to see him back in Cleveland. This city has so many great people, and they deserve some good news!

When there is a knock at my door on this quiet street, it's usually Joe Wooley, the son of my lawyer, Jim Wooley. Joe is a medical student who is about my age, and he gets me. He is funny and makes me laugh. We never talk about the past but about what's happening today and what we are planning for tomorrow. He's always fixing something in the house, or putting up the Christmas tree, or assembling a trampoline for Jocelyn. Once he came with his girlfriend, and they played with Jocelyn for hours.

When I see flyers of missing children that come with the ads in the newspaper, I memorize what the boy or girl looks like and focus on some feature that would not change with age. I think we all need to do more for missing children. Many people drive by a billboard with a missing kid's photo or walk by a flyer on a store door and don't really even pay attention to them.

When the police first came to my house, my mom was sure I had been kidnapped, but they didn't take her seriously. That's just wrong. Even if a lot of teens do run away, when a mother says her kid is in trouble, the police should listen and not tell her they know better. As the years dragged on, most people thought I was dead. So why should there be an ongoing all-out investigation, especially when bank robberies and other crimes occur every day? Why spend the time? I am why. Gina and Michelle are why.

I spend a lot of time being grateful. Especially to all the kind people, many I don't even know, who have helped me. I am grateful that every day I see Beth, Teddy, and their kids. Beth hasn't been well, and I am grateful to be able to help take care of her now. The Courage Fund gave me enough money to buy her a new car that is big enough for all seven of us. Her old car broke down all the time, and it's great to be able to solve that problem for her. I take her to doctors' appointments and I help out with her kids when she isn't strong enough. I can never, ever pay her back for all she did while I was gone, but I am going to spend the rest of my life trying.

I think a lot about the rest of my life, and I still don't know what it's going to look like. Now that Jocelyn is in school, I need to get working on my high school diploma. I want to get a job, hopefully doing something that will help other people. Maybe I can get some training so that I can become some kind of counselor.

I have noticed something interesting about myself over the past year: I'm becoming less afraid of life. Before I was taken, I didn't even go to school dances. I stayed in my safe zone and was afraid to try new things. Now I push myself. I was terrified about getting on an airplane, but I did and had a wonderful trip to Washington. I pushed myself to get my driver's license and now I love the freedom of picking up the car keys and, without telling anybody, walking out the door and driving anywhere I want.

One of these days maybe Joce and I will get in the car and go to New York. I've always wanted to see it after all those years watching the Macy's Thanksgiving Parade, first with my mom and then when I was locked inside Seymour Avenue. New York has always been this magical place that just existed on TV. Now it's not a dream anymore, it's a destination.

I can get there.

Gina

I recently got my first job and love it. I work in a restaurant. I walked into the place not long after I got out of Seymour Avenue and just got a good feeling there. So months later I went back, filled out an application, and right after my interview they made me a hostess seating people. I answer the phones, too. Every time I walk in the door of the restaurant I'm excited. My boss is great, and it's nice to meet new people. If any customers have recognized me they haven't said anything.

I was also able to move out of my old neighborhood and buy a house in the Cleveland suburbs. I'm glad I was able to do that for my family. We have a yard now for Lala and our other dog, Oreo, and my mom has room to plant a garden. She has always wanted to grow her own tomatoes and cucumbers.

The new house has two entrances, and I live on the side that's like an in-law suite. Everyone else—my parents, my brother, my sister, and her two kids—are on the main side of the house. We eat together, and I hang out over there all the time, but I also can escape when my nieces get too loud and crazy. For the first time in my life, I have my own bedroom and bathroom. In my old house we had one bathroom for seven people, so someone was always yelling at someone else to hurry up. Now we have three and a half bathrooms! I feel lucky.

I've reconnected with Chrissy, too. She's busy with a boyfriend and a job and she lives on the opposite side of Cleveland now, but we send funny texts to each other. People ask me what I think of men, and I say my dad and my brother are great and I would like to meet a wonderful guy someday and have kids. But for now most of my time is spent studying for my high school diploma and working.

Every day I try to keep thinking about now and next, and not about the past. I am trying new things and going new places that make me feel like I have a fresh start on life. Some days it's easy. Others, not.

I used to blame everybody for what happened to me. I blamed Arlene and Arlene's mother for not figuring out who kidnapped us. I blamed the people who came into that house and didn't figure out that we were there. I thought the neighbors on Seymour were so dumb for not realizing what was going on. I was upset that the police and FBI couldn't find me. It even got to the point where I was mad at my own family, because they were living their lives while I was stuck. But I don't think like that at all anymore. I know that nobody is to blame for this except Ariel Castro. Not me, not my family, not anybody else. Just one very bad man.

But enough of him. I'm focused on the future. I'm going to travel. I want to see Europe and visit Spain and Italy. I would like to go to Puerto Rico and to the pyramids in Egypt. I want to go skydiving, maybe even bungee jumping. I would never have even thought about doing something like that before I was kidnapped, but now I want to try things that make me feel like I am living every minute to the fullest.

And then I can come back to my cozy new house, where I can find peace and pray to God to watch over my family and keep us all safe.

Acknowledgments

First and foremost, I want to thank my beautiful mother, Louwana, the strongest person I have ever known. She never gave up hope and fought for me with everything she had. I know she's watching me now, and she knows I'm safe. I think about her every waking moment and miss her in ways I can't put into words. It is because of her, and my beautiful sister Beth, that I never gave up hope. I owe them everything.

My mother and my sister were not the only ones who fought for me while I was gone. Our family was at their side, as were countless friends and supporters, including wonderful people like Judy Martin, Art McCoy, the DeJesus family, Pastor Dave Shinault, Bill Safos, Bill Martin, Regina Brett, and many more. People who came to the vigils, who prayed for me, who stayed at my mother's side. People who never quit on me. I knew you were there. I saw what you were doing for me. You have no idea how important that was. I thank you all from the bottom of my heart.

I also want to thank the good people with Black on Black, the Polly Klaas Foundation, the BairFind Foundation, and Project Jason who supported my family so they did not have to fight alone. I would like to thank the National Center for Missing & Exploited Children, not just for what they did for me and my family, but also for what they do for families everywhere. Thank you for the Hope Award, and an unforgettable trip to Washington.

I also am grateful to those police officers and investigators who worked to find me, including Detective Laura Parker, Detective Rich Russell, Detective Brian Heffernan, and FBI agents Phil Torsney, Tim Kolonik, and Andrew Burke. They—in particular, my friends Jennifer Meyers and Lisa Hack from the FBI—also helped my family and me after we were free. Thanks to you all.

After we escaped, there was an outpouring of support for me and my family from people I had never met. I was—and still am—completely blown away by the kindness of people who were complete strangers to me. Thank you to the people who created and donated to the Cleveland Courage Fund, and the numerous businesses that held fund-raisers for it. Your generosity has helped put me and my daughter on a path to a wonderful future. I also appreciate the numerous gifts and cards from people who sent messages of support. I have read and saved every single one.

I want to think Mary and Russ Khouri, whose generosity amazes me. I wouldn't have my house without them. I'm also grateful to the Milam family for all their support. And a very special thank you to George Sheikh, Paul Irwin, and every volunteer who make a house into our *home*. I cannot imagine more selfless and generous people.

Thank you to Northern Trust, Westgate Resorts, and to the Cleveland Clinic for all the dental and medical care.

Jim Wooley is one of the greatest friends I've ever made. He and his law firm, Jones Day, have given me their time and skills in a way that I can't fully describe. There is nothing Jim hasn't done for me and my family. He has helped us rebuild our lives. I'll be forever grateful. I also want to thank the whole Wooley family, especially Deb and Joe, for their friendship, love, and totally selfless support. They are my family, too.

To our other wonderful lawyers, Heather Kimmel, Henry Hilow, Ben Beckman, and Chris Kelly, I want to tell you how much I appreciate your time, hard work, and pure hearts. You are all amazing.

Thank you to Charles Ramsey for helping me on that crazy day.

Thank you to Bob Barnett, Clare Ferraro, and all the wonderful people at Viking. I am grateful to Mary Jordan and Kevin Sullivan for helping me tell my story, for all the boxes of tissues, and becoming friends for life.

And finally, thank you to my friend and coauthor, Gina DeJesus. We are now living *our* lives the way we should!

—*Amanda Berry*

I want to thank my mother, Nancy Ruiz, and my father, Felix DeJesus, for never, ever giving up the search for me and for keeping hope alive. It is because of your love that I was strong enough and courageous enough to endure my decade away from you.

My parents did not have to wait alone. I'm so grateful for all my friends and family who provided love and support over the years—you are too numerous to name but you know who you are. Thank you especially to Judy Martin, who stood by my parents at every vigil, and to Bill Safos, who became a real friend to my family over the years. For all the prayers, I thank our family pastor and his wife, David and Carol Shinault. And I also appreciate the support of Mary Rose Oakar.

Thank you to those who brought awareness not just to my disappearance, but to missing children all over this country. Dennis Bair, founder of BairFind Foundation, thank you for your BringHome100 campaign and for being a friend to my parents. Tara Pretends Eagle Weber, thank you for helping my parents raise the level of public awareness of my disappearance, and for your efforts to promote the legislation that could become AMINA's Law. Finally, thank you to the dedicated people at the National Center for Missing & Exploited Children—for your work over the years and for giving me the Hope Award. It was a week I will always remember.

Over the years, many police officers and investigators were involved in my case. I appreciate all of your efforts, especially those of Phil Torsney, Tim Kolonick, and Andrew Burke of the FBI. Please don't give up on all of the other missing children out there.

So many people stepped forward to help me and my family after I escaped. You all have my heartfelt gratitude—especially all of the people who created the Cleveland Courage Fund and donated money to it, and all the businesses that held fund-raisers. Your generosity is amazing and has helped me in ways that you cannot even imagine. I would especially like to thank my cousin Sylvia Colon, who was a calm voice in the midst of the craziness and acted as the spokesperson for my family; Charlene Milam, who taught me to drive, giving me a real sense of freedom; Margo Funk, for helping me to start to heal. Thank you to Betsy Martinez. And to Jennifer Meyers of the FBI, for her support and guidance. Also, thank you to the generous people at Westgate Resorts.

I want to express my gratitude to my lawyers for giving so generously of their time and resources and for never asking for anything in return. From helping me navigate the media storm after my escape to helping me find the right way to tell this story, their guidance has been instrumental. They are: James Wooley of Jones Day; Heather Kimmel of the Office of General Counsel of the United Church of Christ; and Henry Hilow, of McGinty, Hilow, & Spellacy.

I would also like to thank Robert Barnett and the good people at Viking for the chance to bring our story to an audience, and Mary Jordan and Kevin Sullivan for helping me to tell it with grace. I hope that it will inspire everyone who reads it.

And finally, I would like to thank my coauthor Amanda Berry. I look forward to many good days ahead.

—*Gina DeJesus*

Thank you, Amanda and Gina, for being so strong and honest and trusting us to help tell your stories. We are forever changed and better for knowing you, Jocelyn, Beth, Nancy, and Felix.

Jim Wooley's support of Amanda and Gina has been wise, unfailing, and ferocious, and we are grateful to him for opening the door for us to this project, and for reminding us of the power of optimism, just as Patrick Jordan would. Pat, a champion of the underdog, would have loved Amanda and Gina.

Heather Kimmel and Henry Hilow and the whole Hilow-Ghazoul clan are the finest of people, as are the great Deb and Joe Wooley, and we are grateful for their help and friendship.

Thanks to Maestro Bob Barnett for putting it all together. Clare Ferraro, who brought this book to Viking, is such a pro and unforgettably kind-hearted, and Rick Kot is nothing less than a brilliant editor.

At the *Washington Post*, huge thanks to Marty Baron, Cameron Barr, Tracy Grant, and David Griffin. We are extremely grateful to David Finkel for sharing his gift with words and ideas when we most needed it, and to our first readers, including Katharine Weymouth, Laurie Freeman, Mit Spears, Andy Burkhardt, Ray and Jennifer Billings, and Julie Jordan.

Thanks to Patti Davis at the National Center for Missing & Exploited Children for her thoughtfulness and deep knowledge of the issues surrounding missing children. Thanks also to Maryanne Warrick for all her great work.

Muchas gracias to Sockie Colon, a gracious host in Puerto Rico, and to Antonio Rodriguez for leaving his Yauco factory to lead us up into the hills.

In Cleveland, a great American city, there are too many people to thank, including many from St. Joseph Academy; please know how grateful we are for your support. A special shout-out to Tom and Mary Ellen Jordan and Maggie and John Keaney, Sharon Sobol Jordan, and Dave Wallace, and all their fabulous kids. And thanks to Patrick Campbell of P.J. McIntrye's for his welcoming pub and his intrepid truck.

We're also grateful to Noreen Jordan and Allen Reiser, Julie Jordan and Jim Cummings, and Kathleen Jordan and Paul Machle for all their support— and Jim's majestic wine cellar.

Thanks and love to Thomas Sullivan and Patricia Laughlin, and to Ed and Marg Sullivan, the best parents anyone could ask for.

Nora Jordan, who turns eighty-eight on the day this book is published, has always been the most excited about this project, a champion cheerleader. Thanks, Mom!

We dedicate this work to Kate Sullivan and Tom Sullivan, who make it all matter.

—Mary Jordan and Kevin Sullivan

Mary Jordan and **Kevin Sullivan** are journalists who write for the *Washington Post*, who write about national and foreign news. They are long-time foreign correspondents who have been based in Tokyo, Mexico City and London. Winners of the 2003 Pulitzer Prize for international reporting, they are also the authors of *The Prison Angel: Mother Antonia's Journey from Beverly Hills to a Life of Service in a Mexican Jail*. They live in Washington, DC, with their two children.